WIVES

OF THE KINGS OF
ENGLAND

By the same author

Great Britain and Europe 1815–1914
Oscar Wilde's Last Chance: The Dreyfus Connection
Prime Ministers' Wives – And One Husband (published by Peter Owen)
The Troubled Century 1914–1993

WIVES
OF THE KINGS OF
ENGLAND
FROM HANOVER TO WINDSOR

Mark Hichens

PETER OWEN
London and Chester Springs

PETER OWEN PUBLISHERS
73 Kenway Road, London SW5 0RE

Peter Owen books are distributed in the USA by
Dufour Editions Inc., Chester Springs, PA 19425-0007

First published in Great Britain 2006
© Mark Hichens 2006

ISBN 0 7206 1271 3
A catalogue record for this book is available from the British Library.

Printed and bound in Great Britain by Cambrian Printers Ltd

CONTENTS

ILLUSTRATIONS

Plates between pages 98 and 99

Sophia Dorothea of Celle (William Faithome Jr; National Portrait Gallery)

Queen Charlotte of Mecklenburg-Strelitz, 1761 (Sir Thomas Lawrence)

George III and Queen Charlotte and their six eldest children (Zoffany, Royal Collection 2005, Her Majesty Queen Elizabeth II)

Marriage of George IV to Caroline of Brunswick (National Portrait Gallery)

Caroline of Brunswick (Henry Meyer after Lonsdale; National Portrait Gallery)

Queen Adelaide of Saxe-Coburg (Thomas Lupton; National Portrait Gallery)

Queen Alexandra When Princess of Wales (National Portrait Gallery)

Queen Alexandra (W. and D. Downey; National Portrait Gallery)

Edward VIII and Queen Alexandra with Children (W. and D. Downey; National Portrait Gallery)

Queen Mary (Bassano; National Portrait Gallery)

George V and Queen Mary with children, 1906 (W. and D. Downey; National Portrait Gallery)

Queen Mary inspecting the Green Cross Corps, 1919 (National Portrait Gallery)

The Duke and Duchess of Windsor (Dorothy Wilding; National Portrait Gallery)

George VI and Queen Elizabeth with Family (Dorothy Wilding; National Portrait Gallery)

George VI and Queen Elizabeth inspecting war damage at Buckingham Palace (Topfoto)

Portraits reproduced on the front cover

Alexandra of Denmark (Walery; National Portrait Gallery); Caroline of Brunswick (Sir George Hayter; National Portrait Gallery); Caroline of Anspach (John Faber; National Portrait Gallery); Queen Mary (Bassano; National Portrait Gallery); The Duchess of Windsor (Dorothy Wilding; National Portrait Gallery); Elizabeth of Glamis (Anthony Buckley; National Portrait Gallery)

INTRODUCTION

B ritain should be grateful for the wives of her kings. Life has seldom been easy for them, often tormented. Most of them have been devoted and dutiful, and their influence in the country has been widespread and benign. In the period covered by this book many European thrones have fallen. That in Britain the monarchy has survived is in no small part due to their dedication and example.

Their characters have been diverse: some have been beautiful and charismatic, others plain and subdued. They have all at times had roles calling for self-sacrifice and courage, and many of them have had to adapt to idiosyncratic and unfaithful husbands. They have also been subjected to malicious ridicule and unfair criticism to which they have been unable to reply. And the fates of some of them have been daunting. Since the coming of the Hanoverians one wife spent most of her life shut up in a bleak German castle, another was arraigned before the House of Lords on a charge of adultery, and another has been described as 'the most wronged wife in Europe'. But they have also had their rewards. They have been at the centre of great events and triumphant occasions and been the object of euphoric love and enthusiasm.

In the eighteenth and nineteenth centuries there was little romance about royal marriages. They were more in the nature of official appointments made by parents. Princes and princesses might be betrothed to someone they had never set eyes on and then married with little or no time to become acquainted. Previously there would have been investigations into the suitability of a candidate, particularly as regards religious beliefs, morals and family reputation; comeliness would also be taken into account, as would an assessment of likely fertility. In England the essential requirements for a princess were that she should be of royal birth and Protestant. Surprisingly, marriages resulting from this selection process have often been fitting and happy. In some cases kings and queens have come to love each other dearly; in others they have come to a practical understanding. Only once among the Hanoverians was there a disaster that erupted into a public scandal.

With this exception (Caroline of Brunswick, wife of George IV), wives have been unfailing in support of their husbands. Caroline of Anspach was more intelligent than George II and not without political ambition, but she was always at pains to conceal these traits and to appear to be entirely submissive and to put her husband's interests first. Charlotte of Mecklenburg-Strelitz, apparently homely and docile, also had a mind of her own but felt bound to put up with the quirks of George III and for his sake to live in virtual seclusion. Similarly Adelaide of Saxe-Coburg kept herself in the background, her only concern being to keep the wobbly William IV as far as possible on an even keel. Queen Alexandra had a different problem with Edward VII: there were no fears as to his mental stability, but his physical appetites were prodigious and she felt she had to come to terms with his multiple infidelities. Queen Mary of Teck also had to make sacrifices: intelligent, erudite and with artistic tastes, she nevertheless subordinated them to George V's interests, which did not extend beyond shooting, yachting and stamp collecting. To Elizabeth the Queen Mother fell a particularly daunting task – to be drawn from a calm, untroubled domestic life and suddenly plunged into the maelstrom of queenship at the time of a major royal crisis and to prop up George VI, who dreaded becoming king and whose frail health was to be put under mortal strain.

A major cause of anguish, especially to the early Hanoverian queens, was the rebellious and often scandalous behaviour of their children. The first three Georges had bitter feuds with their eldest sons, and the younger ones, too, were apt to go their own ways, while their daughters, most of them unmarried, led confined and frustrated lives. Later queens also did not always have ideal relationships with their children. Queen Alexandra was too possessive and indulgent, Queen Mary too aloof and unbending. Most successful was Queen Elizabeth the Queen Mother, who created a relaxed and happy family atmosphere and later maintained a loving and undemanding relationship.

Of the wives since 1700 who have not been loyal to their husbands Sophia Dorothea of Celle, in the course of a bitterly unhappy marriage to the future George I, then Elector of Hanover, had a romance with a roaming Swedish count as a result of which she was divorced and put into confinement for life. She never came to England. The case of Caroline of Brunswick was more brazen. At their first meeting the future George IV called for brandy and could only get through the marriage service in a state of intoxication. Somehow a child was begotten, but thereafter they developed a deep hatred for each other, Caroline eventually breaking loose and leading a licentious life abroad. The most notorious of kings' wives was Wallis Simpson, later Duchess of Windsor, twice divorced, American and with a dubious past, but her marriage to Edward VIII, which caused such a furore at the time, although not entirely plain sailing, survived and ran more smoothly than expected.

There is a danger that queens may become power-hungry and bent on undue political influence. History shows several cases where this has been fatal, notably Henrietta Maria and Charles I, Marie Antoinette and Louis XIV and Marie Federovna and Tsar Nicholas II. But since the eighteenth century there has been only one English queen who has sought to be 'the power behind the throne'. At one time Caroline of Anspach did have considerable influence, but she exercised it moderately and on the whole benignly. Nevertheless it was noticed and resented, and there were loud outcries against 'pettycoat government' which served as a warning to other queens who might have similar ideas.

Poignant visions are conjured up from the lives of the queens contained in this book: of Sophia Dorothea serving her life sentence in the fortress of Ahlden; of Caroline of Anspach on the receiving end of a barrage of abuse from George II but untroubled, knowing that it signified nothing and that she would get her way in the end, and later of her dying an agonizing death under the surgeon's knife without anaesthetic; of Charlotte of Mecklenburg-Strelitz, between giving birth to fifteen children, listening to the playing of Mozart and then subjected to the ghastly ordeal of seeing her husband lapsing into dementia; of Caroline of Brunswick traipsing defiantly around Europe with a disreputable entourage and then standing trial before the House of Lords and trying to force her way into her husband's coronation service; of Adelaide of Saxe-Coburg sitting placidly at her sewing after dinner while William IV either dozed or let forth a stream of irrelevant and incoherent conversation; of Alexandra of Denmark, marvellously beautiful, outshining all other women, pouring out heartfelt sympathy to the sick and wounded and playing practical jokes on visitors to Sandringham; of Mary of Teck, upright and changeless as ever whether in an Indian durbar or an English village bazaar; of Elizabeth of Glamis amidst a bomb-battered Buckingham Palace and then over the years on parade for her hundredth birthday celebrations.

Truly a remarkable pageant.

1
SOPHIA DOROTHEA OF CELLE
WIFE OF GEORGE I

Few queens have had such a tragic life as Sophia Dorothea, the divorced wife of George I. The only offspring of a morganatic marriage, she had a lonely childhood and at the age of sixteen was married to a man she disliked.[1] After twelve years of marital discord there was a brief interlude of happiness and romance with a glamorous adventurer which was terminated by his disappearance in mysterious circumstances. For the rest of her life (thirty-two years) she was confined in depressing and humiliating circumstances.

Even by the standards of German royalty Sophia's upbringing was peculiar. Her father, George William, had become Duke of Hanover at the age of seventeen and with a generous state allowance had led a roving, philandering life; but there came a time when his subjects expected him to settle down, marry and produce an heir, and it was intimated to him that unless he did so his income would be cut. He therefore felt obliged to cast around for a wife, and his choice fell on Princess Sophia, daughter of the ex-King of Bohemia and his English wife Elizabeth (daughter of James I of England and known in history as the 'Winter Queen').

Sophia was a lady of considerable accomplishments, said to be able to speak five languages and to be well versed in philosophy and divinity. She was the twelfth child of her parents and at the age of twenty-eight was eager to marry and responded readily to George William's overtures. At the last moment, however, the latter had cold feet; the thought of giving up his free-ranging bachelor life for one of family domesticity was too much for him and he sought desperately for a way out. To dump Sophia unceremoniously was impossible; it would incur too much odium; so he contrived a plan whereby she would marry instead his younger brother Ernest Augustus. Ernest was willing but only on certain terms, and these took two years to agree. In the first place there had to be a generous financial settlement, and more importantly George William had to renounce marriage for ever and accept that Ernest and his descendants would inherit the dukedom and estates of Hanover.[2]

It might have been expected that Sophia, a lady of strong character, would object to being bandied about in this way. She was always conscious of her superior rank as the daughter of an ex-king, granddaughter of another and sister of the Elector Palatine (ruler of one of the larger German states). But she longed to be married, with an establishment of her own and an assured future.

As she put it succinctly in later memoirs: 'I would be only too happy to do anything considered advantageous to my interest.' So she and Ernest were married and lived together reasonably happily. They were never seriously in love, but Sophia was a dutiful wife and in time gave birth to a family of six boys and one girl, which included the future King George I of England. Ernest for his part was an attentive husband but made no pretence of being a faithful one, which Sophia, ever a pragmatist, accepted as inevitable and to which she turned a blind eye.

For a time she and Ernest lived together with George, but after three years Ernest became Bishop of Osnabruck (and Sophia Madam Bishop) with an establishment of their own. Soon afterwards, however, a crisis arose. For the first time in his life George William fell deeply in love; now he longed to abandon his old ways and settle down to an orderly married life, but this he was precluded from doing by the terms of his agreement with Ernest. The object of his love, Eleonore d'Ombreuse, was the daughter of a French nobleman who had been driven into exile because of his Protestant beliefs. She was a lady of great charm and beauty but also of virtue, which made it impossible for her to accept the role of *maîtresse-en-titre*.[3] George William would have liked to marry her but felt bound by his pledge of renunciation, and Ernest and Sophia were not going to let him renege on it. But he was not to be denied, and he and Ernest entered into another prolonged negotiation, as a result of which it was agreed that George William and Eleonore were to bind themselves to each other in a service of commitment and would live together as man and wife. Eleonore's financial future would be assured, but this arrangement was not a legal marriage recognized by the Church. Eleonore became known as Madame Harburg and was treated with disdain by some royalty, including her sister-in-law, Sophia.

In due course Eleonore gave birth to several children, but only one survived – a daughter, Sophia Dorothea, a lively and attractive girl to whom her parents became devoted. Her position, however, was ambiguous as officially she was illegitimate. George William did what he could to atone for this by lavishing wealth on her and doing everything possible to make her secure against future trouble. The French King Louis XIV was persuaded to grant her French citizenship, and the Emperor of Austria invested her with the order of the Female Slaves of Virtue (a bondage from which she was later to emancipate herself). Because of her wealth and royal connections, at an early age Sophia aroused the interest of several impecunious German princelings, but there was always the disadvantage of her illegitimacy. This was not, however, insuperable and would be overcome if George William and Eleonore were to be officially married in church. To this, as might be expected, there was adamant opposition from Ernest Augustus and Sophia, but it became evident that they might be persuaded to agree to a morganatic marriage. Once again the terms had to be right, and negotiations over them were long drawn out, but finally there was agreement and George William and Eleonore were at last married. Sophia Dorothea became legitimate.

She was engaged to marry her cousin, Prince Augustus Frederick of Wolfenbüttel, but almost at once he was killed in battle and another husband had to be found. As was the custom of the time, Sophia Dorothea had little say as to whom this should be. The decision was left to her parents, who decided that the best possible match for her would be to her first cousin, George Louis, eldest son of Ernest Augustus and Sophia. This would have certain advantages: it would mean the reunification of nearly all the family lands of Lüneburg, which would greatly strengthen the claim of the Duke of Hanover to be admitted to the body of German rulers which elected the Holy Roman Emperor and which carried the title of Elector, one of great prestige in Europe.[4] The two brothers therefore entered into negotiations once more, as always with much financial haggling, until it was finally agreed that George Louis, later Elector of Hanover and King George I of England, should marry his first cousin, Princess Sophia Dorothea of Celle.

There was only one hitch to this otherwise advantageous betrothal: the two parties had a strong dislike for each other, which was not unusual in arranged marriages but not considered of major importance. They were expected to come to a working arrangement and avoid an open rupture.

They might even come to love each other. But this did not happen in the case of George Louis and Sophia Dorothea. George had shown himself to be an able and courageous soldier and had earned a glittering reputation in wars against the French in the Netherlands and the Turks outside Vienna; but he was narrow and boorish, and his interests did not extend beyond horses, women and food. Literature and the arts he abhorred, and he had a dread of anyone who made intellectual demands of him.[5] Sophia, on the other hand, had a lively mind and a wide range of interests. She took after her French mother rather than her German father. It should have been possible for her to fashion for herself a congenial lifestyle. Certainly her residence was splendid enough. The palace of Herrenhausen, built some twenty years earlier by her father-in-law Ernest Augustus, was an imitation of Versailles for which no expense had been spared. It was complete with moat and gondolas, formal gardens, an open-air theatre, the busts of twenty-three Roman emperors and the largest grove of orange trees in Europe. But life there was formal and flat. Not even the Electress Sophia, with all her accomplishments and vitality, had been able to breathe life into it, and for Sophia Dorothea the boredom was suffocating.[6, 7] In addition she was shocked to find that the palace was to a large extent dominated by her husband's wilful and predatory mistresses, whom he showed no signs of renouncing after marriage. If she had been wise like her mother-in-law she would have accepted the situation and made no objection, but she remonstrated and made scenes, which alienated her further from her husband. And then, recklessly, she took a lover of her own.

In 1690, some eight years after marriage, there appeared on the scene a dashing, handsome Swedish count, Philip Christopher von Königsmarck, whom Sophia Dorothea found irresistible. They fell deeply in love and made little secret of the fact. If there had been any discretion the affair might not have caused trouble. But there was none; rather, it was flaunted brazenly and there was even talk of an elopement. What happened next is shrouded in mystery, but it is known that Königsmarck suddenly disappeared, almost certainly murdered. Who by and at whose instigation is not known. George Louis can be exonerated as he was abroad at the time, but the finger of suspicion points to his father, Ernest Augustus, or his evilly disposed mistress, Countess Platen (perhaps in a fit of jealousy, as Königsmarck had once been her lover). For many years afterwards the circumstances of the murder became the subject of gossip throughout Europe.

At the same time Sophia Dorothea was arraigned before a Consistory Court to face an action for divorce. The charge of adultery did not stand, so the cause had to be wilful desertion, and before this could be levelled a pantomime had to be enacted whereby George Louis invited Sophia to resume conjugal relations (which was the last thing he wanted) and Sophia had to refuse, which she did readily. At the time she was in a state of shock following the murder of the man she loved and was desperate for a divorce which would, she hoped (although vainly as it proved), bring her freedom from the court of Hanover. She therefore cooperated fully with the lawyers in charge of the matter. By law she should then have been able to go where she liked, but her father-in-law and husband were fearful of the danger she might pose if she were at liberty. She could have stirred up trouble among Hanover's enemies, and if she was to marry again there might be major complications. In Hanover the word of the Duke could override the law, so she was consigned by her father-in-law, Ernest Augustus, to what amounted to house arrest, a sentence that was to prove lifelong.

The conditions in the place of her confinement, the castle of Ahlden, were severe but not brutal. She was not imprisoned in a dungeon. She lived in comfort with some sort of a court, complete with marshal, ladies-in-waiting, gentlemen-at-arms, pages and footmen, but these were not appointed by her, and most of them were sent to spy on her and report anything suspicious. And there were rigorous restrictions: she could have no visitors, her post was censored, and on the rare occasions she was allowed beyond the castle moat it was always under heavy escort.

During her imprisonment there were few to befriend her. She might have expected support from her father, George William, but he tended to be under the thumb of his younger brother Ernest and agreed that for the sake of the family's honour Sophia should be kept in custody. Moreover the general opinion among European royalty was that whereas it was no disgrace for a husband to have his infidelities a wife was fatally dishonoured by them, so Sophia Dorothea had got her just deserts.

The only person to remain faithful and loving to Sophia was her mother, the Duchess Eleonore. At first she was not allowed to visit, but eventually permission was granted and she kept Sophia in touch with the outside world. She also never gave up in her efforts to obtain Sophia's release, but these were unavailing. On this matter Ernest Augustus and George Louis were obdurate. Sophia remained confined for the rest of her life, altogether thirty-two years.

It seems that in time Sophia became inured to castle life. She became deeply religious and concerned herself with many works of charity which she was able to do as she had control of her own money. She also wrote long letters, and, although these were supposed to have been censored or suppressed, some were smuggled out with the connivance of her custodians. She also took a keen interest in her investments and saw to it that these were placed to the best advantage on Europe's stock exchanges.

What Sophia missed most during her years of captivity was any contact with her two children. Her son, George Augustus (later King George II), was aged eleven at the time of his parents' divorce. He was said to have been devoted to his mother and to have pleaded her cause, which could have been one of the reasons why he was on such bad terms with his father. When he became King of England a portrait of his mother was hung in a prominent position in his palace. Sophia's daughter, also called Sophia Dorothea, was much sought after in marriage because of her wealth and beauty. She finally was to make a not altogether fortunate choice of husband in Prince Frederick William of Brandenburg, later King Frederick William II of Prussia, who was a ruthlessly efficient ruler but a difficult husband and a vicious father. Lord Macaulay wrote of him that 'his character was disfigured by odious vices and his eccentricities were such as had never before been seen out of a madhouse'. His great passion in life was the marshalling of an army of giants, for which he scoured Europe and of which he was inordinately proud, so much so that he could never commit them to battle; they were for show only. This proved an expensive hobby, and to pay for it rigorous economies were enforced, particularly in the family where food was always scarce and often inedible. His treatment of his son, the future Frederick the Great, was brutal, and his subjects lived in terror of his outbursts.[8]

In 1701, after the death of Queen Anne's last surviving offspring, in order to preserve the Protestant succession the English Parliament passed the Act of Settlement by which Queen Anne was to be succeeded by the Electress Sophia and her issue. As Sophia was thirty-five years older than Anne it was not likely that she would ascend to the throne, but in the event she predeceased her by only fifty-six days – a pity as she would have made her mark as Queen of England. So it was that in 1714 George Louis became King George I. This was to bring him little pleasure, as he had no love for England and showed it. The turbulent politics, the religious strife and the rebelliousness of the people (noted throughout Europe for the rough treatment of their monarchs) filled him with dread – so different from Hanover, where he exercised a more or less benevolent despotism over orderly and submissive subjects. However, the crown of England was too great a prize and he could not let the opportunity go by.

After the death of Queen Anne he travelled to England, although none too hurriedly; he brought with him an entourage of over 150 Hanoverians, which included ministers of state, physicians, twelve footmen, eighteen cooks and one washerwoman but no wife.

Among this mixed bag of hangers-on the greatest interest was focused on the King's two principal mistresses, Melusina Schulenburg and Sophia Charlotte Kielmansegg (soon to become Duchess of Kendal and Countess of Darlington respectively). People wondered that they should be quite so unsightly – the former tall and scrawny, the latter large and voluptuous.[9] They became known as the Maypole and the Elephant, and in one broadsheet were described as 'ugly old trulls such as would not find entertainment in the most hospitable hundreds of Old Drury'. But it was soon apparent that, hideous though they might be, their influence with the King was paramount, and those seeking favours from him found it necessary to pay court to them. Their venality was all too blatant, and in the streets of London they were constantly being mobbed. Once one of them tried to pacify her tormentors by telling them in broken English that they should realize that 'she had come for their goods', prompting the immediate retort of 'Too true, and for our chattels.' It was not only the King's mistresses who did well for themselves; there were many other fellow countrymen who found rich pickings. In the words of a contemporary: 'A flight of hungry Hanoverians like so many famished vultures fell with keen eyes and bended talons on the fruitful soil of England.'

There was, of course, much curiosity about George's missing wife. For some reason the divorce was never mentioned, perhaps because it carried some stigma or perhaps because it was of dubious legality and did not bear close investigation. But, whatever the reason, Sophia Dorothea was enveloped in silence and mystery, it being inferred at times that she was out of her mind or even dead. It was seen to be a delicate subject, best not mentioned. Actually Sophia did not die until 1726, and in her last years on the orders of George she was attended by the best physicians in the country. This was not, however, because of care for her or pangs of conscience but, rather, because he had become aware of a prophecy by a seer that he would die within a year of her (which as it happened he did). On Sophia's death the courts of Hanover and Prussia went into deep mourning, but in England her passing went unnoticed, the King making no change to his normal routine and apparently showing no emotion.

Married at the age of sixteen, divorced at twenty-eight and then thirty-two years in custody, Sophia's life might seem to have been tragic and wasted. Tragic it certainly was but not altogether wasted. Through her son she became the ancestress of the Hanoverian line of monarchs in England and through her daughter the grandmother of Frederick the Great, King of Prussia, described by Lord Macaulay as 'the greatest king that has in modern times succeeded by right of birth to a throne'. So perhaps her life had not been in vain.[10]

2
CAROLINE OF ANSPACH
Wife of George II

Caroline of Anspach, wife of George II, was the ablest and most powerful of all Queens Consort. She was Queen of England for only ten years, but during that time and before as Princess of Wales she imposed her will not only on her husband but also, by her association with Robert Walpole, on Parliament. This she achieved quietly and inconspicuously, without histrionics or bouts of temper. Insidious persuasion was her *modus operandi*.

Caroline had an unsettled childhood. Her father was the hereditary ruler (margrave) of one of the smallest German states, that of Brandenburg-Anspach. He had died when Caroline was three and had been succeeded by her half-brother, an unsympathetic character who coerced her into an unhappy marriage with the Elector of Saxony. Soon afterwards, however, the Elector died, as also did Caroline's mother, so that at the age of thirteen she found herself a widow and an orphan. This might have been a desperate plight, but it proved a blessing in disguise as she was then taken under the wing of one of the great ladies of that time – Sophia Charlotte, Electress of Brandenburg (later first Queen of Prussia). Sophia was the daughter of the redoubtable Electress Sophia of Hanover (see p. 13). Like her mother, Sophia Charlotte was a lady of strong character and intellectual prowess: she spoke a number of languages, read widely and discerningly and delighted in presiding over discourses among great scholars of the time in which all talk was open and uninhibited. It was into this stimulating milieu that Caroline was introduced in her teens, and it made a profound impression on her. She had a lively mind and developed into a considerable scholar with a fund of wisdom and acumen.

As Caroline's intellectual attainments were combined with charm and beauty she was much sought after in marriage. Her guardian, the King of Prussia, wanted her for his son, Frederick William, but of him, mercifully, she was spared. His behaviour was always odd and in middle age verged on lunacy (see p. 17). The most glittering prize in Europe was hers for the taking – the hand of Archduke Charles, heir to the Holy Roman Emperor and nominal King of Spain. She must surely have been tempted by this offer, which would have brought her all she had ever dreamed of in wealth and power, but there was an insuperable barrier: it would have been necessary for her to convert to Roman Catholicism. Generally in matters of religion Caroline was open-minded and flexible. She had been brought up a Lutheran but would have been ready to adapt to other Protestant sects (as she did later to the Church of England), but for her the Roman Church was too dogmatic and authoritarian and she could not conform to it. Besides, there was at that time another potent force at work, that of the Electress Sophia who was determined to get her for her grandson, the Electoral Prince George Augustus, later King George II of England. There was much to be said for such a connection. In recent years the stature of Hanover in Germany had been rising steadily, and then in 1701 the English Parliament in the Act of Settlement had nominated the Electress Sophia and 'the heirs of her body as long as they were Protestant' to be the successors of Queen Anne. It was unlikely that Sophia herself would succeed, as she was thirty-five years older than Anne, but her son George Louis, Elector of Hanover since 1698, and his son George Augustus were heirs presumptive to the throne of England. So Caroline would have every expectation of becoming Queen of England as well as Electress of Hanover.

In 1704, when she was twenty-one, Caroline suffered a tragic blow when Sophia Charlotte, Queen of Prussia, died; of all the people in her life she was closest to her. But she was not left alone for long, for soon afterwards she found herself being wooed by George Augustus. This was an unusual courtship in that it was carried out in great secrecy. It seems that George Louis, the Elector, was anxious that his son should not like himself be saddled with an unhappy marriage; nor did he want George Augustus to be rejected publicly like the Archduke Charles. Great pains were taken to pave the way and prevent any setbacks. George Augustus was ordered to travel to Anspach incognito so that he could inspect the Princess with a view to marriage and then come to a decision. The result of this clandestine operation was that he fell in love with Caroline at first sight and wanted to marry her at once, but his father advocated caution and sent an ambassador to ascertain whether Caroline was free from all commitments and would look kindly on advances from his son. Only when these enquiries proved satisfactory was George Augustus permitted to make his suit, which was accepted.

When Caroline arrived in Hanover for married life she was not inexperienced in the ways of German courts. She had already lived in three (Anspach, Saxony and Berlin), and she soon became aware that in Hanover, as in the others, there were cross-currents and tensions to which she would have to adapt. In the first place her father-in-law, the Elector, was not an easy man. Dour, reclusive and penurious, he cast a pall over a court which in the days of his predecessor had been festive and bright. His wife had been divorced and shut away in a remote castle (see p. 16) and he was consoling himself with three mistresses – Melusina Schulenburg and Sophia Kielmansegge (see p. 18) and Countess Platen, younger and more beautiful but less influential.

Caroline also realized early that marriage to George Augustus would not be easy. There was no doubt that he was in love with her, but his love often manifested itself in strange ways. He was for ever snubbing and rebuking her and flying into passions about nothing much. But Caroline was quick to see that his bark was worse than his bite. His petulance and rages could be ignored for he was *au fond* malleable, and by a blend of patience, tact and guile she could bend him to her will. She endured his tantrums, never answered back and agreed with everything he said, confident that in time he could be manipulated. Above all, she never lost sight of the fact that her fortunes were inextricably bound up with his, and if she was ever to attain the power and influence she sought it would be through him. So in all situations she was ready with unqualified support.

At an early stage in their marriage Caroline accepted that George Augustus had taken a mistress. At that time mistresses were almost *de rigueur* among German royalty, the view being that, if a man married for reasons of state, usually someone chosen by his father, he was entitled to console himself with a lady of his own choice. In the case of George Augustus this was an unusual one – no voluptuous German siren but a demure, cultivated English lady, Henrietta Howard. Henrietta was married to a feckless, ne'er-do-well husband of noble birth (he later became Earl of Suffolk) who had run through both his own fortune and his wife's and had come out to Hanover, like other fellow countrymen, to curry favour with the future monarch. In this he had had little success until Henrietta attracted the attention of Caroline, who appreciated her intelligence and ladylike manners and appointed her lady-in-waiting and admitted her to the intellectual seminars which she held with the Dowager Electress. It was not long before Henrietta was noticed by George Augustus, who appropriated her and became intimate with her, although the degree of intimacy was always in some doubt, as she was not a *maîtresse-en-titre* (see p. 171) like Schulenburg and Kielmansegge. However, intimacy there certainly was, and to this Caroline made no objection. Unlike her mother-in-law Sophia Dorothea, she showed no resentment, made no scenes and never played the role of injured wife; nor did she take a lover of her own. Then and throughout her marriage her conjugal fidelity was never called into question.

One person at the court of Hanover with whom Caroline had no difficulties was her grandmother-in-law, the Dowager Electress. She and Sophia had much in common, notably their worldly-wise views and their artistic and intellectual tastes (not shared by many in Hanover). As heiress to the throne of England Sophia had much prestige abroad, but at home she was kept firmly in the background by her son, the Elector, and allowed no part in government; but her scholarly activities were unrestricted, and Caroline took a full part in these.

The subject of the English succession caused great anxiety in Hanover. As has been seen, Sophia had been nominated Queen Anne's successor by Act of Parliament, but this could be repealed. If Sophia's supporters, the Whigs, were to fall from power and be replaced by the Tories (as did happen at the end of Anne's reign), there would be a strong movement to bring to the throne James

II's lawful son by his second marriage (and Anne's half-brother), James Edward, known to history as the 'Old Pretender'. By birth he had a much stronger claim than Sophia, as did others then living, but as long as the Whigs were in power these were excluded because they were Roman Catholics. However, the situation was precarious and would change dramatically if James Edward or other offspring of James II were prepared to become Protestant. Then the Jacobite movement, as it came to be called, might be unstoppable. Even without conversion James Edward had many supporters, particularly among Tories, and Queen Anne herself was said at times to be sympathetic. The Electress Sophia was aware of the uncertainty of her position and how vital it was not to upset Queen Anne, who had it in her power to change the succession if she so wished.

Anne is one of the tragic figures of history: mild, placid, frumpish and easily put upon, she found herself perforce at the centre of bitter political intrigue. It had been a terrible decision for her in the revolution of 1688 to side with her sister Mary and brother-in-law William of Orange against her father James II, and she had only done so because of her devotion to the Church of England, which, she had been persuaded, was in danger. She had had a reasonably contented marriage to the dull but innocuous Prince George of Denmark, but in the course of it she had lost at birth or in infancy no less than fifteen children.[1] In late middle age she had become ever more obese and inanimate but was still a force to be reckoned with and on certain subjects had strong, intractable opinions. And it was to become evident that she had no love for her Hanoverian cousins. Certainly she had no wish to meet them and firmly rejected the idea that any of them might visit England. 'It would', she said, 'be like viewing my coffin.' At the end of her life she fell under the influence of Tory ministers who were secretly plotting a Jacobite restoration, but she died just before their plans came to fruition, and the oligarchs of the Whig party were able to ensure the succession of George Louis as George I.

Few kings have entered into their inheritance with such ill grace. Among his few good qualities was a rugged honesty and inability to dissemble, and he made no attempt to conceal the fact that he had little wish to become the English king and had only done so because he believed it would be of benefit to Hanover. In spite of rumours of Jacobite plots he made no haste to come to England to claim the throne, and when he did he made a minimal response to the joyous greetings that awaited him. He was to be king for thirteen years, and during that time made little effort to make himself agreeable to his subjects. He did not adapt to English ways, did not learn the language and kept himself to himself. The only matter in which he showed any eagerness was finding well-paid sinecures for the Hanoverian hangers-on he brought with him.

It was not long before George became seriously unpopular. The English expect their monarch to make regal public appearances, to be accessible and to give generously to public causes; and on all these counts George failed. For most of the time he kept out of sight and when he did hold court the proceedings were mean and dreary. Here Caroline could have been a great asset as she had everything needed for the part – warmth, charm, beauty and sparkling intelligence – but she had to be careful of pushing herself forward as the King would be jealous of anyone seeming to upstage him. His relations with his eldest son, now Prince of Wales, became increasingly hostile, made worse by the growing popularity of the Prince and Princess. Both had gone out of their way to be generous and affable. The Prince was profuse in his praise of everything English and claimed to be every inch an Englishman. 'I have not a drop of blood in my veins', he once declared (quite untruthfully), 'that is not English.'[2] Caroline was heard to say that she would 'as soon live on a dunghill as return to Hanover'. As might be expected, such sentiments were much appreciated by the English but strongly resented by the King who did all he could to keep the Prince and Princess in the background and out of the business of government. A notable example of this occurred during the Jacobite rebellion of 1715 when George Augustus was eager to take the field against the Old Pretender, an undertaking for which he was well qualified, having gained a military reputation for himself at the battle of Oudenarde under the Duke of Marlborough. But his father forbade it, and 'Hanover Brave', as he was known, was compelled to stay in London on the sidelines.

The years following 'The Fifteen' were a harrowing time for Caroline. In 1716 she gave birth to a dead baby. In the same year relations between the King and his son became markedly worse when George I announced his intention of visiting Hanover, and there arose the question of a regency while he was out of the country. The Prince of Wales was the obvious person to assume this role, but the King tried hard to make some other arrangement. In the end he had to agree to it but did so with an ill grace and insisted on imposing strict and humiliating restrictions on the Prince's powers. In the following year Caroline gave birth to a son, and this led to an open breach between King and Prince. It all arose out of an absurd incident at the baby's christening when, to the Prince's fury, the King insisted that one of the godparents should be a man the Prince particularly disliked, the Duke of Newcastle. As he always did, the Prince submitted to his father's demand but then vented his rage on the Duke with words which the latter mistakenly took to be a challenge to a duel, whereupon the Duke, who was only obeying royal commands, complained to the King who lost his cool completely and in what followed showed himself at his most ruthless and brutal. He immediately ordered the Prince, along with Caroline, to be put under house arrest in their apartments in St James's Palace. He would have liked to commit them to the Tower of London but was dissuaded from this by being told of the provisions of Habeas Corpus.[3] Instead he banished the Prince from the palace, while Caroline was told that she could stay with her three young daughters and newly born son but that these were to be placed under the guardianship of the King. She refused these terms, saying that wherever her husband went she went, too, and that her children were not a grain of sand compared to him. The King would have liked to take more drastic action against his son, even barring him from the throne, but this he did not have the power to do, nor could he interfere with his financial grants which came from Parliament and which only Parliament could rescind. The Prince wrote an abject letter of apology to his father, saying he had been misunderstood, regretting past differences and promising to mend his ways in the future, but the King was not to be appeased and far from forgiving him made impossible demands – that he should formally assign to him guardianship of his children and that he should have no communication with or hold in service anyone of whom he disapproved; terms the Prince and Princess had no hesitation in rejecting. Now there was open strife between the King and the Prince. The Prince was banned from the Chapel Royal, and his guard of honour was withdrawn, and everyone of note – peers, peeresses and foreign ambassadors – was warned that if they accepted invitations from the Prince they would be barred from the Court of St James. Cast out from the palace, George and Caroline took up residence in a house in Leicester Fields (now Leicester Square), then a murky district, a haunt of cut-throats, footpads and whores, and there they set up court, a court that was altogether more lively and alluring than that of the King: there were balls, assemblies and masquerades, attended by the brightest and cleverest of the day – poets, artists and scholars.[4] They were also attended by the leading political malcontents, those who, lacking the favours of the present King, were pinning their hopes on his successor. A party of the Prince's friends came to be formed in Parliament which included at first the most formidable political figure of the time, Sir Robert Walpole. In this way began a partnership that in time was to become all-powerful – that of Walpole and Caroline. But before this developed there was a setback when Walpole made his peace with George I's ministers and took office with them.

In this confrontation between King and Prince the great advantage of the former was his control of the latter's children. Over them he established a 'guardianship', confirmed by a court of servile judges, whereby the Prince could not see them at all and the Princess only by appointment, which, of course, caused misery to the children and may have contributed to the death of the newborn Prince. But the Prince of Wales was not powerless. His party in Parliament was able to make a nuisance of itself, so much so that Walpole urged on the King a reconciliation. He saw that the conflict with his son was becoming a public scandal of benefit only to the Jacobites, as the Hanoverians' reputation became more and more tarnished. Indeed, at times the Prince's party in Parliament posed a serious threat to the government. A rapprochement was not easily achieved, as there was mistrust and resentment on both sides, but eventually, after nearly three years, some sort of settlement was patched up whereby the Prince was allowed back into the King's Court and his privileges were restored, and he and the Princess were allowed access to their children, although these were still kept under the guardianship of their grandfather. There were other matters that were not attended to, such as the payment of the Prince's debts and his inclusion in the Council of Regency when the King was abroad. In nearly every way the agreement favoured the King, and for this Walpole bore much of the blame.

During the last years of George I's reign little changed at Court, which remained as dismal and dull as ever – the King surly and ungracious and ever more reclusive, his English courtiers kept at a distance, his personal needs being attended to by two Turkish servants (captured in war) whose company he seemed to prefer; his meals were usually taken in private, and it was rare that he made a public appearance; he did make occasional visits to the theatre and the opera but as often as not incognito, carried stealthily in a sedan chair and then hiding away in the back of his box. Until his death relations with his son remained cold and minimal; with Caroline, too, there was tension, and he was heard on one occasion to make reference to 'cette diablesse de la Princesse', but he was prepared to converse with her, sometimes quite amiably, often during the sermons in the Chapel Royal of which he understood not a word and through which he tended either to sleep or talk, not at all inaudibly, to his neighbour.

George I died suddenly in 1727 on a visit to Hanover.[5] Apart from his mistresses and a few others, his death was unlamented. He had never set out to be popular. However, he perhaps deserved more credit than he has been given. He had been a terrible father and husband but had not been a bad king. With all his faults he had been bluff and straightforward and had exercised his kingly powers (still considerable) with discretion, accepting the will of Parliament and making no attempt to extend the royal prerogative; and, in contrast to his treatment of his family, he was neither vengeful nor vindictive towards his political opponents. He may have done little good, but, unlike some Hanoverians, he did little harm.

With the accession of George II came the opportunity Caroline had long been awaiting – that of exercising power. She knew she could always prevail on her husband to do what she wanted. It required patience and artifice, but she seldom failed. Outwardly she was all deference and obedience with apparently no great interest in public affairs, knowing George's strong disapproval of feminine interference in politics; but all the time she was manipulating him and leading him on, blustering and blaspheming, the way she wanted him to go.

The first matter of which he had to be persuaded was the need to keep Walpole as chief minister or, as it was coming to be called, prime minister. As has been seen, George had been angry with Walpole when he deserted him to take office under his father and then failed to obtain for him the concessions he wanted, and he was looking forward to getting rid of him; but Caroline was aware of Walpole's outstanding abilities and was convinced that he best could cope with the Jacobites, who were still active; and he was also the man most likely to persuade Parliament to provide the King with the increased finance he needed so badly. So she set about coming to terms with him, which proved not difficult as he had become aware of the strong hold she had over the King, and had as high an estimate of her as she had of him. During the following years they developed a close partnership, so close that there was talk of a love affair, but this is improbable: Walpole, obese and malodorous, was hardly a romantic figure, while Caroline's loyalty to George was always absolute. What they set out to do, and achieved, was to rule the country together, Walpole controlling Parliament and Caroline the King. Since his masterly handling of the chaos resulting from the South Sea Bubble, Walpole's reputation in Parliament stood high; and, besides, most members were in his pay (either by direct bribery or as placemen).[6] Even so he was not always able to impose his will, although he usually could in financial matters.[7]

Sometimes in order to obtain the agreement of the King Caroline and Walpole would enact a little charade. Caroline would interrupt a meeting between the King and Walpole and would apologize humbly and offer to withdraw. Then, when this was refused, as she knew it would be, she would be asked her opinion and would declare that she had no knowledge of political matters and was always guided in them by her husband. Then, with sign language from Walpole who throughout remained silent, she would contrive to make out that her ideas had always been those of the King, who would usually end up by asserting them vociferously. Few people at the time realized the extent of Caroline's influence, as she never flaunted it and was quite content that her husband should have all the display of power provided she had the reality. It could not, however, be kept entirely under wraps, and in broadside ballads on sale in the streets ribald rhymsters made mock of it:

> You may strut, dapper George, but t'will all be in vain;
> We know 'tis Queen Caroline, not you, that reign –
> You govern no more than Don Philip of Spain.
> Then if you would have us fall down and adore you,
> Lock up your fat spouse, as your dad did before you.[8]

Unfortunately this particular doggerel fell into the hands of the King, who became more than usually expletive, but, as always, he subsided in time, and Caroline's influence was undiminished.

The means by which Caroline and Walpole ruled the country may have been discreditable, but some of the consequences were beneficial: there was a long period of peace abroad and greatly increased prosperity at home; also religious strife died down and politics became less violent and vengeful. But all was not well: as a result of the debasing of Parliament public life became more corrupt as venal placemen strove ever more for private gain rather than the public interest.

When George II succeeded his father it was expected by many that there would be a new style of monarchy. As Prince of Wales he had been generally friendly and sociable, mixing freely among people and full of praise for everything English. But on becoming king this changed. He became cantankerous and parsimonious, given to snubbing people and turning his back on them in public.[9] He also took to finding fault with England and, like his father, openly showed a preference for Hanover and expected that English resources would always be available for furthering Hanoverian interests. Of course such conduct was greatly resented, and it gave rise to a revival of Jacobitism. Of this Caroline was aware and did all she could to counteract it: at audiences, in drawing-rooms and on all public occasions she went out of her way to be charming and gracious; she also made herself accessible to as many people as possible, taking walks in London parks and reviving the old custom of the King and Queen dining in public view on Sundays. She knew that what the British people expected from royalty was display and ceremonial, and whenever she and the King went out – to church, to the theatre or to and from royal residences – it was usually in state. She was also generous with money, giving it away freely, sometimes recklessly: hospitals, orphanages and schools were founded by her and there were numerous hand-outs to extraneous individuals – victims of fire, indigent haymakers, religious refugees from abroad, anyone with a hard-luck story; and she had a special feeling for insolvent debtors, longing to be able to release them from the horrendous prisons in which they were incarcerated.

Brought up first in the court of Sophie Charlotte in Berlin and then in that of the Electress Sophia in Hanover, Caroline was intent on introducing into the English Court some element of culture and sophistication, which it certainly needed as both George I and George II were illiterate philistines who never read books and whose taste in art was for overweight females ('monstrous fat Venuses', as George II called them). She managed on occasion (usually during her husband's visits to Hanover) to introduce some great works of art into royal palaces, but these were often replaced when he returned with pictures more to his taste. She was able to assemble scholars and philosophers both from England (including Isaac Newton) and abroad (including Voltaire). She would have liked to be a great patroness of English writers, but there were difficulties here, for although she read widely English was not her native language and she never mastered it sufficiently to have a sound judgement of English literature. Also it was not only her husband who despised writers; Walpole, too, cold-shouldered them and gave them no patronage, with the result that most of them (Pope, Swift and Gay among others) took sides with the political opposition and wrote scurrilous pieces about the Court and government. But there were still lesser writers (most of them long since forgotten) whom Caroline did help, and she was a regular visitor to the theatre where she had a catholic taste in plays including (perhaps especially) the more salacious.

Another part of English life in which Caroline took great interest was the religious establishment. This was surprising as her own views on religion were unorthodox. She had been brought up a Lutheran but later had been greatly influenced by free-thinking European philosophers, notably Leibniz and Voltaire, as a result of which she had become an extreme Protestant. She believed strongly in liberty of conscience, was sceptical of dogma and was in agreement with the latitudinarians that religious belief should be settled by reason and personal judgement rather than by divine or supernatural revelation; the Bible for them was not infallible. To these convictions Caroline was faithful: as has been seen, she had declined marriage to the most exalted prince in Europe because it would have meant converting to Roman Catholicism. She had been able in conscience to convert to the Church of England as it was not so different from Lutheranism, but she was not in full accord with it; in her judgement it was still too positive and liturgical. But it was necessary for her to keep these views under cover, as her husband was titular head of the Church of England and it was required of both of them that they should regularly attend the services of the Church, which they did scrupulously but without enthusiasm. But although Caroline had little interest in the doctrines of the Anglican Church she was keenly interested in the appointments to high office within it. Officially these rested with the monarch, but George II would not be concerned with them. For bishops he had a blistering contempt, once describing them as 'a pack of black, canting, hypocritical rascals . . . who, while preaching that the kingdom of Christ was not of this world, were yet prepared as Christ's ambassadors to receive large annual stipends'. Walpole, too, was a sceptic: in the appointment of bishops his only concern was that they should be of the right political persuasion so that he could be sure of their votes in the House of Lords. So in the matter of ecclesiastical preferment Caroline had the field almost to herself, and by her influence free-thinkers were appointed to high office even though their beliefs were not necessarily in accordance with the Church of England or even, in some cases, with basic Christianity.

This anomalous situation was exacerbated by the strong influence exerted over her by one of her women of the bedchamber, one Mrs Clayton (later Lady Sundon), a lady of obscure origin and no great learning who professed strong and enlightened views on Church affairs. Her ascendancy over the Queen, for which it is difficult to account, became well known with the result that clergymen seeking preferment felt obliged to come meekly to her with their respects and supplications – not the least of the quirks of the Anglican Church at that time. The influence of Caroline and Walpole on ecclesiastical appointments must have contributed to the malaise of the Church of England in the eighteenth century: cynical, worldly bishops who rarely visited their dioceses were matched by avaricious humbler clergy who followed their example and were mainly concerned with accumulating as many livings as possible and leaving their parochial duties in the hands of impoverished curates. Caroline's interest in Church affairs, however, was not entirely harmful: she made many generous donations to churches as a result of which they were restored, their funds bolstered and indigent clergy relieved. One noticeable exception to her charity was in the missionary field. It might be that 'o'er heathen lands afar thick darkness broodeth yet' (*English Hymnal*), but Caroline showed no compulsion to disperse it.

It can, perhaps, be accepted that as 'the power behind the throne' Caroline's influence was generally benign, but there was one matter in which she had no success: she was quite unable to establish a reasonable relationship between the King and his eldest son, Frederick Prince of Wales. Here history was repeating itself, and there was much rancour. Frederick had had an abnormal childhood even by the standards of royalty, beginning with his birth which was surrounded by mystery. He was born in Hanover, and as at the time he was heir apparent to the thrones of both Hanover and England the birth should have been witnessed by dignitaries of both countries. But, unusually, it took place in secrecy, which later gave rise to wild rumours about his legitimacy. Was he really the son of his alleged parents? Or was he a 'changeling' introduced to fulfil their urgent need for a son and heir?[10] Not many people believed this foolishness, but credence was given to it by the lack of love there had always been between the child and his parents. When in 1714 they left Hanover for England Frederick, aged seven, was left behind. The reason for this is not clear; it was said to have been on the orders of his grandfather, George I, who had a strong aversion to heirs apparent, but there is no evidence for this. And during the next fourteen years his father and mother made no objection to the arrangement. So Frederick remained in Hanover, apart from his family, solitary and unloved. With the accession of his father to the English throne he became Prince of Wales and was then brought over to England, but almost at once he fell foul of his parents. For this George II was mainly to blame. Like all Hanoverians he had a deep mistrust of his eldest son and wanted to keep him under his thumb, and one way in which he attempted to do this was by appropriating to himself the Prince's parliamentary grant of £100,000 a year and handing out to him such meagre instalments as he thought fit, while at the same time keeping him under a watchful eye at St James's Palace.[11] Of course Frederick bitterly resented this, and the rift between him and his parents became ever greater. In time he set up a rival court, just as his father had done twenty years before, and in the same way, too, it became the focal point for all discontents. Opponents of the government, including writers and artists, flocked there all the more readily, as Frederick, unusually for a Hanoverian prince, had a genuine interest in literature and the arts. And in the same way, too, his court began to outshine that of his father, for, as has been seen, George had lost much of his charm and affability and as King become more aloof and pompous. His only interest seemed to be in military matters and points of etiquette; he had become obsessed with punctuality and seeing that everything proceeded as it always had done. In spite of all Caroline's efforts, his Court had become dull and lifeless, as one courtier (Lady Pomfret) wrote at the time: 'All things seem to move in the same manner as usual, and all our actions are as mechanical as the clock which directs them.' The same jealousy and resentment that had existed between George I and his son now existed between George II and Frederick. As always when her husband was in dispute with anyone Caroline stood firmly behind him; and her aversion to her eldest son became vitriolic: 'My dear first-born is the greatest ass and the greatest liar and the greatest *canaille* [scoundrel] and the greatest beast in the whole world, and I most heartily wish he was out of it.'

In 1736, when the Prince was twenty-nine years old, the King at last agreed to his insistent requests that he should be married and maintain his own estab-lishment. The choice of bride, made of course by the King, was for Princess Augusta, daughter of the Duke of Saxe-Gotha, a minor German principality. It was a fortunate choice as Augusta proved to be a lady of character who played a significant role in English history, although mainly as the mother of George III rather than as the wife of Frederick.

In 1737, not long before Caroline's death, there was an open breach between King and Prince, occasioned (as between George II and his father) by a royal birth. The facts of the case are not entirely certain, but it seems that while Frederick and Augusta were staying with the King at Hampton Court Palace Augusta, who was pregnant, went into labour prematurely. Her husband bundled her into a coach and insisted on driving her in great pain and distress to St James's Palace. Here no preparations were in hand for the birth of a baby, which occurred soon after their arrival in makeshift and inadequate con-ditions.[12] Later that night the King and Queen were informed of what had happened, and Caroline lost no time in setting out for St James's to see that all was well and to make sure that the newly born baby was indeed that of Frederick and Augusta, as it was in direct line to the throne and she had always had doubts about her son's potency.[13] The Prince's motive for his extraordi-nary behaviour can only be surmised. Maybe it was to show his independence of his father and to infuriate him. If this was so he succeeded completely, for the King was beside himself with rage and, like his father before him, banished the Prince from St James's and let it be known among ministers, peers and Privy Councillors that anyone visiting the Prince at his house in Kew would not be received at Court. He did not, however, go to the same lengths as his father twenty years before when he and his wife were separated from their children.

Posterity has not been kind to Frederick. It has generally been accepted that he was weak and ineffectual, and he is still known by the sobriquet given him at the time of his death of 'Poor Fred'. This harsh judgement derived largely from the hostility and spitefulness of the two great gossip writers of that time, Horace Walpole and John Lord Hervey. Certainly he did behave fool-ishly, but he was treated terribly by his parents and was not the weakling usually portrayed. He died in 1751 at the age of forty-four.

Caroline's relations with Frederick were a tragedy, and she was not altogether blessed in her seven other children. Of her two younger sons one died in infancy and the other, William Augustus Duke of Cumberland, her favourite whom at one time she was said to be contriving to supersede Frederick as king, was to acquire for himself the unenviable sobriquet of 'butcher' following the massacre of Highlanders after the Battle of Culloden. Of her five daughters two remained unmarried. Of the others the eldest, Princess Anne, was wedded to the Prince of Orange, almost a dwarf and humpbacked, but so desperate was she to escape the boredom of her father's court that she declared she would marry him if he were a baboon – and in the event the marriage proved reasonably happy. The same could not be said of her younger sister Mary, who married Prince Frederick of Hesse-Cassell, a cruel and unfaithful husband who made her life a misery; but the worst fate was that of Princess Louisa, the youngest daughter who was married to the half-crazed King of Denmark and was to be imprisoned for adultery with a Court physician.

When her husband became king Caroline must have had all the power she had dreamed of, but even more was in store for her when in the third year of his reign George announced his intention of going on a prolonged visit to Hanover and nominated Caroline as Regent while he was away. His visit was resented by his English subjects, who were hoping he would not follow his father's example in this matter, but indeed on becoming king he decided that Hanover was where he truly belonged and he spent as much time there as his father had done. As might be expected, Caroline in conjunction with Walpole carried out her duties as Regent with great style and capability, giving her assent to Acts of Parliament, appointing bishops and judges and negotiating treaties with foreign powers. All these duties she relished, but there was one she detested – the signing of death warrants – and whenever she could she granted a royal pardon.

The King's trips abroad became a regular occurrence, and he had no qualms about investing Caroline with full powers. It was no doubt a satisfaction to him to be thwarting the Prince of Wales, who felt strongly that it was he who should be Regent. On one of the King's visits a complication arose when he became infatuated with a Hanoverian beauty, one Amelia von Walmoden. As was his wont he made no effort to conceal his passion from Caroline; indeed he told her about it in detail, expecting her to be as sympathetic as before.[14] But this time Caroline was wary. She suspected at once that this attachment was something different, and on George's return to England she became aware of a change in his attitude to her. In her anxiety she consulted Walpole, who was no comfort, telling her bluntly that at her age (fifty-two) and growing stout she could not expect to depend upon her person to retain her influence over a vain and vigorous husband; rather, she should rely more on her personality. Her fears that her hold over George might be slipping were increased when he arrived back from Hanover in a vile temper, finding fault with everything

English – cooks, actors, jockeys, coachmen, everyone – in contrast to Hanover, where he maintained that peace and prosperity reigned, men were patterns of politeness and gallantry and women of wit and beauty.[15] In a typical outburst he ranted: 'I wish with all my heart that the devil may take all your bishops, and the devil take your ministers and the devil take your Parliament and the devil take the whole island provided I can get out of it to Hanover.' And this he did soon afterwards. By then Caroline had become seriously alarmed, but she did not lose her cool and, albeit reluctantly, followed Walpole's advice to urge George to invite the Countess von Walmoden over to England, which he did, but the lady had the prudence to decline, having no wish for a confrontation with Caroline.

By Hanoverian standards George had been a reasonably faithful husband. Passing affairs there had been, but nothing serious, and his *maîtresse-en-titre*, Mrs Howard (see p. 21), had been maintained in position for nearly twenty years, long past her first bloom. However, by the time he became king George's relationship with Mrs Howard was beginning to fade, and at the same time her husband, always with an eye for the main chance, tried to play the part of injured husband and demanded the return of his wife to her marital duties; but, of course, what he really wanted was not his wife but an increased allowance for his complaisance. At first the King was not unwilling to let his lover go, but at the same time felt he must protect her from a husband known to be 'brutal as well as a little mad and seldom sober'. In this he was strongly supported by Caroline, who had become accustomed to Mrs Howard and feared that a replacement might be less agreeable and less amenable. So a bizarre arrangement was made whereby George paid an increased fee for a mistress he no longer wanted to a husband who did not want her back, while the unfortunate mistress was longing to be rid of both of them.[16] In allowing himself to be persuaded George did not lose the opportunity of firing a broadside at Caroline: 'What the devil did you mean', he demanded of her, 'by trying to make an old, dull, deaf, peevish beauty stay and plague me when I had a good opportunity of getting rid of her?'

Caroline was to be Queen of England for no longer than ten years. Her health had never been good: she was always beset by some affliction – gout, ague, pleurisy and a general debility known at that time as 'the vapours'. Of these she made a point of never complaining, although once in a moment of great anguish she was heard to exclaim: 'I can say since the hour I was born I have not lived a day without suffering.' She knew that her husband had a horror of sickness and was infuriated when anyone around him became ill. So however bad she was feeling, Caroline forced herself to go through with all the royal duties expected of her. In 1734, three years before George became king, she suffered a serious mishap when on the birth of her last child she had a minor internal rupture, but this she kept secret as she thought that news of it would upset her husband. For a time it did not give her undue trouble, and she learned to live with it, but it never healed and without medical treatment it would only become worse and in time serious. This it did three years later when at the end of 1737 she collapsed under the pain of it, but still for fear of angering the King and losing her hold over him (this was at the time of the Walmoden affair) she kept the true cause of her illness to herself and pretended it was due to other things. The doctors applied all the usual horrific remedies – bleeding, emetics, aperients, blistering, as well as such quack cures as snake root and Daffy's elixir – which made her much worse. But the truth at last came out: the rupture could no longer be concealed and she had to undergo the agony of an operation without anaesthetic which she bore with the greatest courage, beseeching the surgeon to take no notice should even a groan of pain escape her.

By then it was becoming clear that her illness was mortal, but she took a long time dying. In her last days the King became frantic with grief; he made little effort to control himself, sobbing ceaselessly, never leaving her bedside and forcing food on her which she did not want and could not keep down but which for his sake she felt bound to take. To all around he never stopped praising her as 'the most wonderful wife ever man had . . . the best mother, the best companion, the best friend and the best woman that ever was born'. At the same time, as he had always done, he fell to scolding and snubbing her, but this worried her not at all; she was accustomed to it and knew now what she had once doubted – that she was the great love of his life, just as he, in spite of his tantrums and infidelities, was the only man she had ever loved and to whom she owed everything. Just before she died she took from her finger the ruby ring he had given her at his coronation, saying to him: 'This is the last thing I have to give you; naked I came to you, naked I go from you.' At the same time she urged him to marry again after her death, but in a flood of tears he blurted out: 'Non. J'aurai des maîtresses.' To which she replied sorrowfully: 'Ah, mon Dieu. Cela n'empeche pas.' ('That need not prevent you.')

News of Caroline's impending death brought word from her eldest son that he wanted to come and make his peace with her; but there was to be no reconciliation. The King, working himself into one of his furies, declared: 'I always hated the rascal and now I hate him worse than ever . . . He wants to come and insult his poor dying mother, but she shall not see him. No, no, he shall not come and act any of his silly plays here, fake, lying, cowardly, nauseous puppy.' And Caroline, although she might have liked a *rapprochement*, felt bound to comply. 'At least I shall have one comfort,' she declared, 'in having my eyes eternally closed. I shall never see that monster again.'

Until the end Caroline's mind remained clear and her spirit undimmed; she was even capable of joking, telling one surgeon as he wielded his knife that he probably wished that it was on his wife (with whom he was on notoriously bad terms), and told another, when his wig caught fire from a candle, to stop his ministrations so that she could laugh. But she grew ever weaker, and on 20

November 1737, eleven days after she first broke down, at the age of fifty-four she was released from her agony.

George never ceased to mourn Caroline. 'I never yet saw a woman fit to buckle her shoe,' he once declared. After her death he had insisted on honouring all her debts and continuing to pay all her pensions. 'I will have no one poorer for her death but myself,' he said. Caroline had certainly made her mark on England. As with all who exercise power, she had her detractors; but there was a general feeling that with her death a benign and moderating influence had been lost.

George was to outlive Caroline by twenty-three years. He kept his promise not to marry again, as he did, too, as regards mistresses. Soon after Caroline's death the Countess von Walmoden was brought over to England where under the title of Countess of Yarmouth she was to exercise widespread patronage and was much sought after by place-hunters.

For a time George continued to rely on Walpole, but the latter was declining and not the same without Caroline. In the year after her death he was pushed by public opinion into an unnecessary and somewhat ridiculous war with Spain known to history as the War of Jenkins' Ear and then two years later into a more general war with France over the Austrian Succession.[17] At the age of sixty George II led his army into battle, bravely and with great style if without much success.[18] If Caroline had lived as long as her husband she would also have witnessed the Jacobite rebellion of 1745 and the panic which it caused in London and finally the waging of one of England's most successful wars, the Seven Years' War, during which an empire was founded. Rarely have British arms been so victorious, and this at a time when the government was in the hands of a bizarre trio – two geriatrics and one man of genius: the King, then in his seventies, deaf, half blind and usually only accessible through his German mistresses; a Prime Minister (the Duke of Newcastle), timid and often absurd but nevertheless exercising a hold over Parliament that could not at that time be broken; and a Secretary of State (William Pitt) who was dynamic and over-powering but in terrible health, verging at times on dementia.

George II was not one of the more lovable nor virtuous of English kings. Generally the tone of his royalty was coarse, and at times he was ridiculous.[19] However, he had redeeming features – courage and patriotism; he reigned according to the laws and customs of the country and did little harm. His grandson, George III, who succeeded him was certainly more virtuous but equally certainly did much more harm.

3
CHARLOTTE
OF MECKLENBURG-STRELITZ
WIFE OF GEORGE III

At the beginning of 1761 the prospects for Princess Charlotte of Mecklenburg-Strelitz were dim. The youngest daughter of the duke of one of the smallest German principalities (about the size of Sussex), without beauty or intellect, she seemed doomed either to a life of obscure and impecunious spinsterhood or possibly marriage to one of the less eligible German princelings. But then, out of the blue, she was informed that she was to be Queen of England, the wife of King George III. Of course she had no say in the matter; it had all been arranged by her elder brother, the Duke and delegates from England. It was taken for granted that she would comply and fall into line, as indeed she did. Never at any stage was there the least trace of romance. It was an official appointment.

The English King had succeeded to the throne in the previous year at the age of twenty-two, and it had been impressed upon him that he must lose no time in finding a wife and making sure of the succession. At the time he was deeply in love with a radiant English beauty, Lady Sarah Lennox, who might seem to have been an ideal wife for him – the daughter of the Duke of Richmond and the great-granddaughter, albeit illegitimately, of Charles II – but those closest to the King (family, courtiers, statesmen) advised him that his bride must be of royal birth, and such was George's sense of duty that he felt obliged to agree, so he made enquiries about a possible candidate from abroad. By the law of the land she had to be Protestant, which meant in effect that his choice was restricted to the princesses of Germany, of which there were many. Otherwise the requirements for the position were not exacting: she must be, so George laid down, of a pleasant disposition and good understanding and, most important of all, be able to bear children; great beauty was not considered essential, nor were intellectual interests; and she must have no inclination to meddle in politics. In the previous reign strong feminine influence had been brought to bear on the monarch, and George was determined that there should be no more 'pettycoat government'.

In the first instance Charlotte was not among the forerunners. There were few in England who had heard of Mecklenburg-Strelitz and even fewer who had heard of Princess Charlotte. There were princesses more gifted and more prestigious, but gradually, for one reason or another, these were eliminated. Some were reported to be 'obstinate and ill-tempered' while another, although amiable, was said to have a taste for philosophy which George did not share. Yet another was ruled out because her grandfather had married an apothecary's daughter and another because her mother was reputed to have had an affair with a courtier of lowly birth. So it came down to Charlotte – plain, uninspiring, worthy – concerning whom there was no breath of scandal; she was not known to have political or intellectual leanings, and there was no reason to suppose she would not be a fruitful bearer of children (as indeed she proved to be). All, of course, was not perfect: she was far from being a beauty, and her religion, while Protestant, was Lutheran, although it soon transpired that there would be no theological difficulties in her switching to the Church of England. Thoughts of Lady Sarah Lennox were not easily put aside, but George's betrothal to Charlotte was arranged with some urgency as it was of great importance that they should be married in time for the coronation, the date for which had been fixed in 1762.

As soon as George's proposal had been accepted, which it was readily, the Privy Council was informed of his choice and a suitable escort, including three duchesses, was dispatched to Mecklenburg-Strelitz to bring Charlotte to England forthwith. Their journey back was exceptionally hard, particularly the sea crossing which was tempestuous. All the Princess's attendants were laid low by seasickness but not Charlotte, who could be heard above the raging of the storm playing on the harpsichord and perfecting her knowledge of some well-known English songs.

On arrival in England Charlotte's stamina was further stretched. After spending one night ashore she was taken off to London. She arrived at three o'clock in the afternoon and after a brief introduction to her future husband was informed that her wedding was to take place that evening.

It had been taken for granted, rightly as it proved, that Charlotte's clothes would be impossibly dowdy, and a large and magnificent trousseau had been assembled for her, including a wedding dress so heavy that she could hardly stand upright in it. As Horace Walpole recorded gleefully: 'An endless mantle of violet-coloured velvet – lined with ermine and attempted to be fastened on her shoulder by a bunch of huge pearls – dragged itself, and almost the rest of her clothes, half-way down her waist. The spectators knew as much of her upper half as the King would himself.' At the ceremony, which took place at nine o'clock at night, Charlotte was attended by ten bridesmaids, none of whom she knew and among them Lady Sarah Lennox; and she was given away by George's elderly and decrepit uncle 'Butcher' Cumberland (see p. 31). Afterwards there was an enormous wedding feast. It was then the custom that the newly-weds should be 'seen to bed' by the assembled company, but this at least Charlotte was spared, although it did become known subsequently that the marriage was consummated at 3.30 that morning. To have come through such an ordeal at the age of seventeen in a strange country with only a few words of English was surely a feat of heroism.

Two weeks later Charlotte had to face up to the coronation. For the young girl from the backwaters of Germany this must have been another daunting experience. There is nothing the crowds of London enjoy more than a royal occasion, and as always they turned out in force, well lit up and in festive mood. Inside Westminster Abbey all the greatest in the land were packed tightly in full panoply, come to pay homage to the new King and Queen. The ceremony lasted for more than ten hours, and for Charlotte, who was suffering from toothache and neuralgia, it must have been an agonizing ordeal; but once again she did not falter, and she won praise for her grace and simplicity.

Inevitably in the first weeks Charlotte came under close scrutiny. Everyone wanted to catch a glimpse of her, to exchange a few words and then go off and gossip about her. Foremost among these was Horace Walpole, fourth son of the long-serving prime minister, prolific author and diarist, sharpest of wits and ever ready to retail and embellish any item of tittle-tattle that came his way. He made sure of an early opportunity of viewing the new Queen and has left this detailed and personal description of her: 'She is not tall, nor a beauty, pale and very thin, but looks sensible and is very genteel. Her hair is darkish and fine; her forehead low, and her nose very well, except the nostrils spreading too wide; her mouth has the same fault, but her teeth are good.'

In time Charlotte came to discover what sort of a man she had married. She must have seen at once that he was kindly, diffident and unworldly. For the so-called high life – racing, gambling, wenching – he had no liking, even a strong distaste. Later she would have learned that he had had a troubled and unhappy childhood. He had been born two months prematurely and was a weak and puny baby and probably only survived because of the sustenance he received from a sturdy wet nurse, the wife of a royal gardener. As a boy he was timid and self-effacing, overshadowed by his younger brother Edward (later Duke of York) who was his parents' favourite. Both boys were dominated by their mother, Princess Augusta of Saxe-Coburg, a formidable and wilful lady who conceived it her duty to bring up her children in the fear and love of God and sheltered from the wicked and profligate life all around them, so they were in effect kept in isolation from most adults and children of their own age.[1] She was a caring mother but not a warm-hearted one. George's father, Frederick Lewis, Prince of Wales, was a somewhat pathetic character known generally as 'Poor Fred'. Openly despised by his mother and father with whom he had a bitter feud, he was regarded by most of his contemporaries as a nonentity, only of interest because he was heir to the throne.[2] But he seems to have been a gentle and kindly father, and when he died suddenly in 1751 George was deeply upset.

George's situation was of course greatly altered by the death of his father. At the age of twelve he became heir to the throne, and his grandfather, George II, was in his sixty-eighth year. At once he became the focus of ambitious and unscrupulous politicians who were looking to the future. His mother did all she could to protect him and saw to it that his education was worthy of a king.

Various governors, precentors and tutors were appointed, all learned men but for the most part without the gift of passing this learning on and without an understanding of a boy with little self-confidence and no great intelligence. As a result he showed little aptitude for book learning and because of his mother's obsession that he should be kept in isolation from other young people he had woefully little knowledge of what his governors called 'the usages of the world'. By the age of seventeen he was still shy, immature and unmotivated. But then a great change occurred when he came into contact with someone for whom he felt a great love and admiration and who for ten years was to be the dominant influence in his life.

John Stuart, Earl of Bute, was once an impecunious Scottish nobleman on the make.[3] Handsome, erudite and plausible, he had been taken into the household of Poor Fred where he had become friendly with Princess Augusta. Contemporary scandal-mongers, notably Horace Walpole, were in no doubt that their association was of an amorous nature, but today this is generally considered unlikely. However, it is certain that he exercised great influence on her, and on the death of her husband she appointed him personal tutor to George. His effect on the boy was fundamental; it is not too much to say that he transformed his life. Although in some ways a stern and haughty character, Bute yet gave the Prince what he had never had before – affection and understanding – and his response was immediate. From being an indolent, ineffective youth he suddenly became highly motivated, with a new and ardent interest in learning and a passionate desire to improve himself in every way. Under Bute's tutelage George was provided with a liberal education he would not otherwise have had, one that included, as well as the usual Latin, Greek and Divinity, such subjects as Science, Art, Agriculture and Architecture. Bute's influence over George was almost entirely beneficial; from him he gained self-confidence and the courage of his convictions as well as an interest in a wide variety of subjects. It was, nevertheless, a pity that his domination was so complete. For nearly ten years all George's ideas came from Bute, and he seemed only concerned in humbling himself before him and justifying himself in his eyes. Just before coming to the throne he wrote to him:

> You shall find me make such progress in the summer that shall give
> you hopes that with the continuation of your advice, I may turn out
> as you wish . . . I beg that you will be persuaded that I will constantly
> reflect whether what I am doing is worthy of one who is to mount the
> throne, and who owes everything to his friend.

Such abject submission was not healthy, and led to trouble when George became king, but, fortunately, as George's character matured (partly owing to marriage) and Bute proved inadequate as a prime minister, his influence faded.

This then was Charlotte's husband – chaste, high-minded, idealistic, but unworldly, prudish and narrow-minded. As a Hanoverian he was an odd man out, with none of his forebears' or successors' uncontrollable libidinous appetites. He set an example of marital fidelity few kings can equal. At no time did he develop a taste for the rip-roaring life of the Whig aristocracy, preferring always a life of quiet domesticity with his plain, unexciting wife. 'The first duty of kings', he wrote to Bute, 'is to lead a moral life and refrain from indulgences and sensual pleasures.' Although these virtuous thoughts may have found favour in some quarters, they were not appreciated by everyone – not by England's full-blooded aristocracy, nor for that matter by the masses, who have always enjoyed a degree of lechery in their rulers. Horace Walpole, seldom charitable in his comments, wrote him off as 'bigoted, young and chaste'. Earlier his grandfather, George II, had been even more scornful: 'fit for nothing but to read the Bible to his mother'.

The first years of Charlotte's marriage can hardly have been agreeable. In the first place there was her mother-in-law, Princess Augusta, who had always dominated her son and then became bent on dominating Charlotte by making life as difficult for her as possible. Then there were her husband's idiosyncrasies. In his determination to keep her clear of all politics he imposed on her a life of almost total seclusion. Social life was kept to a minimum and visitors were strictly vetted and usually prohibited. A large and formidable German lady, Madame Schellenburg (known as Cerberus), was installed to see that no intruders made their way through to the royal presence. Of her life at that time a contemporary wrote: 'Except for Ladies of the Bedchamber for half an hour a week or a ceremonious drawing-room, she never had a soul to speak to but the King.' Retiring domesticity was no hardship for her as, like her husband, she had no taste for high life and grand social occasions; and she certainly adapted herself to George's style of life rapidly, busying herself reading, sewing, learning English and, her great love, music. She herself had a pleasing voice and was no mean performer on the harpsichord, taking lessons at times from J.C. Bach (son of the great Johann Sebastian) and listening to the playing of the child prodigy Wolfgang Mozart, who dedicated a piano sonata to her. Looking back later on this circumscribed life she had no complaints:

> I am most truly sensible to the dear King's great strictness at my arrival in England to prevent my making many acquaintances, for he always used to say that, in this country, it was difficult to know how to draw a line on account of the politics of the country and that there never could be kept up a society without party, which was always dangerous for any woman to take part in, but particularly so for the Royal Family; and with truth do I assure you that I am not only sensible that he was right, but I feel thankful for it from the bottom of my heart.

There were, however, other aspects of Charlotte's life for which she must surely have been less grateful. Some of George's ways must have been very trying. In the first place there was his conversation, which was incessant, repetitive and inconsequential (as well as being interlarded with endless 'what whats' and 'hey heys'). Dr Johnson said of him: 'His Majesty is multifarious in his questions but thank God he answers them all himself.' Then there was his taste in literature and the arts which was, to say the least, unsophisticated. He seems to have had an unerring instinct for the second rate (except music where his devotion to Handel was absolute), whereas Charlotte was more discriminating and her tastes more mature, but, submissive as ever, she kept these to herself. Most exasperating of all must have been George's passion for penny-pinching economies. He was not an ungenerous man and at times gave liberally both to people and to worthy institutions (notably the Royal Academy), but he could become prepossessed about such matters as the price of cheese and cabbages. His own meals were austere and meagre and his hospitality of the most parsimonious. This was not to Charlotte's liking, but, as always, she made no complaints and went along with her husband's abstinence and petit-bourgeois tastes.

In time Charlotte became less constricted and was able to have more of a life of her own. With marriage and kingship George became more mature and self-confident and less subject to the influence of Bute and his mother. Charlotte must have known that he was never deeply in love with her, but he was an affectionate husband and a dutiful one: in 1762 their first child was born, a son, the future George IV, and from then on additions to the family came thick and fast so that by the time Charlotte was forty she had given birth to no less than fifteen children of whom, remarkably for that age, thirteen survived into adulthood.

His growing family was a great comfort to George, and he was much in need of this in the early years of his reign when political troubles crowded in on him. His great objective on becoming king had been to free the monarchy from the dominance of the Whig oligarchs, but it soon became clear that this could not be achieved by himself and Bute alone. Control of Parliament was essential, and for this he must beat the Whig magnates at their own game and outbid them in the purchase of members' votes – a sordid business which he and Bute were too inexperienced and too fastidious to undertake themselves; for this task hard and cynical operators were needed. To George, who had declared on coming to the throne that his great object was 'to discountenance and punish all manner of vice, profaneness and immorality in all persons of whatsoever degree and quality within this our realm', this was a humiliating climb-down, but as he declared candidly: 'We must call in bad men to govern bad men.' The men he called in for this purpose were indeed a shameful lot. Henry Fox, whom he made Secretary of State, was an ambitious parvenu who came to be known as 'the public defaulter of unaccounted millions'.[4] An even more outrageous choice was Sir Francis Dashwood, whose Rabelaisian orgies in his Hellfire Club shocked even that licentious age and who besides knew nothing of public finance and who had declared openly that he was equally fit to be Archbishop of Canterbury as Chancellor of the Exchequer. But these men set about their business with a will and with considerable success. The aged Duke of Newcastle, who had been in office for most of the last thirty years, was edged out, as also was the great William Pitt (the elder), which caused great popular anger as he had become a national hero after leading the country to one of its most successful wars; and George, and more particularly Bute, came in for vociferous abuse. Soon afterwards Bute found the strains of office too much for him and retired, and George was compelled to accept the services of a competent but bigoted and overbearing Whig lawyer, George Grenville. His popularity then took a further plunge when tumult broke out over the alleged wrongs of a notorious character, one John Wilkes.

Wilkes, a scurrilous rogue if ever there was one, was Member of Parliament for Aylesbury, and like most MPs at that time he had his price, but so disreputable was he that George and Grenville forbore to pay it and so, like most politicians left out in the cold, he resorted to making such a nuisance of himself to the government that ministers would come to terms. Being a natural demagogue and a man of wit and charm, he did this brilliantly, so much so that he found himself hailed as a champion of liberty and freedom of the press, and became the hero of the London mobs. The inept handling of the Wilkes affair by the government gave rise to violent turmoil, but much greater trouble was to be caused by another of Grenville's acts at that time, the imposition of a Stamp Tax on the colonies in America which resulted in a long-drawn-out dispute culminating in the colonists declaring their independence and setting up the United States of America, an event which caused George the greatest anguish and which perhaps more than anything contributed to the breakdown of his health.

The Wilkes affair with its seething, angry mobs must have opened Charlotte's eyes to the true nature of her adopted country. At first, perhaps, the landscapes and rural idylls of Gainsborough and other great artists, as well as the cultivated and richly apparelled men and women around her, might have led her to believe that England was a country of elegance and refinement. But this was misleading. Beneath the surface were the lives depicted by Hogarth, brutal and festering. London at that time was the most turbulent city in Europe. Poverty and depravity were rife; and since the city had become awash with cheap gin (drunk for a penny) most Londoners were vicious and aggressive. They drank and brawled and amused themselves with cruel and bloodthirsty sports and were always ready to go on the rampage. Usually this was because of unemployment or the high price of bread, but they could also be whipped into frenzy by such extraneous matters as reform of the calendar, concessions to Roman Catholics or the alleged wrongs of a member of the Royal Family.[5]

On a number of occasions Charlotte had close encounters with London mobs, and never failed to comport herself with dignity and courage, and at times she gave back as good as she got. Once, when assailed by hooligans while travelling in her sedan chair, she turned on them strongly. 'I am an old woman of seventy; for over fifty years I have been Queen of this country, and I have never been so insulted in my life.' Her tormentors retreated, abashed.

During Charlotte's years of 'gilded captivity' her life followed much the same pattern – unobtrusive, domestic, fecund. Secluded though she might have been, she was yet provided with ample accommodation. Soon after marriage the King acquired for her a house in St James's Park belonging to the Duke of Buckingham (on the site of present-day Buckingham Palace), and there were country houses for her at Windsor, Richmond and Kew. Here, as well as begetting her large family, she spent her time reading, sewing, knitting,[6] playing and listening to music, engaging in works of charity[7] and developing an interest in botany, becoming quite an expert in the subject and taking part in the setting up of the Royal Botanical Gardens at Kew. Her circle of friends was always small and mainly confined to the royal household. One to whom she became particularly attached was the novelist Fanny Burney, who for four years was the Second Keeper of the Queen's Robes. She was the most devoted and loyal of royal servants and has left a vivid portrait of Charlotte, describing her as 'the most charming woman, full of sense and graciousness mingled with delicacy of mind and liveliness of temper'. Not everyone, however, took such a favourable view. Lady Anne Hamilton, a lady about Court and a notorious scandalmonger, wrote that she was 'one of the most selfish, vindictive and tyrannical women that ever disgraced human nature'. But this was hardly an objective judgement. Few others spoke in such terms. And if at times her temper was 'quick and rather warm', she had much provocation. She was often in poor health, partly as a result of her frequent pregnancies, and suffered much from headaches and digestive troubles. Her husband, too, could be vexatious, and her children in adulthood caused her much grief and anxiety. Her eldest son, the Prince of Wales, was soon kicking over the traces – in true Hanoverian fashion hobnobbing with the parliamentary opposition and conspiring with them against the King's ministers as well as running up huge debts and forming liaisons with unsuitable middle-aged ladies. In time most of Charlotte's other sons (apart from the two who died in infancy) followed suit, while her six daughters were kept cooped up, unmarried on the insistence of their father until middle age in what came to be known as 'the nunnery'. Certainly Charlotte had her tribulations early on, but these were as nothing compared to the ghastly ordeal which was in store for her later.

There had been a foretaste of George III's dementia as early as 1762 and again in 1768 when during bouts of flu he had shown signs of mental instability; in the words of his doctor 'his countenance and manner were a good deal estranged'. But these had been short-lived and were hushed up so that they were not known outside the Palace.

For the next twenty years the King enjoyed good health, with no serious

illnesses or any signs of derangement. During this time his way of life was
wholesome and bracing, with plenty of fresh air and exercise and moderate
eating and drinking habits. However, he was subject to great nervous strain
caused mainly by the loss of the American colonies and the irresponsible behaviour of his eldest son. On 16 October 1788, at the age of fifty, he was taken ill
with a chill and cramp and a fit that rendered him speechless and which caused
Charlotte to come running from their bedroom calling for someone to fetch
the local apothecary (chemist). At first there was not undue alarm, and a week
later he was able to attend a levee without disaster. But then his condition
declined critically: he was subject to violent rages and floods of tears and
chattered incessantly and incoherently; he was also for much of the time in
great physical pain, but his greatest agony was the realization that he was going
mad, and like King Lear he was aghast at such a prospect:

> O let me not be mad, not mad, sweet heaven!
> Keep me in temper; I would not be mad!

Matters came to a head on 5 November when he became manifestly out of
his mind: his eyes became swollen and were, according to Charlotte, 'like black-
currant jelly'; he foamed at the mouth and ranted ever more deliriously; and
he attempted violence on the Prince of Wales. From then on he had to be put
under restraint, often in a straitjacket, and in the charge of various doctors.
This was perhaps the worst that could happen to him, as no doctor at that time
had the ability to deal with porphyria, which was the disease from which he
was suffering. Today it is known that this is a physical rather than a psycho-
logical disorder caused by metabolic imbalance which gives rise to mental
derangement. But the doctors then could only rely on conventional cures for
all diseases, and these could be horrific – repeated bleeding, purgatives,
emetics and, worst of all, blistering, all of which were hit-or-miss guesswork.
Sometimes they had a beneficial effect but more often the reverse. The next
four months were a torment for the unfortunate King.

And they were agony, too, for Queen Charlotte. Her husband's behaviour
terrified her so that at times she became hysterical. It became necessary at once
for her to move into another bedroom, but he pursued her and burst in upon
her, eyes aflame and gabbling desperately so that she thought he was going
to murder her. It seemed that she aggravated his condition, and the doctors
made her move further away, but not before she had become aware that in his
babbling the King had uttered what a courtier described as 'many indecen-
cies', including some highly offensive things about her – that he had never
liked her, that he preferred another, that her children were afraid of her and
that she had been mad these last three years. At the same time he could not
bear to be parted from her and said that she was his best physician.

Another cross Charlotte had to bear was the dreadful behaviour of the

Prince of Wales, who was doing everything possible to have his father declared permanently insane and himself appointed regent with full sovereign powers. In this he had the support of his friends among the Whigs, notably their leader Charles James Fox, who were confident that if this happened the Younger Pitt, who had been in office for the past five years, would be ousted and they would take his place. But Pitt, who was a man of great abilities and enjoyed a majority in Parliament, was not easily shifted, and when it became necessary to introduce a Regency Bill nominating the Prince of Wales it was with considerably restricted powers. This gave rise to furious debates in Parliament as well as angry disagreements among the King's doctors, those appointed by the Prince ready to declare that the King was insane with no hope of recovery and those appointed by Pitt saying that the King's illness was basically physical and he would in time recover from it. Into this unseemly wrangle Charlotte could not avoid being drawn, feeling it her duty to protect her husband from the rapacity of his son and, as she put it, 'to keep the crown upon his head'. For the first time in her life she found herself in the midst of politics. By the terms of the Regency Bill she was put in charge of the King's treatment and general welfare and all household matters. This made her the King's principal guardian, and as such she came under great pressure from the Prince of Wales and his coterie to give them her backing, and when she did not do so she came in for vicious and scandalous abuse. The Prince's doctors snubbed her and humiliated her and tried to keep her as far away as possible from the King, and it was intimated that she was as mad as he was. A scurrilous and ludicrous rumour was also put abroad that she was having an affair with the asexual William Pitt. During these traumatic months it was seen that her hair turned from auburn to grey, and it must be doubtful that she would have survived without the love and support of her ladies-in-waiting, of Fanny Burney in particular.

Charlotte's agony began to come to an end when in February 1789 the King showed signs of improvement, and in the following month he was formally declared to have recovered and the doctors were withdrawn. This gave rise in the country to great scenes of rejoicing. The King had never been so popular. For the next twelve years he remained free of his malady, and he and Charlotte were able to resume their previous lifestyle, sometimes at the Queen's House and sometimes at Windsor or Kew with occasional visits to Weymouth for sea bathing (which Charlotte did not enjoy). But all was not well between them. George's derangement had put a strain on Charlotte from which she never recovered. Outwardly they lived together peaceably and contentedly, but there was an estrangement which was to become ever greater.

And these were turbulent years. A few months after George's recovery the French Revolution broke out, leading three years later to the execution of the French King and Queen and war with England which was to last with one short break for twenty-three years. Revolutionary ideas were abroad, especially as regards kings and queens, and George and Charlotte were often in danger of their lives. Riots and assassination attempts were not infrequent. These perils George and Charlotte, whose physical courage was never in doubt, could bear stoically; but there were troubles at home which were harder to bear.

Charlotte's seven surviving sons were bringing her little joy. It was, of course, always unlikely that these young men – full-blooded, lustful Hanoverians – would be content to follow the example of their father and mother in lives of virtuous domesticity. Siren voices beckoned and they were ready to respond. The Prince of Wales (the future George IV) led the way with reckless abandon. As soon as he was old enough he broke loose and gave himself over to a life of pleasure – drinking, gambling, seducing relentlessly. His association with his father's political enemies was maintained, and Carlton House, the gorgeous palace he built for himself, became a centre of Whiggery and dissipation. When he was twenty-two the Prince fell desperately in love with a Mrs Fitzherbert, a lady of grace and character but seven years his senior, twice widowed and a Roman Catholic. There was therefore no question of the King giving his consent to their marriage, which Mrs Fitzherbert as a strict Catholic insisted was the only liaison there could be between them. The Prince, however, wilful and self-ish, was not to be denied, and a secret marriage took place, orthodox in the eyes of the Roman Church but not of English law. Later great pressure was brought to bear on the Prince, as heir to the throne, to make a lawful marriage, but he refused to be fobbed off, like his father, with a plain German princess, and for a time he held out against any such idea. But in the end he had to give way owing to the size of his debts, which would only be paid off if he married. His hand being thus forced he then sulked and took no interest in whom his wife should be, leaving the choice entirely to his father who selected the Prince's first cousin, Princess Caroline of Brunswick. How disastrous this was will be seen in the next chapter.

The King had hopes that his second and favourite son, Frederick, Duke of York, would be different from his elder brother. He appointed him at the age of seven months Bishop of Osnaburgh, not with a career in the Church in mind but in order to keep the emoluments of that office within the family. Later he destined him for the army and, partly to keep him out of the clutches of his elder brother, sent him abroad for a military training in the formidable army of Frederick the Great, King of Prussia. But it was to no avail, for on his return to England Frederick at once joined the Carlton House set and combined with the Prince of Wales in tormenting his father and adapting to the Whig way of life. At the age of thirty-two he was appointed commander-in-chief of the British army and presided over an unsuccessful campaign against the French in Flanders where he incurred much ridicule.[8] Later he contracted a marriage (loveless and childless) with a princess of Prussia, but this did not change his ways, and he became involved in a serious scandal when one of his mistresses, Mrs Mary Anne Clarke, was found guilty of turning a dishonest penny by trading in army commissions. There was no evidence that the Duke had profited from her activities, but his relationship with her was brought to light in humiliating detail and he suffered the worst of all punishments – 'the indignation of the moral, the sympathy of his friends and the titters of the vulgar'.[9] It was necessary for him to resign his command. However, in spite of these somewhat flamboyant faults, unlike his elder brother he was a popular figure.

George and Charlotte's third son, William, Duke of Clarence, was not highly regarded by his parents, particularly his mother who once referred to his 'little, nonsensical, volatile head'. He had had a naval upbringing but could not be entrusted with high command. How for much of his life he cohabited with a well-known actress and begat a family of ten illegitimate children before becoming King William IV is told in a later chapter.

George III's fourth son, Edward, Duke of Kent, had spent most of his early life abroad in the army where he had acquired the reputation of a brutal martinet, sentencing soldiers under his command to hundreds of lashes for minor offences. During this time he had formed an attachment to a French-Canadian lady, Madame de St Laurent, with whom he lived contentedly for nearly thirty years. Then on the death of Princess Charlotte he took a legal wife, Princess Victoria of Leiningen, Madame de St Laurent agreeing compliantly to retire to a nunnery.[10] A few years later the Princess gave birth to the future Queen Victoria.

The fifth son of George III, Ernest, Duke of Cumberland, was a sinister character. Boorish, cold-hearted and of extreme right-wing political views, he inspired great hatred and mistrust. In 1810 at the age of thirty he was implicated in a flaming scandal when his valet was discovered with his throat cut. At the enquiry into his death the jury returned a verdict of suicide, but such was Ernest's reputation that it was put abroad that he had murdered him in order to cover up some sex scandal (possibly homosexuality) in his life. Four years later he was again in controversy when he married a German princess who had once been engaged to his youngest brother, Adolphus, Duke of Cambridge, and who had jilted him in favour of an obscure German prince, and in consequence was *persona non grata* in England. Queen Charlotte for one was outraged and refused to receive her at Court. On the accession of Queen Victoria Ernest became King of Hanover (where queens were barred), but in England he was always to remain an ogre, and there was great relief when Queen Victoria embarked on her large family and so removed him effectively from the line of succession to the throne.

Compared to their elders the two youngest sons of George and Charlotte caused their parents little worry. Augustus, Duke of Sussex, was an amiable, easy-going, liberal-minded individual and always well liked. His only fall from grace occurred when at the age of nineteen on a visit to Rome be fell in love with Lady Augusta Murray, a commoner and thus precluded from marriage by the provisions of the Royal Marriages Act. Augustus, however, wedded her secretly, although unlawfully, and they lived together for eight years until they separated, apparently quite agreeably.

Adolphus, Duke of Cambridge, the youngest son, was the only one not to cause his parents any anxiety or distress. For much of his life he served abroad in the Hanoverian army and remained unmarried until he was over forty when, on the death of Princess Charlotte, he, too, made haste to make a lawful marriage. He found himself a suitable German princess by whom he was to have three children who, but for the fecundity of Queen Victoria, might have been close in the line of accession to the throne.

Some comfort and support did come to George and Charlotte from their six daughters. Owing to the selfishness of their father, who had insisted on keeping them closeted at home in 'the nunnery' until they were into middle age, only three of them married and none had issue.

Great as had been Charlotte's troubles in middle age, her last years were even more distraught. In 1801 symptoms of the King's derangement returned – biliousness, aching limbs, non-stop talking and general incoherence. However, it was not certain that he was out of his mind, and he seemed to have recovered after a few weeks. But three years later the symptoms came back in a more pronounced form, and the agonizing decision rested with Charlotte whether or not to call in the doctors again with their terrible cures. 'How cutting it is to my feelings', she declared, 'to do that which if the King recovers may perhaps for ever make me forfeit his good opinions.' Already by then relations between the King and Queen had come under severe stress, as noted by one of their sons (the Duke of Kent) who wrote of 'a great coolness on the part of the King towards our mother'. Charlotte believed, rightly or wrongly (probably wrongly), that George's recovery from his first derangement had been due to the ministrations of a parson turned lunatic keeper, the Reverend Francis Willis, and his sons. In 1804 the King's derangement was still ambiguous, but on the advice of the Prime Minister, Henry Addington (himself the son of a doctor), the Willis family were called to administer their harsh strong-arm methods, and once again the King recovered. He enjoyed another six years of relative sanity until in 1811 he went completely and irretrievably out of his mind. By then he was both blind and deaf, and coherent communication with him was impossible. He withdrew into a world of his own imagination, conversing with angels, raising people from the dead and finding some solace playing on his flute and harpsichord. For the last eight years of his life Charlotte had no contact with him.

In old age Charlotte became a tragic and forlorn figure. Someone close to her described her as 'an old, sick, frightened woman'. She had never been a beauty, but now she became positively ugly. As was unkindly remarked of her: 'the bloom of her ugliness is going off'. She also became inordinately fat. But she deserved well of the British people. She had had much to put up with. In exceptionally difficult circumstances she had remained placid and level-headed and had offered her husband loyal support. In a lax and licentious age she had given society an example of which it was sorely in need. Her behaviour never gave rise to the slightest breath of scandal. Early in her marriage she had declared: 'My anxious desire is to preserve society upon a respectable footing which it has ever been my own and the King's study to maintain.' Plain and unprepossessing though she might have been, such influence as she had was benign.

4

CAROLINE OF BRUNSWICK
Wife of George IV

No British queen has come in for such calumny and been steeped in such scandal as Caroline Amelia Elizabeth, Princess of Brunswick. Her husband, George IV, described her once as 'the vilest wretch the world ever was cursed with', while she regarded him with equal contempt and did all she could to humiliate and infuriate him. Her behaviour at times passed all bounds – disporting herself vulgarly and brazenly, flirting shamelessly with disreputable lovers and being arraigned before the whole House of Lords on charges of adultery. George IV, unworthy king though he may have been, hardly deserved such a wife.

In the eighteenth century royal marriages were seldom romantic, but none was as cynical and heartless as that between George and Caroline. In 1794 the affairs of the Prince were in deep crisis. Nine years before he had been married secretly to Mrs Maria Fitzherbert, a Roman Catholic lady, twice widowed and six years his senior. Secrecy had been necessary as the marriage had not received the royal assent (as required by the Royal Marriages Act of 1777) and so was unlawful; but as it had been solemnized by a Roman Catholic priest it was regarded by Mrs Fitzherbert as sacred and binding. At the time the Prince was passionately in love with her, but his passions were always transitory and by 1794 he had become deeply enamoured of another lady, the Countess of Jersey, also older than himself and by then a mother of nine children and a grandmother.[1] The Prince at the time was thirty-two, and it had been expected of him for some time that he would make a lawful marriage, settle down to a respectable married life and produce an heir to the throne. This was especially the wish of his father who himself had had fifteen children but, as yet, no legitimate grandchildren. But the Prince, in thrall to Lady Jersey, was unwilling to comply. By temperament he was unsuited to family domesticity, his lifestyle being splendid, extravagant and entirely selfish. However, his hand was to be forced. He had incurred immense debts – some £600,000, equivalent to about £30 million today – and these were ever increasing as he continued to live beyond his means and pay increasing interest charges. A crisis was reached as creditors closed in and tradesmen refused to serve him except for ready money. In this situation the only person who could rescue him was his father, but he had made it clear that he could expect no help from him unless he were to marry a suitable wife and live a reformed life. Such a prospect daunted the Prince, but in the circumstances he felt he had no alternative but to acquiesce. Having taken this decision he then behaved in a way that was foolish and contemptible – sulking, holding aloof and showing no interest in the choice of a bride which he left entirely to his father, who chose disastrously.

There were many reasons why Princess Caroline of Brunswick was unsuitable. In the first place she was close in consanguinity, being the daughter of George III's elder sister and so the Prince's first cousin. Her family also seemed ill-fated and none too respectable. Her father, a brave soldier and hoary old reactionary, lived apart from her mother, a light-hearted gossip given to scandal and scatological stories. Two of her brothers were insane, and her sister had disappeared in mysterious circumstances in Russia. Caroline's own reputation was not untarnished. In 1794 she was twenty-seven and past the first bloom of beauty, which had never been great, and stories abounded of impropriety and loose behaviour, sometimes with men of low degree. If the Prince had been at all circumspect he would have given her a wide berth, but he seems not to have cared, his attitude being that, as his heart would always be elsewhere, one German princess was as good (or bad) as another. As his financial straits were becoming ever more desperate he was anxious that the matter should be settled quickly. So a diplomat of high standing, Lord Malmesbury, was dispatched to Brunswick to make formal application for the Princess's hand and, if this was accepted, to escort her back to England.

On arrival in Brunswick Malmesbury could not but be alarmed by what he found there: the Duke was surly and reclusive, taking a gloomy view of his daughter, the Duchess voluble and eccentric and Caroline herself unseemly and gauche. It was clear to him at once that she was not the ideal wife for the Prince of Wales. Glaring as were the Prince's faults, he was a man of elegance and charm, his taste in literature and the arts was of the highest quality, and his manners and deportment were impeccable. It was not without reason that he had become known as 'the first gentleman in Europe'. Malmesbury could not imagine him married to the uncouth Caroline. Later he was much blamed for keeping his fears to himself and not warning the Prince of what awaited him; but he maintained that his mission was solely to offer the Prince's hand in marriage and did not include passing judgement. However, he did record his impressions in his diary, and these showed deep unease. The entries included a detailed and candid description of Caroline's person: 'pretty face – not expressive of softness – her figure not graceful – fine eyes – good hand – tolerable teeth but going – fair hair and light eyebrows, good bust – short, with what the French call "des épaules impertinentes"'. Not an attractive proposition, and he could not fail to notice other drawbacks: 'lack of poise and conversation that was usually vulgar and trivial'. Nevertheless, he did not entirely despair of her. He found that she was also 'well meaning and well disposed and had good humour and a good nature'. He also found that when advice was kindly and tactfully proffered, she was ready to listen to it. He was hopeful that in time something might be made of her.

For the refining of the Princess he had more time than expected as, owing to the invading armies of Napoleon, there was a delay of over a month before they could set out for England. During this time Malmesbury went to work, gently intimating to Caroline how she should behave: to think before speaking, not to ask personal questions and not to be too free in expressing opinions of people and things. He recommended that for her first six months in England she should be totally silent. Advice and words of warning poured in on the unfortunate Princess from all quarters, including a letter from her future father-in-law (and uncle) King George III, expressing the hope that when she arrived in England 'she would not be too vivacious and would be prepared to lead a life both sedentary and retired', advice which must have dismayed her as nothing could have been less in her nature. There also came from England a letter from a total stranger relating in detail the present state of play between the Prince of Wales and Lady Jersey which needed all Malmesbury's diplomatic skills to explain away. Altogether it would not have been surprising if Caroline had wanted to call the whole venture off. But this did not occur to her, and when eventually the party set out she was in the highest spirits and longing to meet her husband whom she felt sure she would adore.

The journey to England was hard and quite dangerous. The winter was exceptionally severe, and Malmesbury wrote that the cold was more intense than anything he had encountered in Russia. Because of the dangers from Napoleon's armies there were frequent delays and setbacks, and contact with England was often impossible. During this ordeal Caroline showed great courage; whatever the frustrations and discomforts it was noted that she was always in good humour. The same could not be said of her mother, who had agreed to accompany the party as far as the Dutch coast. She was the most fractious of travellers, always complaining and wanting to turn back. Even in good moods she caused embarrassment with her foolish chatter and vulgar humour. Amid all these tribulations Malmesbury remained calm and in control and took the opportunity to give Caroline further lessons on how she ought to behave in England. He warned her that, whatever her husband did, she must make no scenes or show any jealousy. At the same time he let her know that by an ancient law if she, the Princess of Wales, had an affair with another man, both of them would be guilty of high treason, which was still punishable by death. 'This', wrote Malmesbury, 'seemed to startle her.'

There was a further matter of a more intimate nature which Malmesbury felt obliged to mention. It was borne in on him that Caroline's personal hygiene was not what it should be: she was unclean and malodorous, and her underclothing was soiled and threadbare. Bearing in mind the immaculate and beautifully perfumed ladies who attended the Prince of Wales, Malmesbury knew how repelled he would be by such seaminess, and he impressed on one of the ladies of her household how essential it was that the Princess should be cleaned up.

Eventually, after a journey of fourteen weeks, the party reached the Dutch coast and was taken on board a British man-of-war, but Caroline's troubles were not over, for when the ship reached Greenwich there was no welcoming party to greet her. It arrived an hour later, delayed apparently by the machinations of Lady Jersey who, incredibly, had been appointed one of Caroline's ladies-in-waiting. It soon became evident she was bent on trouble. For her own devious reasons she had commended Caroline as the Prince's bride, as in order to protect her own position it suited her book that his wife should be unattractive and graceless. Once the matter had been arranged, however, she changed her tune and did all she could to find fault with the Princess and to exacerbate relations with her husband. On arrival at Greenwich she immediately started throwing her weight about, insisting that Caroline's clothes were unsuitable for her entry into London and that she was looking seedy and needed more rouge on her face (an excessive amount, according to some observers). Other troubles, too, she stirred up and, not surprisingly, Caroline took a strong dislike to her and showed it.

But the contretemps in Greenwich was as nothing to what awaited the Princess in London. Her introduction to her future husband could not have been more disastrous. It seems to have been a case of spontaneous aversion. When she was presented to him the Prince reeled and called for brandy and then withdrew abruptly. Not unnaturally Caroline was aghast at such treatment. 'Mon Dieu!' she exclaimed. 'Is the Prince always like that? I find him very fat and nothing like as handsome as his portrait.' At dinner that evening the situation was tense. The Prince had eyes only for Lady Jersey and, as always in an unfriendly atmosphere, Caroline was at her worst. Malmesbury was appalled by her behaviour: 'it was flippant, rattling, affected raillery and wit, and throwing out coarse, vulgar hints about Lady Jersey'. It seemed that all his wise advice had been to no avail. The wedding was due to take place three days later and had to go ahead. It was a bizarre occasion. The Prince was strongly fortified by brandy and according to one observer 'looking like death and full of confusion'; the Princess, on the other hand, was apparently untroubled, cheerful and chatty.[2]

That night a prurient crowd gathered outside Carlton House to watch the lights go out in the nuptial chamber and to speculate on what was going on inside. In their wildest dreams they could not have guessed. Later the Princess was to reveal that the Prince, then almost totally intoxicated, lay for most of the night in the fender. However, he seems to have rallied, as somehow the marriage was consummated and a child was conceived.

Unpropitious as was the marriage ceremony, relations between the Prince and Princess for some time afterwards were reasonably tranquil. Certainly there was no love between them, but they were able to maintain the façade of a happy marriage, and this was enhanced by the news of Caroline's pregnancy and the birth in January 1796 of a daughter, Princess Charlotte. But the situation could not last. The antagonism between them was too great. Only three days after the birth of his daughter the Prince of Wales, fancying that he was dying, drew up a long and detailed will, brutal in its frankness. This showed that his unstable emotions were moving away from Lady Jersey back to his first love, Maria Fitzherbert, described extravagantly as 'the wife of my heart and soul', 'my second self', 'my dearest angel'. To her he bequeathed all his estates, property and monies (not as generous as it sounded, as most of these would be pre-empted by creditors). As for his legal wife, referred to here as 'she who is called the Princess of Wales', she was specifically excluded from all care and responsibility for their daughter's upbringing; she was to give up all the jewellery he had given her and for herself was left one shilling.

Already by then the Prince's dislike of Caroline was turning into a frenzied hatred; her uncouth ways and vulgar chatter disgusted him. He could not bear to be alone with her or to eat with her. 'I had rather see toads and vipers crawling over my victuals than sit at the same table with her,' he wrote. In his loathing he became unbalanced, describing her in a letter as 'a fiend, an infamous wretch and the most unprincipled and unfeeling person of her sex'. Yet at the same time as hating her and keeping away from her he sought to control her life: she must only see people of whom he approved; she must not go on visits in the country on her own; her household must be regulated as he thought fit. Such unreasonable and brutal treatment astounded many people, including some of his friends. Lord Melbourne, the wisest and most broad-minded of men, later told Queen Victoria when he was her Prime Minister: 'He cared as much about what she did as if he had been very much in love with her . . . His conduct to her was quite madness.' Madness it was, for at the same time the Prince could declare in all solemnity: 'I can on my sacred oath affirm that I have neither used an expression nor acted in a manner that can ever savour of the smallest degree of harshness.'

For the Prince of Wales his marriage had, indeed, been a disaster. It had brought him not only unhappiness but even greater unpopularity, as well as much ribaldry and abuse. It had also failed in its main purpose, which was to bring relief to his desperate finances. He had hoped that when he sacrificed himself to a correct, loveless marriage Parliament would respond with a generous settlement, but Parliament had proved tight-fisted, laying down strict conditions on which money was granted, so that he found himself little better off than before.

Caroline's plight, too, was miserable. She had expected that as Princess of Wales she would have a dazzling and exciting life, surrounded by brilliant people and with a loving, or at least affectionate, husband who would treat her kindly with the honour that was her due. Instead she found herself cooped up with her ladies-in-waiting – middle-aged, fusty and in the case of Lady Jersey snide and hostile, hemmed in by petty restrictions and formalities, treated with coolness by the female members of the Royal Family and only ever seeing her husband when he was the worse for drink and in boorish and truculent mood.

To someone as wilful and high-spirited as Caroline such an existence was intolerable, and three months after the birth of Princess Charlotte she rebelled against it. As she and the Prince had no verbal communication, she wrote him a letter in which she asked to be relieved of the company of Lady Jersey, to whom she referred bluntly as 'your mistress'. This led to a long and acrimonious correspondence between them, the Prince pompous and self-righteous, the Princess querulous and demanding. The Prince wrote to her: 'Our inclinations are not in our power, nor should either of us be held answerable to the other because nature has not made us suitable to each other. Tranquil and comfortable society is, however, in our power; let our intercourse be restricted to that.' She replied: 'Since I have been in this house you have treated me neither as your wife, nor as the mother of your child, nor as the Princess of Wales: and I tell you that from this moment I shall have nothing more to say and that I regard myself as being no longer subject to your orders or to your rules.'

Soon afterwards the Prince asked his father for a legal separation from Caroline, but this George III would not allow. 'You seem to look on your disunion with the Princess', he wrote, 'as merely of a private nature, and totally put out of sight that as Heir Apparent of the Crown your marriage is a public act wherein the Kingdom is concerned.' If a legal separation was barred, greater apartness was clearly necessary. By 1797 Caroline could put up with life at Court no longer and in August of that year she took herself off to live in a house near Blackheath, then a picturesque village five miles out of London. She was to live there for the next sixteen years.

Of the many ways in which Caroline infuriated her husband, nothing baited him more acutely than her ability to attract popularity. To the people, particularly Londoners, she became a wronged heroine cruelly used by a selfish and insensitive husband; while at the same time he was being ever more reviled, so much so that at times it was unsafe for him to venture into the London streets. In his fury the Prince became obsessed with the idea that Caroline was deliberately stirring up public opinion against him. When on one occasion she visited the opera and was given a rapturous reception he was convinced that this had been specially orchestrated as an insult to him. And when in a rancorous and hard-fought by-election in Westminster the Whig leader, Charles James Fox, defeated the government candidate and Caroline joined in the general rejoicings, he solemnly warned his father that she was plotting with revolutionaries to overthrow the monarchy. Certainly Caroline did have democratic tendencies and was always ready to play to the gallery in an uninhibited way, but she was no revolutionary, nor was she able to sustain convincingly the role of a martyred princess. She was not cut out for the part; she was too raucous and tactless, too rough and ready, so completely without charisma. Nevertheless, at her new home in Blackheath her standing as Princess of Wales ensured that she was able to attract distinguished visitors. At first these included respectable members of society, including members of the Royal Family, but later the nature of her parties, which tended to be unruly, put off all but the raffish and the self-seeking. Still, she had some unexpected admirers including the Tory leader Spencer Perceval and the brilliant and up-and-coming young politician George Canning.[3] She also attracted the roving eye of that stalwart old warhorse Admiral Sir Sidney Smith.[4] It was not long before a major scandal erupted.

For a time in Blackheath Caroline occupied herself reasonably happily in rural and domestic pursuits such as gardening, painting and sewing, but it was unlikely that these would satisfy her for long. Her craving for drama and excitement was too great, and her behaviour became ever more eccentric. She longed to love and be loved, and in her unhappiness withdrew into a world of fantasy haunted by demon lovers and heroic escapades. But it was also haunted by small children whom she adored and loved to have about her. Her natural daughter, Charlotte, had been removed from her care at an early age into the safe keeping of her grandfather and grandmother at Windsor, which might have been a great sadness to her but in fact was not, as she liked to treat children in a way that would have been unsuitable for a princess. She looked on children in the same way as some people look on puppies or kittens – cosseting them and making toys of them. As this was not possible with her own child she consoled herself by adopting children from destitute families in the neighbourhood. At first these were housed at a distance in separate accommodation and only allowed into Caroline's presence when she was in the mood for them, but things got out of hand.

In 1802, five years after Caroline had arrived in Blackheath, a Mrs Austin arrived on her doorstep with a baby, William, whom she was desperate to have adopted. As was usually the case Caroline agreed to take him under her wing, and all might have been well if he had been assigned to the orphanage with the other children and treated as one of them. But almost at once Caroline became besotted by the child, keeping him with her at all times of day and night and proudly displaying him on all occasions and making him play up. She also insisted on attending to all his basic needs herself and not in private, so that fastidious guests might arrive in her drawing-room to find it festooned with nappies and other babyware. Even this behaviour, although startling, might have been harmless, but it did not stop there. Caroline came to believe that Willikin, as she called him, was her natural son. This she first confided to a neighbour of hers at Blackheath, a Lady Douglas, with whom for a time she had formed a passionate friendship. But this had ended in tears and recriminations when Caroline came to believe that Lady Douglas was spreading scandalous gossip about her. Their quarrel became intense, and Lady Douglas in retaliation informed the Duke of Sussex, a younger brother of the Prince of Wales, of Caroline's affairs with various men, notably Sir Sidney Smith, as well as her avowal that she was the mother of Willikin. The Duke of Sussex lost no time in apprising his elder brother of these stories. At first the Prince was inclined to take them lightly, but when it was impressed upon him that Caroline was also letting it be known that he, the Prince of Wales, was Willikin's father, the matter became more serious, as in that case Willikin would be heir apparent to the throne of England. This could not be allowed to pass, and King George III was persuaded that it was necessary to set up what became known as the 'Delicate Investigation' into the behaviour of the Princess of Wales. This was conducted in 10 Downing Street by the Prime Minister, Lord Grenville, and three other eminent noblemen. One of the first witnesses to be examined was Lady Douglas, who was venomous about her old friend, describing her 'loose and vulgar' talk and her absurd fantasy about being pregnant. Most of the other witnesses were domestic servants who recounted backstairs gossip of 'strange goings-on' and mysterious figures in the corridors and the Princess in compromising situations. None could say for certain that she had ever been pregnant, and her doctor was prepared to swear that she never had been. In the end the members of the Commission pronounced definitely that Willikin was not Caroline's son but that of an unemployed Deptford dock labourer and his wife. They also said that charges of adultery were unproved but added that the Princess had for some years been behaving 'in an unseemly and improper manner such as must, especially considering her exalted rank and station, necessarily give rise to very unfavourable interpretation'. In spite of this sharp backhander, however, Caroline considered that she had been vindicated and lost no time in writing to George III asking to be received once again at Court, but the King demurred, saying that the whole story had not yet been told and that Caroline had been guilty of 'so much levity and profligacy'. Up to then he, of all members of the Royal Family, had been her main devotee. Indeed on occasions his attentions to her had been excessive and embarrassing, but now his favour was withheld, causing her great anguish.[5] She felt she was being treated unjustly. The Commission had cleared her of all impropriety but the Court, notably Queen Charlotte and her four unmarried daughters, continued to ignore her and keep her at a distance.

Once again, when unhappy and frustrated, Caroline took refuge in fantasy. She put it about that Willikin, far from being of humble birth, was the illegitimate son of a Prussian prince who had been smuggled into the country clandestinely and swapped with William Austin. She also deluded herself that she was a gifted musician and, to the great discomfort of her ladies-in-waiting, spent hours pounding the piano and singing discordantly. At the same time she took into her household two stray Italian musicians, father and son, with whom she not only made music but also treated with great familiarity.[6]

In 1806 the pattern of Caroline's life was temporarily disturbed when her mother arrived in England, a refugee from the invading armies of Napoleon which had overrun Brunswick following a battle in which Caroline's father, at the age of seventy-two, had been killed leading his troops into battle. The Duchess, who had been lucky to escape, was treated with kindness and generosity by her brother, George III, and with some consideration by her daughter, although relations between them were never cordial, each regarding the other as crude and slightly mad.

In 1811 came a turning point in Caroline's life. George III was finally declared by the doctors to be incurably mad, and the Prince of Wales was appointed Prince Regent. This meant that his powers and influence were greatly extended and Caroline's position became more insecure. People became wary of accepting her invitations, and one-time friends kept their distance. At the same time the Prince Regent did all he could to make life difficult for her and reopened the 'Delicate Investigation' to look into allegations of her immoral behaviour. However, this brought him no joy as the Commission reported again that there was no evidence of serious misconduct by the Princess. Flirtatious she had certainly been but not, as far as could be ascertained, adulterous. Once more Caroline regarded herself as completely vindicated and determined to fight back, in her own words 'teasing and worrying the Royal Family by endlessly making trouble'. For this her main opportunities lay in her relations with her daughter Charlotte.

As has been seen, Charlotte had been removed from her mother's care at an early age. Visits between them had then been strictly regulated and supervised, and Caroline had had no part in her daughter's upbringing and education, which did not distress her unduly as there was no great warmth between mother and daughter; none the less both, for their own ends, made a great grievance of it.

The unfortunate Charlotte had had a dismal childhood, closeted at Windsor with her grandparents and four maiden aunts and overshadowed by a somewhat harsh and unaffectionate father. At an early age she had been subjected to a battery of governesses and tutors (led by a bishop), few of whom she had found sympathetic. She was a lively and intelligent child but no great scholar and found too much education oppressive. Her father, although in no strong position himself to take such a stance, was particularly concerned about her morals and was anxious, not without reason, that on her visits to her mother she would not meet people who would have a pernicious influence on her, so he insisted on vetting everyone she would meet there. When she came of age at eighteen Charlotte expected that she would at last be rid of governesses and tutors and have an establishment of her own with ladies-in-waiting and other attendants, but her father took a hard line and laid it down that this would not happen until she married. On the question of her marriage her parents were, as always, divided. Her father was keen for it to happen soon as she would then be less trouble and probably out of the country, which he would welcome as, like all Hanoverians, he tended to feel resentment towards his heir apparent. Caroline, on the other hand, was against an early marriage as she would then lose one of her main means of making trouble.

When the Prince of Wales became Regent it was generally expected that he would dismiss the Tory government favoured by his father and give office to the Whigs with whom he had once been very friendly; but when it came to the point he felt unable to do so mainly because of the Whigs' opposition to the war against Napoleon. In consequence a group of Whigs became bitterly opposed to the Regent and sought every opportunity to humiliate him, and nowhere were they able to do this more successfully than in his treatment of his wife. The leader of this group was a shrewd, unscrupulous, ambitious lawyer, Henry Brougham, who constituted himself as Caroline's protector and legal adviser. The relationship between them was uneasy as both were fully aware that they were being 'used' by the other for ulterior purposes. Nevertheless they made a formidable combination and caused the Prince and his ministers endless annoyance. Caroline was of no great intelligence, but she had her wits about her and one thing she had been careful to do in recent years was to preserve all written correspondence between herself and her husband and other members of the Royal Family. Soon after the setting up of the regency she felt the time had come to make use of these documents and with the adroit help of Brougham compiled a formidable indictment of the heartless way she had been treated. In the first instance a letter was sent to the Regent, who refused to read it or even acknowledge it; then, on Brougham's advice, it was sent to the editor of a well-known Whig newspaper, the *Morning Chronicle*, who was only too ready to publish it. As might be expected it caused a furore. In some quarters, especially among those unacquainted with the Princess, there was furious indignation at the way she had been treated. 'A truly virtuous and illustrious female' was how she was described in one newspaper. 'A pure and innocent Princess,' wrote another. But not everyone believed in her righteousness. There were those who had seen her close to who thought otherwise. 'If not mad, a very worthless woman,' declared Lord Holland.

The conflict between Prince and Princess was to last several years and at times became intense, but it was evident that the odds against the Princess were too great. She may have been supported by vitriolic Whig politicians on the make and a London mob that was always ready to rise on her behalf, but she was fighting a losing battle. The Prince had behind him all the might and majesty of royalty, the executive power and the fount of great honours and high places. Moreover his grace and charm (irresistible when he chose to exert them) contrasted starkly with Caroline's *gaucherie*. Caroline became aware of her growing isolation as people kept their distance and found excuses for declining her invitations. At the same time her behaviour became increasingly odd. She was obsessed with the idea that she was surrounded by spies and informers, and she quarrelled, sometimes violently, with servants and courtiers.

She dallied recklessly with her Italian musicians and other peculiar characters. She also took to a form of witchcraft and spent time sticking pins into wax images of her husband. In addition she was beset by misfortunes. She fell heavily into debt and had to move from Blackheath into a house in Bayswater which she never liked. Altogether life in England was becoming intolerable, and her thoughts began to turn to a life abroad – a freer, more exhilarating life where she would be less hemmed in and less surrounded by hostility.

She might have been restrained from this by feelings for her daughter, but they had never been intimate and of late had been growing further apart, Charlotte disapproving of her mother's strange ways and Caroline thinking Charlotte too submissive to her father and not supportive enough of herself. In any case she was now of an age to be married, in which event they would have even less need of each other. Charlotte was eager for this to happen; her life in England was tedious and confined, and she longed to be set free. As was the custom, her father took the choice of a marriage partner on himself, and as he cast his eye round Europe after the downfall of Napoleon it seemed to him that a likely candidate was the Hereditary Prince of Orange, who would in time become King of the Netherlands. Reports of him reaching Charlotte were somewhat mixed. He was said to be 'amiable and sensible' but also 'excessively plain and thin as a needle'. She was not put off and at their first meeting took a liking to him, and before she quite knew where she was she found herself engaged to him. But almost at once she had second thoughts, especially when she learned that she would have to spend half the year in Holland. She was also influenced by the discovery that the Prince was a heavy drinker and could not hold his liquor.[7] Then she fell in love with someone else – Prince August of Prussia. August was certainly good-looking and had a reputation for bravery on the battlefield, but in love he was fickle and his affair with Charlotte, as with others before, came to nothing.

The reaction of the Prince Regent to Charlotte breaking off her engagement to the Prince of Orange was heavy-handed. He could not compel her to marry him, but he could apply pressure, and this became so oppressive that Charlotte was driven to run away from home and take refuge with her mother. This put Caroline in a difficult situation. At one time she would have welcomed an opportunity to stir things up between father and daughter, but she had just taken the decision, as yet secretly, to live abroad, and at that moment did not want her daughter on her hands. She therefore supported Brougham and other advisers who urged Charlotte to return home and make some sort of peace with her father.

When Caroline made known her plans for leaving England there were those who tried hard to dissuade her. Surprisingly Charlotte was upset because, although she and her mother rarely saw each other, she felt she could rely on her for support in clashes with her father; without her the Prince Regent was liable to be more autocratic and overbearing. Strong opposition, too, came from Brougham and the Whigs because they had no wish to lose their most effective weapon in tormenting the Regent and his Tory ministers. They also feared that if Caroline was living abroad she would let herself go even more uninhibitedly than in England and provide her husband with grounds for divorce, in which case he might marry again and sire a son who would then supplant Charlotte as heir to the throne. But Caroline was not to be put off. She had made up her mind and was looking forward to a colourful and extrovert life far away from the stuffiness and persecutions of life in England. The one person who was in entire agreement with her decision was her husband, who could not have been more pleased at the thought of her being in distant lands and was ready to facilitate her departure in any way he could.

Thus on 9 August 1814, after nineteen years of troubled life in England, Caroline and various attendants (including Willikin, now a somewhat vacuous teenager) embarked on a British warship in Worthing for pastures new. For the next six years she led a wandering life, always on the move, indulging every whim, looking for pleasure in any quarter. Etiquette and formality were kept to a minimum, dignity was thrown to the winds, and no heed was given to what people might think; they had to accept her on her own terms.

Her first objective was Brunswick, where she was warmly welcomed by her brother the Duke (soon to be killed at Waterloo). She then made her way to Switzerland, where she met up with the ex-Empress Marie-Louise, the second wife of Napoleon. She had little in common with the stately, humourless Austrian Princess, but they struck up a friendship of a sort and sang duets together – to the dismay of their attendants as neither had much idea of how to sing in tune.

Caroline and her entourage then set off across the Simplon Pass into Italy. The hardships and dangers of this journey were intense, but Caroline was undaunted. Rivers in spate, thunderstorms and dirt-tracked roads held no terrors for her, and, although she was forty-six, she faced up to rickety transport, nights in the open and rat-infested inns without complaint. Once in Italy she soon found enchantment. The verve and brio of Italian life were much to her taste. In this ambience her behaviour became ever more unbridled. In Genoa she drove through the streets in a mother-of-pearl phaeton, resembling a seashell, drawn by two piebald horses driven by a child dressed like an operatic cherub in flesh-coloured tights. And at parties she dressed, or rather half dressed, in whatever took her fancy and danced uninhibitedly with all and sundry regardless of rank or decorum. Foreigners were amazed by her ways, and English people were scandalized. The aristocratic Countess of Bessborough (sister of Georgiana, Duchess of Devonshire) could not believe what she was seeing at a ball given in her honour:

> a short, very fat, elderly woman with an extremely red face in a girl's
> white frock-looking dress, but with shoulders, back and neck quite
> low (disgustingly so), down to the middle of her stomach; very black

hair and eyebrows, which gave her a fierce look, and a wreath of light
pink roses on her head . . . I was staring at her from the oddity of her
appearance, when suddenly she nodded and smiled at me, and not
recollecting her, I was convinced she was mad till William [Lord William
Bentinck] pushed me, saying, 'Do you not see the Princess of Wales
nodding to you?'

Thus at balls, masquerades and assemblies throughout southern Europe
Caroline disported herself – bewigged, painted, often topless and always
unashamed.

In March 1815, seven months after Caroline had left England, all Europe
was set alight by the news that Napoleon had escaped from Elba and was
gathering an army and advancing on Paris. This sent most English tourists
on the Continent scurrying back home but not Caroline. At the time she was
in the Kingdom of Naples, then ruled by Joachim Murat, one of Napoleon's
marshals and his brother-in-law. He had given Caroline a magnificent reception and had been carrying on a mild flirtation with her, but on the news of
Napoleon's escape he had at once pledged his support to his old chief, and it
was necessary for Caroline to make a hurried exit into the neighbouring
Papal States where she was paid the signal honour of a visit to her house in
Genoa by Pope Pius VII, on whom she seems to have made a marked impression as in later days he was to be one of her strong protagonists.[8] From Genoa
she proceeded to Sicily where the rugged country made a great impression
on her, and she was able to pursue a growing interest in visiting classical sites.

By now Caroline's retinue had altered in character. When she left England
she had been accompanied by a respectable group of attendants including a
distinguished archaeologist, but most of these had fallen by the wayside, unable
to keep up with her pace and style. Their places had been taken by a motley
crew of French, Italian and Arab personnel of dubious reputation and with their
eyes fixed firmly on the main chance. In due course one of these superseded
all others. Bartolomeo Pergami was fourteen years younger than Caroline, with
swarthy good looks and flamboyant braggadocio. Although alleged to be of
aristocratic descent he had at first been taken into the Princess's household in
the humble capacity of a courier; but he was soon promoted. He became first
valet de place and then chamberlain in charge of all the Princess's business affairs;
and soon afterwards it became evident that she was besotted with him and could
refuse him nothing. In due course through her influence he was invested with
a number of nebulous titles – Baron della Franconia, Knight of Malta and Grand
Master of the Order of St Caroline of Jerusalem. He saw to it that his next of
kin were also well provided for, places being found in the Princess's household
for his mother, two brothers and two sisters, while Caroline doted on his baby
daughter and treated her as though she were her own. The only person omit-
ted from this flow of favours was his dim and self-effacing wife.

With this group in attendance Caroline set out in 1816 on a Mediterranean odyssey. Her first port of call was Tunis, where she was received in great state by the Bey. Sumptuous banquets were provided for her, as also were archaeological expeditions to the ruins of Carthage. She was also allowed the unusual privilege of being admitted into the Bey's seraglio where she met his three immense wives (one so large she could not get out of her room). A potentially critical situation arose when British warships arrived in Tunis with the object of freeing all slaves and threatening to bombard the city if this was not carried out. However, the danger was averted when the Bey, while outwardly refusing to yield to force, was ready to agree to a request from Caroline that the slaves, or some of them, should be released.

When they left Tunis the Princess and her party set out on a pilgrimage to the Holy Land. The voyage there was hazardous – through pirate-infested seas and sudden squalls which might result in shipwreck. But they arrived eventually, and Caroline was given a tumultuous welcome. In the following weeks she showed herself again to be a hardy and indefatigable traveller. Religion had had no great part in her upbringing, but now she became absorbed by the Gospel story. With an entourage which with camp followers at times numbered over two hundred she visited Nazareth and Bethlehem ('a wretched habitation indeed'), and when she entered Jerusalem she insisted on riding on a donkey rather than in the comfortable litter which had been provided for her. Later she followed the Via Dolorosa to Calvary and made a long detour to collect water from the Jordan to take home with her and would have liked to go on to Egypt but was persuaded, with difficulty, that this was too dangerous. Before leaving Jerusalem she instituted the Order of St Caroline with Pergami as its Grand Master and William Austin an Honoured Knight.

On her return to Italy after another parlous voyage Caroline found herself confronted with an array of dangers and difficulties.[9] Prominent among these were financial troubles. Egged on by Pergami, she had been spending money recklessly. The Mediterranean excursion had cost a fortune, and before leaving she had acquired a large villa on Lake Como, Villa d'Este, which she had ordered to be enlarged and embellished. While she was away the cost of this had escalated out of control and she found herself heavily in debt. Like her husband, Caroline had little idea of economy, and her debts continued to grow.[10] She did decide, however, that she must sell Villa d'Este and move to another villa on the Adriatic coast, the Villa Cassiella in Pesaro.

Soon afterwards she was faced with a grievous family tragedy, the death of her daughter Charlotte. Since leaving England she had had no correspondence with her at all, only the information formally delivered that she was to be married to Prince Leopold of Saxe-Coburg. But the news of her death in childbirth in November 1817 hit Caroline hard. Apart from the personal loss, her death meant the end of Caroline's dream of becoming the progenitor of a line of English sovereigns. It also portended, as she had no doubt, a hardening in the Prince Regent's attitude towards her. Until then consideration for his daughter had restrained him, but now that she was dead he would be more determined than ever to divorce Caroline and maybe marry again. There were soon signs of this determination. At an early stage in her meanderings the Prince had set on Caroline's trail a Baron Ompteda, Hanoverian representative at the Vatican, who had spent much time snooping around Villa d'Este on the look-out for scandal, and in due course had reported back to the Prince of his wife's 'very incongruous conduct which had created general astonishment and justly merited indignation'.

From another source came word of 'her indecorous public and private conduct and her glaring very intimate connection with a certain Pergami'. On receipt of these reports and after consultation with his legal advisers the Prince became convinced that he had grounds for divorce, and in 1818 he set up a commission of three (later known as the 'Milan Commission') to investigate his wife's conduct. The commission arrived in Italy in July and immediately set about examining a mixed bag of witnesses – domestic servants, innkeepers, sailors, gardeners – who might be able to help them in their investigation. In this they did not always have full cooperation, as, for all her quirks, Caroline inspired some loyalty and respect among her staff; they might have been more forthcoming if the commissioners had offered them a bribe, but this they had been specifically forbidden to do. Nevertheless tongues did wag and sleazy stories were told, and it soon became apparent that there was a body of evidence of 'a continued adulterous intercourse between the Princess and Pergami'.[11]

With all this evidence to hand, the Prince, and more particularly his ministers, were none the less hesitant about instituting divorce proceedings. For a divorce to be granted clear proof of adultery would have to be established, and this might be difficult: most of the witnesses were of low quality, could speak no English and were unlikely to stand up to interrogation in a court of law. A further consideration, of which the government was very much aware, was that in spite of her peccadilloes the Princess was still regarded in England as a heroine, and proceedings against her would be liable to stir up popular feeling which might constitute a threat to public order. And there was another factor which could not be overlooked: a close investigation into Caroline's conduct might provoke an equally close one into her husband's, which was far from unimpeachable. The last thing he wanted was a spotlight to be turned on his secret marriage to Mrs Fitzherbert and his subsequent relations with Lady Jersey and Lady Conyngham.

In view of this situation there seemed much to be said for a deal between the Prince and his ministers on the one hand and the Princess and her Whig advisers on the other. After a visit to the Princess in France, James Brougham (brother of Henry; see p. 58) was convinced that she had no wish to return to England and no ambition to be queen. All she wanted was enough money to continue leading the rambling, irregular life she liked so well. Henry returned to England with little doubt that she could be 'bought off' and that this was the best solution to the problem. Unfortunately it was to prove impossible. At heart the Regent would settle for nothing less than divorce so that he would at last be rid of 'his hated wife', while Caroline for her part was unwilling to be exposed publicly as an adulteress.

In January 1820, after years of dementia, George III at last died, the Regent at fifty-seven became king, and Caroline, five years younger, found herself queen. Her situation for a queen consort was bizarre: of no settled abode, heavily in debt, surrounded by a ragbag court and living in intimacy with a stray adventurer of dubious provenance.

When the news first reached Caroline that her father-in-law was dead and she was Queen, it did not seem to affect her determination to stay away from England and renounce the title. Certainly she was offered generous terms to do so – an annual income of £50,000 (worth well over £1 million today) along with a pledge from the government that 'she should be acknowledged and received abroad by all diplomatic agents according to her rank and station'. Nearly everyone hoped she would accept these terms, including her close adviser Henry Brougham. This astute politician, much as he appreciated her value as a stick with which to beat the Tory government, yet realized that she might well run out of control and commit follies that would backfire on him. 'I earnestly implore you', he wrote to her, 'to refrain from rushing into certain trouble and possible danger.' But it was to no avail. Caroline had now made up her mind to return to England, and nothing would shift her. It is not clear what caused this change of heart, but she had recently fallen under the influence of an even more ambitious and unscrupulous politician, one Alderman Matthew Wood, who thought he saw in Caroline and her troubles a means of political advancement; and he may have persuaded her that popular feeling in England was running so strongly in her favour that if she were to appear there the government could deny her nothing.[12] She turned the government's terms down flat and demanded a warship to bring her back to England, and when this was ignored, along with Alderman Wood and other hangers-on, she travelled by ordinary packet boat. She arrived in Dover on 5 June 1820.

The reception awaiting Queen Caroline on her arrival in England exceeded even the expectations of Alderman Wood. She was accorded a twenty-one-gun salute from Dover Castle (presumably not on the orders of the government), and a large, exuberant crowd was there to greet her. It was the same all the way to London. Her suite was not impressive – three modest carriages containing no one of distinction – but all the way crowds gathered, shouting 'Long live Queen Caroline and her son King Austin' (seated in one of the carriages, as uncouth and inane as ever). Her entry into London was recorded by the diarist Charles Greville:

> The road was thronged by an immense multitude the whole way from
> Westminster Bridge to Greenwich. Carriages, carts and horsemen

followed, preceded, and surrounded her coach the whole way. She was everywhere received with the greatest enthusiasm. Women waved pocket handkerchiefs and men shouted wherever she passed.

On arrival in London she went first to the house in New Bond Street of Alderman Wood, who lost no opportunity of pushing himself forward and stealing the limelight. For several days the crowds surged around her and rampaged through the streets so that cabinet ministers and supporters of the King went in fear of their lives. The King, himself, somewhat ignominiously, withdrew to Brighton from where he ordered his ministers to lose no time in initiating proceedings against the Queen. The report of the Milan Commission (contained in a green bag which for some reason became an object of great hilarity) was then studied by a government-appointed committee including the Archbishop of Canterbury and the Lord Chancellor, who in due course reported that the papers contained allegations of 'scandalous conduct on the part of the Queen which called for a solemn enquiry'. Following this up, the government decided that it would not be, as before, a 'Delicate Investigation' but a full-scale public inquiry by the House of Lords. The medieval law pronouncing infidelity on the part of the Princess of Wales to be treasonable and punishable by death was still on the statute book, but, partly because Pergami was Italian and therefore not subject to English law, this was not advanced. Instead the government resorted to a Bill of Pains and Penalties which was introduced into the House of Lords. This accused the Queen of 'having conducted herself towards Bartolomeo Pergami with indecent and offensive familiarity and freedom and of having carried on a licentious, disgraceful and adulterous intercourse with him'. It sought 'to deprive Her Majesty, Caroline Amelia Elizabeth of the title, prerogatives, rights, privileges and pretensions of Queen Consort of this realm and to dissolve the marriage between His Majesty and the said Queen'.

On 17 August 1820 in front of 250 peers of the realm the inquiry, or trial as it was in effect, was opened. The Queen herself arrived in great state in a magnificent carriage drawn by six bays, attended by liveried footmen and accompanied by a wildly enthusiastic crowd, and was received with all deference and escorted to her seat. It was not expected that she would want to attend the entire proceedings as some of these would be long drawn out and abstruse, so she was provided with a retiring-room where she could relax and, among other diversions, regale herself with a game of backgammon with Alderman Wood.

The trial lasted for twelve weeks, which caused distress to some peers as it overlapped with the grouse and salmon season, but unless they could provide a plausible excuse their presence was mandatory. As the trial proceeded it became evident that the Queen's counsel, Henry Brougham and Thomas Denman, were of great ability and flair and usually outshone the Attorney-General and Solicitor-General, who were acting for the King. Brougham's opening speech, lasting eight hours over two days, was generally considered a histrionic masterpiece. He then had little difficulty in demolishing the ragbag of Italian witnesses – domestic servants, tradesmen, seamen and sundry hangers-on – who had been summoned by the prosecution. These unfortunates were, indeed, in a sorry plight. Since arriving in England they had been subjected to the fury of the populace and for their own protection had been closely confined under armed guard. Now, overawed by the majesty of the House of Lords, speaking no English, trying to recall events of five years ago, and with quick-witted lawyers tripping them up, it was no wonder they were at a loss. Not that the witnesses called by the defence fared much better. These included two upright officers of the Royal Navy who had been co-opted on to Caroline's staff and were determined to do all they could to uphold her honour. However strongly they contrasted with the illiterate and incoherent Italians, they were easily deflated and made to look foolish. It seemed that nearly all the witnesses called proved to be of greater benefit to the opposing side. However, there were some who stood their ground, and a picture did emerge of scandalous goings-on between the Queen and Pergami, although not actually of adultery, proof of which was necessary for divorce. The only witness who had testified before the Milan Commission to having encountered the couple *in flagrante delicto* refused to come to England, as did several others when they heard of the treatment being meted out to their fellow countrymen who did come.

During the course of the trial London was in uproar. Seldom has popular feeling run so high. Ministers boarded up their houses and lived in a state of siege, and no one was booed more loudly or stoned more insistently than the great national hero of five years ago, the Duke of Wellington. Day and night excited crowds roamed the streets with cries of 'The Queen for ever', 'We'll give our blood for you' and 'No Queen. No King!' Anyone suspected of sympathy for the King was manhandled, and all passers-by were compelled to join their ranks, as Princess Lieven discovered in Bond Street:

> when I met the Queen in a state coach with six horses, being led at walking pace, and escorted as usual by some hundreds of scallywags. As soon as they saw my carriage they stopped it and ordered my servants to take off their hats, and me to let the window down. Neither I nor my servants obeyed. I was surrounded by people shouting abuse, whistling and booing. Meanwhile the Queen passed by throwing me a withering glance. I saw two enormous black eyebrows, as big as two of my fingers put together: the contents of two pots of rouge on her cheeks: and a veil over everything. She looks completely brazen.

It was not only the scallywags ('radicals, mechanics, artisans and hooligans') who demonstrated their support for the Queen. The sober and respectable middle classes also came out, at times with loyal addresses, at times in orderly processions down Piccadilly. Even among the aristocracy the Queen had supporters. It seemed to make not a rap of difference that her behaviour had been, in the words of her old admirer Sir Walter Scott, 'abandoned and beastly'. People were able to persuade themselves that she was an 'angel of innocence'. Even the Quakers, the strictest of Christian denominations, turned a blind eye and processed in her favour, convinced that the whole case against her was a conspiracy.

Not often in London's history has law and order been so threatened. People talked seriously of 'a Jacobin revolution more bloody than that of France'. Perhaps the most sinister feature was the mood of the military, then the principal guardians of the peace. Here, too, the rank and file seemed imbued with the Caroline mania and were joining in the cheering and the heavy drinking to her health. 'Dangerous indeed it is,' someone remarked at the time, 'when the extinguisher is taking fire.'

Throughout the trial there were always crowds outside the House of Lords and the house where the Queen was staying. In the past Caroline had never been averse to publicity, but now it became too much even for her and she took refuge in a house in Fulham, on the river and not easily accessible; but there was to be no escape for her there, as people came in boatloads to shout and get a glimpse of her.

There was talk of little else – which is hardly surprising as it is not often that a queen is arraigned on a charge of adultery before the entire House of Lords.[13] Among the aristocracy some affected boredom with the subject, but they were not convincing, as Charles Greville reported: 'Since I have been in the world I never remember any question which so exclusively occupied everybody's attention and so completely absorbed men's thoughts.'

Among the 250 peers of the realm sitting in judgement sentiment ebbed and flowed for and against the Queen. Certainly there were few who were not convinced that she had behaved indiscreetly, even disgracefully, but most felt nevertheless that her treatment at the hands of her husband had been shameful and that proceedings should not have been brought against her, especially in view of the very strong popular feelings they had aroused. At the end of the trial there was a somewhat ludicrous moment when Sir Thomas Denman, who with Brougham was leading for the defence, made a passionate oration in which he applied to Caroline the words of Christ to the woman taken in adultery, 'Go and sin no more', which was hardly apt as the burden of his speech had been that she had not sinned at all. Nevertheless, when the Bill of Pains and Penalties was put to the vote the government had a majority of no more than twenty-six, which some regarded as 'tantamount to a defeat'. When four days later, after some amendments, it was again put to the vote the majority was down to nine, and the government had to accept that the Bill was doomed; there was no hope of its being passed in the House of Commons, and therefore it had to be abandoned.

As might be expected, this gave rise to the wildest rejoicings: bonfires were lit, guns fired and fireworks let off. Never since the news of victory at Waterloo had there been such exultation. At the centre of it all was a graceless, overwrought figure, neither beautiful nor virtuous, but the wrongs allegedly done to her had moved the British people to a fury, and the popular will had prevailed. The King, his ministers and most of the House of Lords had been forced into retreat. Caroline had played a significant role in the coming of democracy to England.

Caroline was of course greatly exalted by the outcome of her 'trial', but at times she was also depressed. She knew that the furore it had aroused would soon die down and her position would be little better than it had been before. She had not been branded an adulteress, but she was still an outsider – not to be crowned queen, not to live in a royal palace and, a matter to which she attached great importance, not to be mentioned by name in the liturgy of the Church of England. She knew that she had been just a pawn in the political infighting. 'No one, in fact, cares for me,' she wrote soon afterwards, 'and this business has been more cared for as a political affair than as the cause of a poor forlorn woman.' Her only satisfaction had been the humiliation of her husband.

Certainly the King was furious. In the comparative safety of Brighton he gave full vent to his rage, inveighing violently against his ministers who, he felt, had let him down and completely mismanaged the affair.[14] A guest at Brighton Pavilion described his language as 'beyond anything indiscreet and improper'. However, he knew that the only alternative to his Tory ministers was the Whigs and he could expect little sympathy from them, so he consoled himself in the only way he knew how – by lavish expenditure, this time on his impending coronation, which he planned to be the most magnificent ever. But here again he was plagued by the fear that it might be marred by Caroline; and, as it transpired, his fears were well founded.

When the 'trial' was over it might have been expected that Caroline would return to Italy and the arms of Pergami; but this she did not do. It seems that there was some fight left in her yet and she was still bent on tormenting her husband; in particular she could disrupt his coronation plans by demanding her right to attend and be crowned queen. These demands were, of course, rejected by the government whose members made light of them, but the King was seriously concerned and insisted that she be kept under constant surveillance and that for the coronation extra guards should be posted at Westminster Abbey to keep her out. They proved to be necessary because on the day she did attempt to make an entry, but her way was firmly barred and she had to make a humiliating retreat. At one time that this would have caused an uproar among the crowds outside but no longer. It was already evident that her popularity was on the wane. The fickle crowd had been beguiled by the splendour and pageantry of the coronation, and she who had once been their darling was now greeted with silence and even on occasions ribaldry.[15]

The coronation ceremony, all five hours of it, proceeded without disturbance. Magnificent it certainly was – a combination of oriental pageantry, European ceremonial and English wealth. On such occasions the King was at his best: he was majestic and gracious. Immersed in ermine, ostrich feathers, velvet, satin and diamonds, he resembled, according to one present, 'some gorgeous bird of the East'. At times in the stifling atmosphere and under the weight of his massive robes he seemed to wilt, but, fortified by doses of sal volatile, he revived and managed to keep going; and at the end was ready to tuck into an immense banquet in Westminster Hall.

Within a month of the coronation Caroline was dead. Nothing could have been more pathetic than her last days. At times she attempted a comeback, attending public functions, waving and curtseying to all and sundry; but the response was not there; her day had passed. At the same time her domestic arrangements seemed to have lapsed into chaos: her servants became demoralized and out of control, and any house she lived in soon became uninhabitable from dirt and disorganization. At the beginning of August she was taken ill with inflammation of the bowels, and her condition soon became critical. All the horrific remedies of the time were applied – bleeding, calomel, opium and huge doses of castor oil – but to no effect, and on 8 August 1821 she died.

At the time the King was embarking on a tour of Ireland which he scarcely allowed to be interrupted by the news of his wife's death.[16] The choice of her burial site might have caused a problem, but fortunately in her will she had expressed a wish to be buried in Brunswick, so the government arranged for her coffin to be conveyed by an inconspicuous route to Harwich. But then once again the mood of the mob changed, and the hearse was seized and borne in state through the City of London, the streets lined with respectful crowds.

Caroline's life had been almost unbroken tragedy. She was despised and abhorred by her husband, kept at a distance by her family and never found the love she craved, only pity and exploitation.

5

ADELAIDE OF SAXE-COBURG MEININGEN
WIFE OF WILLIAM IV

Queen Adelaide, wife of William IV, is one of the most underrated queens of England. In her time she was regarded as dull and colourless, and even today few people are aware of her and the important role she played at a crucial time in English history. She was always self-effacing and retiring and the last person to seek publicity.

Adelaide was the daughter of the Duke of Saxe-Coburg Meiningen, a minor German state about the size of an average English county. Of quiet, unassuming disposition with neither great wealth nor beauty, she seemed in her late twenties to be heading for spinsterhood; but then out of the blue she attracted the attention of Queen Charlotte of England who was looking for a suitable wife for her third son, William Henry, Duke of Clarence. Such a matrimonial prospect was hardly inviting. William at the time was fifty-three, overweight, eccentric and with a large family of illegitimate children.

His life had been irregular and undistinguished. When he was thirteen his father, George III, had put him into the Navy as a midshipman with no special princely privileges,[1] and he had had to rough it as a junior naval officer, travelling the world, acquiring bluff salty ways and sowing wild oats freely. By most of his fellow officers he was well liked, notably by Horatio Nelson with whom he became a close friend and at whose loveless marriage to Mrs Nisbet he was best man. As to his abilities as a naval officer there were differing opinions. Nelson rated him highly, but the Lords of the Admiralty considered him unsuitable for promotion to flag rank; he was a competent seaman, brave and conscientious, but unreliable; he was too indiscreet and his behaviour at times could be raucous and unseemly. Their opinion, which was shared by George III, was that he should retire from the service, as it would be undignified for a royal prince to remain over-long as a mere captain. So when he was twenty-four William's naval career came to an end until nearly forty years later when he was recalled with the grandiose title of Lord High Admiral. At the same time he was created Duke of Clarence with an adequate, if not generous, pension from Parliament.[2]

From then on William led a life of enforced idleness which did not suit him as he was no layabout and longed for some prestigious occupation; but his mental powers were not highly rated and the general opinion was that he was unemployable. He was therefore shunted into the sidelines and even during the Napoleonic Wars was not recalled to the colours.

As he faced up to retirement William's great wish was for a settled domestic life with a wife and family. But in this he was restricted. He was not free to marry whoever he chose. By the provisions of the Royal Marriages Act he had to have the consent of the King, and this would only be granted for a marriage with a Protestant princess of royal birth. But William was not minded to be so limited, for he had fallen in love with a well-known actress and was determined to make his life with her. Marriage might be impossible, but cohabitation, although frowned on in some quarters, could not be prevented.

The actress, whose stage name was Mrs Jordan, was a remarkable lady. Born out of wedlock, Dorothy Bland had come up the hard way. Her father was the disinherited son of an Irish judge, and her mother the daughter of a Welsh clergyman. They were never legally married but had lived together as man and wife for some thirteen years, giving birth to a number of children of whom Dorothy (or Dora, as she came to be called) was the eldest. When she was thirteen her father absconded, leaving the family in dire financial straits so that it was necessary for Dora to go to work in a milliner's shop. It was not until she was seventeen that she went on the stage, where her mother had been striving to earn a precarious livelihood for several years. Dora then led the life of a 'strolling player', mainly in the north of England. This could be extremely rigorous – long journeys on foot between the larger towns, insalubrious lodgings and insecure employment as well as the jealousy and malice of fellow players. Dora's life was made more difficult by the birth of a baby out of wedlock. It soon became apparent, however, that as an actress she had special gifts, notably in comedy, so much so that she was persuaded to try her luck in London. She arrived in the capital in 1785 at the age of twenty-four, along with her mother, brother and sister who were largely dependent on her. At first money was desperately short, but then Dora's talents became recognized, for it was not just that she was a gifted actress, she had also what is known today as 'star quality'. The poet Hazlitt wrote of her:

> Her face, her tones, her manner were irresistible. Her smile had the effect of sunshine, and her laugh did one good to hear it. She was all gaiety, openness and good nature. She rioted in her fine animal spirits, and gave more pleasure than any other actress, because she had the greatest spirit of enjoyment in herself.

Samuel Coleridge Taylor was also a fan, writing of 'the exquisite witchery of her tones'. In time she became included in the most illustrious of London theatre companies, that of Richard Brinsley Sheridan at Drury Lane.

It seems that Dora first caught the attention of William, Duke of Clarence in 1790 when she was twenty-nine and he was three years younger. At the time she was semi-engaged to one Richard Ford by whom she had given birth to three children, while William had had various attachments when he was in the Navy and had fathered at least one offspring. Overtures from a son of the monarch were not to be taken lightly, but Dora hesitated for some time before succumbing and agreeing to set up house with him. When their liaison became public knowledge there was at first much ribaldry, and there was little expectation that it would last long.[3] But in the event it was to endure for twenty years, during which time they begat no less than ten children, who were known as the FitzClarences. Certainly Dora was a lady of exceptional stamina (as well as fecundity), for in addition to raising a large family and acting as consort to the third son of the monarch she also continued with her career as an actress, making frequent appearances not only in London but in such far-flung places as Edinburgh, York and Cheltenham.

During their years together William and Dora led a simple, contented, domestic life with no attempt at subterfuge, and their relationship came to be generally accepted, even eventually by the prudish King and Queen. But it was not to last for ever. After twenty years they began to drift apart and their financial position became untenable. Mrs Jordan's earnings from the stage, on which they largely depended, began to dwindle, and William was still kept on a tight rein by his father. The FitzClarences became more demanding as they grew older, and William, always a generous father, wanted to do his best for them. Eventually he came to the conclusion that he and Mrs Jordan should part and he would find himself a rich heiress who would keep them all going. Heartless though this might have been, it seemed to him the best course, and even Dora recognized the inevitability of some sort of separation, although she hoped that it could be achieved with due consideration for her feelings and her finances, including a proper arrangement for her younger children. But this did not happen. William did not behave with his usual kindliness, leaving negotiations to others and showing little interest in making a fair and reasonable settlement. The story ended in tragedy. Mrs Jordan put her trust in one of her sons-in-law (not a FitzClarence) who defrauded her, and she felt obliged to flee the country to avoid being arrested for debt. There was no helping hand from William. She died in France in 1816 at the age of fifty-five in poverty and unsupported by any of her family.

Meanwhile William was having little success in his quest for a rich heiress; these were proving either unwilling or unsuitable. In 1817, however, six years after he had parted from Mrs Jordan, his position changed radically when Princess Charlotte, the lively and popular daughter of the Prince Regent, died in childbirth. He then became third in succession to the throne after his two elder brothers, the Prince Regent and Frederick, Duke of York, neither of whom seemed likely to live much longer. So it became urgently necessary for one of George III's fifteen children to produce a legitimate heir, of which at that time there was none. This duty was acknowledged by William, who was ready to marry a suitable Protestant princess but only on condition that Parliament made ample financial provisions for him. The choice of a bride was of less importance; he was prepared to leave this to his mother, Queen Charlotte. And so it came about that Princess Adelaide came into consideration.

On being presented with William as a possible husband Adelaide at first held back, as well she might. William was twice her age, by no means handsome, trailing behind him a reputation for eccentricity and crudity and lumbered with massive debts, to say nothing of ten FitzClarences. Why then did she succumb? Certainly not because of the prospect of becoming Queen of England, for she had no worldly ambitions. Nor was there anything to attract her to the English Royal Family at that time. King George was totally and hopelessly out of his mind; his wife Queen Charlotte was sharp-tempered and strait-laced; and their eldest son, the Prince Regent (the future George IV), once brilliant, had degenerated ignominiously into a monstrous, obese figure held in general contempt. One cannot be certain of Adelaide's reasons, but in view of her character as it later manifested itself it can be surmised that she looked on William with pity (rather as Beauty did the Beast) and thought she could change him into something nobler and better. And in this, as will be seen, she was to have some success.

There was never to be anything in the nature of romance in William and Adelaide's betrothal. It was a business deal. William's interest was to obtain an increased grant from Parliament to pay off his debts as well as to become the father of a future sovereign. Adelaide for her part wanted to avoid spinsterhood and, as has been seen, looked on William as a challenge. In Parliament the leader of the House of Commons, George Canning, spelled it out explicitly, stating amid derisive laughter that His Royal Highness 'entered into this alliance not for his own private desire and gratification but because it was pressed on him for the purpose of providing for the succession to the throne'. At the last moment there was a danger that the marriage would be called off because of the inadequacy of the parliamentary grant, but in the end William could not afford to let Adelaide go. She was in every way so suitable, but it was with no great optimism that he embarked on matrimony. 'She is doomed,' he wrote, 'poor dear innocent young creature, to be my wife. I cannot, I will not, I must not ill use her.'

Their wedding could hardly have been more prosaic. Adelaide and her mother arrived in London without formal greeting and were compelled to bide their time in a hotel until William or another member of the Royal Family took notice of them. The wedding ceremony, which took place a week later, was plain and low-key – no enthusiastic crowds lining the streets, no bevy of distinguished guests, instead a simple service at Kew, shared for reasons of economy with William's younger brother Edward, Duke of Kent, and his German Princess, Victoria Maria Louisa of Saxe-Coburg (parents-to-be of Queen Victoria).

For the time being economy was to be the watchword for William and Adelaide, necessary because of the size of William's debts and the paucity of his parliamentary grant; and for a time they were obliged to take up residence in Hanover where the cost of living was cheaper and creditors not so near at hand. To this regime Adelaide made no objection. She may have had no love for Hanover and found some of the economies oppressive, but she saw it as her duty to face up to these trials and did so relentlessly. She was always clear that the main expectation of her was to bear an heir, but in this, sadly, she was doomed to disappointment. In the first year of her marriage she gave birth prematurely to a daughter who survived only a few hours, and in the same year she miscarried another child. Soon afterwards a daughter was safely delivered, apparently sound in wind and limb, only to catch an infection a few months later of which she died.

Although frustrated in child-bearing, in other ways Adelaide was an ideal wife for William. She checked his drinking and profane language, curbed the more blatant of his eccentricities and generally made him more presentable. In other ways, too, her influence was beneficial: she took the FitzClarences under her wing and treated them as her own. She not only kept clear of all family feuds and tensions but did what she could to ease them; and in public she was always accessible and sympathetic, and her works of charity were numerous. Nevertheless, in spite of her kindness and goodwill Adelaide did not became a popular figure. She did not catch the public imagination. Her virtues were undoubted, but they were unrelieved by charm or humour. She had no great personal appeal or charisma. The great ladies of the time treated her with scornful condescension. 'She never did anything that history is aware of save hold her tongue and help the poor,' scoffed one, and another described her disdainfully as 'a small, well-bred, excellent little woman'. Certainly she was not given her due and all too often came in for ridicule and abuse.

Nine years after William's marriage his elder brother Frederick, Duke of York died, so that he became heir apparent to the throne, and as the health of his eldest brother, now George IV, looked precarious, it seemed virtually certain that in time he would become king. This was appreciated by government ministers, who thought he should be brought out of obscurity, polished up and made as ready as possible for kingship. An ancient, honorific title was resurrected – that of Lord High Admiral – once held by the somewhat dim-witted husband of Queen Anne, Prince George of Denmark. The idea was that the appointment would be entirely ceremonial: all important decisions regarding the Navy would be taken by the Lords of the Admiralty to which the Lord High Admiral would give formal assent. But this was not how William saw it. He might have been retired from the Navy for nearly forty years, but his heart was still there, and he had no intention of being a mere rubber stamp. At once he started acting on his own initiative without reference to their Lordships, which caused them such concern that the post of Lord High Admiral had to be hurriedly abolished, and William once again retired. As might be expected this caused him some offence, but, good-natured as ever, he did not allow it to become a lasting grievance. Two years later George IV died and, amid trepidation in some quarters, William became king.

It soon became evident to the British people that their new monarch was very different from his predecessor. Instead of the self-obsessed sensualist, aloof from his subjects and unloved or forgotten by them, William's hallmark was informality and gregariousness. He lost no time in putting himself on public view and would plunge into crowds enthusiastically, shaking hands with everyone and inviting people to dinner indiscriminately (sometimes as many as two thousand a week). Of course such extravagant behaviour caused consternation in some quarters not only because of the lack of decorum but also because of the possible dangers (from footpads as well as prostitutes wanting favours). But William was not to be put off. More than any other monarch he had the common touch and there was nothing he enjoyed more than direct contact with his people. At the Royal Pavilion in Brighton, particularly, he was always ready to let himself go. There was something about the sea breezes and nautical atmosphere there which went to his head. Charles Greville, the broad-minded diarist, was shocked by what he saw: 'He lives a strange life at Brighton with ragtail and bobtail about him and always open house . . . Very active, vulgar and hospitable. Kings, Queens, Princes, Princesses, bastards and attendants constantly trotting about in every direction.'

In other ways, too, William showed his democratic instincts. He thought there was too much majesty about the monarchy and sought to cut it down. On his accession Buckingham Palace was just being completed in its present form, but neither he nor Adelaide had any wish to live there, so he tried to offload it first as a barracks for the Guards and then as a replacement for the Houses of Parliament which had recently been burned down – in neither case availingly. He had more success when he did away with the royal stables behind St James's Palace to make way for Trafalgar Square and Nelson's Column.

On formal state occasions William was an agitated, incongruous figure. Gravitas and dignity were not his strong points, and for etiquette and protocol he had little time, much preferring to go his own way as he thought fit. This could sometimes result in embarrassing and unseemly outbursts, although Adelaide could usually exert some measure of control over him. For most of the time life at Court was deadly dull. Adelaide was no sparkling hostess and after dinner she would sit placidly with her needlework making the tritest conversation while William would make little effort to stay awake, occasionally rousing himself to make an irrelevant comment before dozing off again. No wonder that in later years his niece, Queen Victoria, was moved to comment that he was 'odd, very odd and singular'.

On becoming king in 1830 William had only a few months to accustom himself to his new position before being plunged into a major political crisis – the passing of the Great Reform Bill. Reform of Britain's electoral system was long overdue. There had been few changes to it since the Middle Ages, and the House of Commons was no longer representative of the country at large. Old towns which had dwindled or, in some cases, disappeared continued to return two Members of Parliament while new industrial cities like Leeds and Manchester returned none. Because of these anomalies, combined with widespread corruption, control of the House of Commons was in effect in the hands of the rich and powerful who were able to obtain the results they wanted. There had been talk of reforming Parliament for many years, but it had not happened. One of the main reasons for this was the French Revolution, which caused a great dread of any form of change, so that during the long war against Napoleon and for years afterwards even modest demands for reform were equated with revolution and were heavily suppressed. But by 1830 they could be suppressed no longer; the case for the reform of the parliamentary voting system was overwhelming, although it was still strongly and obstinately opposed in some quarters. And so William found himself in the middle of this great controversy and having to play a crucial role in it. For this he was not well qualified: he was strongly conservative by nature, with no intellectual pretensions and a temperament that was sometimes seriously unbalanced. That he survived was due to a rough common sense and straightforwardness and, vitally, the strong and steady support of Adelaide. During the next two tumultuous years the country came as close to revolution as it has ever been, with widespread violence and disorder; and although William did not always play his part with discretion, he stayed on course and it was in no small measure due to him that revolution was avoided.

During this period the part played by Adelaide was crucial, but she was nevertheless inadvertently the cause of some agitation. Normally she took no part in politics, but she did have an obsessive dread of revolution and was convinced that giving way to the outcry for reform would open the floodgates, as had happened when Charles I summoned the Long Parliament in 1640 and Louis XVI convened the States General in 1789. These were the views of the High Tories, and Adelaide was careful not to express them in public, but rumours leaked out and it became widely believed that she was a strong reactionary influence on her husband. How far this was true is not clear. She was silent when others were present; what she said in private is not known, but it is surely unlikely that she was another Marie Antoinette or Empress Marie Fedorovna of Russia breathing pernicious advice into her husband's ear.

It took Adelaide some time to live down her alleged reactionary views, and for some years she continued to be regarded as a sinister backstairs influence. When in 1834 William on impulse dismissed the Whig government of Lord Melbourne, even though it had a majority in the House of Commons, the immediate reaction was that it was Adelaide's doing.[4] 'The Queen has done it all' was placarded over London, as were crude depictions of her in breeches and William in petticoats. In fact she knew nothing of the matter until it was all over.

In the midst of all the commotion about the Reform Bill William and Adelaide had to undergo the ordeal of a coronation. William had wanted to miss out on it, saying that it was extravagant and out of date, but on this he was overruled, even Adelaide maintaining that the religious element was all-important. However, it was agreed that it should not be on a grand scale, costing one-eighth of the sum spent on George IV's coronation.[5] In agreeing to it, William tried to insist that he should not be kissed by the bishops, but even here he had to give way. It might have been expected that the public would be grateful to William for limiting the expense of the ceremony, but instead there was discontent; people apparently felt that they were being done out of a splendid public spectacle, and there were murmurings about 'a mere half-crownation'. During the ceremony William could not control his restlessness, and the great Whig historian Lord Macaulay wrote caustically that 'he behaved very awkwardly and his bearing made the foolish parts of the ritual appear monstrously ridiculous'. But for the Queen he had nothing but praise: 'she behaved admirably with wonderful grace and dignity'. Other observers agreed. A foreign diplomat wrote at the time: 'Though she is in reality not too good-looking, she appeared so that day undeniably, for the beauty lay in something beyond mere outward loveliness. It was the beauty of her soul that seemed to shine out from and impress itself upon her whole person.'

There must have been times, when she was Queen, that Adelaide wished she was back in the comparative calm of Germany. She had, indeed, suffered rough treatment and ingratitude in England. During the passing of the Reform Bill she had behaved correctly but had nevertheless been the target of hysterical abuse. She had also received no appreciation for her economical way of life; her court expenses were a fraction of those of George IV, but in return Parliament had treated her with parsimony, questioning every pound granted to her; and when she cut back she was criticized for the dowdiness of her outfits. While some found fault with life at her court for being dull and prudish, others blamed her for being too tolerant, especially of the crude and boisterous behaviour of her FitzClarence stepchildren. It seemed she could do no right. Few recognized her undoubted talents; for she was more than an old frump sitting at her needlework all day. According to Princess Lieven, a shrewd and acerbic critic, she was 'far cleverer than generally believed'. She had musical gifts above the ordinary and was an accomplished horsewoman and graceful dancer. Amid all this lack of appreciation, however, she always had the love and support of her husband. He had faithfully kept the pledge made at the time of his betrothal not to ill-treat her. After the bleakest of courtships their relationship had developed into a deep love, so that they could hardly bear to be parted.

In his last years William regained much of his old popularity. His genial eccentricity and lavish entertaining had always been appreciated, particularly by poor people. By 1835, however, when he reached seventy, his health began to fail markedly; he suffered from terrible asthma, was liable to fainting fits and his legs sometimes gave way under him. His mind also became more unsteady, especially, it was noted, in springtime when his speeches rambled on for ever, most of them unintelligible but every now and then containing some breathtaking indiscretion. There were those who had serious fears that he would end up, like his father, in a straitjacket; that this did not happen must in large part be due to Adelaide, for in certain moods only she could soothe him and control him.

In spite of his afflictions William insisted on continuing with his public duties until the end, which came on 20 June 1837. Like other English kings he was to be a long time a-dying, and for the last week of his life Adelaide never left his bedside, and he died in her arms. Except among the smart and sophisticated there was genuine grief at his death. Simple people overlooked his failings and remembered only his warm-heartedness and patriotism.

Adelaide lived on for twelve years after William's death. The role of Queen Dowager she filled with grace and discretion. She had by then become a deeply respected figure. People were at last becoming aware of her qualities. As always her life was quiet and retiring; she had never sought the limelight, and her relations with her niece, Queen Victoria, were of the warmest. On the death of William Victoria addressed her in a letter as Queen of England, which was incorrect, and when this was pointed out to her she said she knew but did not want to be the first to draw her aunt's attention to the fact. Adelaide's letters to Victoria always ended: 'your most affectionate and faithful Friend, Aunt and Subject'. When she moved out of Windsor Castle Victoria told her to take with her anything she wanted; others might then have helped themselves liberally, but Adelaide took no more than a picture of the FitzClarence family and a silver cup from which she had given her husband soothing drinks in his last days.

For some time she had been dogged by ill health, particularly a cough that would not go away and then became worse. To find relief she travelled to warmer climes but to no lasting effect. Wherever she went she left behind marks of her liberality – in Malta the foundation of an Anglican cathedral, in Madeira a new road for the fishermen. In England it might be a new font or chalice for the church or coal and blankets for the poor.

Adelaide died in 1849 at the age of fifty-seven. It is likely that she was ready for death. Her mission in life had been accomplished. She had transformed an elderly, dissolute, unstable prince into a popular monarch and kept him on course through a critical period of English history. Almost as important was the example she set of philanthropy and generosity. The transition from rakish Regency to Victorian respectability was in some measure initiated by her. This was no mean feat for a once disregarded princess from a tiny German principality.

6
ALEXANDRA OF DENMARK
Wife of Edward VII

Of all the queens of England, Alexandra, wife of Edward VII, was the most beautiful and most widely acclaimed. From the moment she arrived in the country she cast a spell not to be broken until her death some sixty years later. No Princess of Wales before her had aroused such enthusiasm, for in addition to beauty and charm she had 'star quality' which meant that wherever she went she was always the centre of attraction. Royalty had known nothing like her for centuries, nor did it again until 120 years later when another Princess of Wales enchanted the country in the same way.

Alix (as she was always known) was the daughter of Prince Christian of Denmark and Princess Louise from the German principality of Hesse-Cassel. Her childhood was happy but impoverished. Prince Christian was not in the direct line to the Danish throne and until elected to the monarchy later in life had to make do on the pay of an army officer, which was barely adequate for the upbringing of a family of five children.[1] Alix was accustomed to a frugal regime with no luxuries, making her own clothes, sharing a tiny attic room with her sister and even waiting at table when there were guests. But she was unworried by such matters. She was of a naturally happy disposition and enjoyed whatever life brought her. She did not have much in the way of education, nor did she want it, as her gifts did not include great intellect. She read few books (except those of her famous Danish contemporary Hans Christian Andersen) and had no academic interests. The life of her family was simple, high-spirited and fun-loving. Few would have guessed that from among them would come a Queen of England, an Empress of Russia, a King of Denmark and a King of Greece.

In 1861 Queen Victoria and Prince Albert, the Prince Consort, were looking (somewhat urgently) for a bride for their eldest son, Albert Edward, known to his family as Bertie. He was no more than twenty at the time, but his way of life was causing his parents anxiety, and it was felt that marriage would settle him down. Europe was being scoured for a suitable princess, and Queen Victoria's requirements were exacting: good looks, health, education, character, intellect, good disposition; and, of course, she must be Protestant. Germany was the usual hunting ground in such a quest, but at that time German princesses did not adequately fit the bill. There were drawbacks to all of them: one was plain, another 'undeveloped', another had skeletons in the family cupboard, while another was reported as being 'shockingly dressed and always with her disagreeable mother'. Bertie's parents were convinced that his wife should be beautiful, otherwise there was little chance of his being faithful to her. And in beauty there was one European princess who transcended all others. Princess Alexandra was no more than seventeen, but all reports of her were glowing and not only for her beauty. Bertie's elder sister Victoria Adelaide, who had just married the Crown Prince of Prussia, wrote of her: 'I never set eyes on a sweeter creature. She is one of the most ladylike and aristocratic looking people I ever saw.'

There were, however, difficulties about a Danish marriage. At the end of the Napoleonic Wars (during which Copenhagen had once been bombarded by a British fleet under Nelson) Denmark had been forced to part company with Norway, with whom it had been united for four hundred years, so it was no longer a European power of great standing. There were other considerations, too. The King of Denmark at the time was a gross, disreputable figure, twice divorced and married morganatically *en troisième noce* to an ex-milliner-cum-dancer with a dubious past. Moreover, the precedents for an Anglo-Danish marriage were not favourable: a daughter of George II who had married a king of Denmark had been dethroned and imprisoned for adultery with a court physician. Of greater import, Denmark was locked in a bitter dispute with Prussia and other German states about its two provinces of Schleswig and Holstein, which were partly German and partly Danish. The rights and wrongs of this matter were complex, but feelings in Denmark ran high, and no one felt more strongly on the matter than Princess Alexandra whose hostility to Prussia was intense. In view of the English Royal Family's close ties with Germany this gave rise to a difficult situation, and at first Queen Victoria was dead against such a marriage. 'It would never do,' she said. 'The German element is the one I want to be cherished and kept in our beloved home.' Besides, she had formed a strong aversion to Alexandra's family. 'Her mother's are bad and the father's foolish,' she declared.

It says much for Alexandra's qualities that these objections were overcome. The first to succumb was the not normally susceptible Prince Consort, who was so delighted by the picture he saw of Alix that he urged his son to pay court to her at once before she was snapped up by somebody else. A meeting between them was then contrived by the Crown Princess of Prussia who, despite her German connections, was strongly in favour of the match: and although the two did not fall in love at first sight they were favourably impressed enough for the matter to go forward. But then came a setback. When in camp with the army in Ireland the previous year Bertie had had a fling with an actress, news of which spread and eventually reached the ears of his father, who was utterly appalled. 'It has caused me the greatest pain I have yet felt in this life,' he told Bertie. There was a long confrontation; eventually Bertie was contrite and his father was inclined to be forgiving. But then within a month he had died of typhoid fever. Whether there was any connection between the two events is doubtful, but Queen Victoria believed there was and that the anguish Bertie had caused his father had hastened his death, something for which she could not forgive him.[2] The Queen's grief at the death of her husband was such that she remained in mourning for more than twenty years.

Although all thoughts of a royal wedding had to be postponed for the moment, Victoria decided that the marriage should go ahead. Albert had wished it, and his wishes were sacred. In spite of strong opposition from her German relatives, who did not scruple to spread abroad scurrilous rumours about the Danish Royal Family, she set the wheels in motion again, and nine months after Albert's death she arranged to meet Alexandra and her family in Belgium. The meeting was less than cordial, and the Queen's description of the Danes as being not *sympathique* was probably an understatement. However, after some pressure had been put on them Bertie and Alix did become engaged soon afterwards. It is doubtful that they were deeply in love at the time, but to Alix it was unthinkable that she should refuse such an amiable, handsome youth who was also heir to the throne of the world's greatest empire, while Bertie must have been thankful that the small number of princesses who were eligible for him included one of Europe's greatest beauties.

The engagement settled, Queen Victoria lost no time in laying down the law. The Danish Royal Family were not consulted and then, as later, were kept at arm's length. She decreed at once that, as the Court was still in mourning for Prince Albert, the wedding should be a comparatively quiet one in St George's, Windsor, rather than a splendid popular affair in St Paul's or Westminster Abbey. She also kept an iron grip on the guests to be invited, excluding all of however high rank whose conduct she thought in any way shady, and confining the Danes to immediate family only. She decided that the date which best suited her was 10 March 1863, which happened to be in the middle of Lent; this drew a mild protest from the Archbishop of Canterbury, but this was swept aside: 'The objection rests merely on fancy and prejudice and one in this case based on no very elevated view of one of God's holiest ordinances . . . Marriage is a solemn and holy act and not to be classed as an amusement.'

In the meantime Bertie was forbidden to visit his fiancée in Denmark for fear that 'the poor weak boy' should become entangled in Danish politics and fall under the influence of Alexandra's 'mischievous' mother. The Queen wanted to see Alix alone in England, so Bertie was pushed off on a Mediterranean cruise, and Prince Christian, who accompanied his daughter, was treated with the meanest courtesy – told he could stay only two nights and left to make his own hotel arrangements. Alix was understandably terrified at the prospect of being closeted with Queen Victoria, 'being inspected on appro', as she put it. But she need not have worried. Like everyone else the Queen fell under her spell. 'I cannot say', she wrote at the time, ' how I and we all love her . . . She is one of those sweet creatures who seem to come from the skies to help and bless poor mortals and light for a time their paths.' At the same time Alix was sternly warned that she must keep out of politics and not involve Bertie in Danish affairs. She was also told that she must not have any Danish ladies-in-waiting, which she found irksome and to which she made objection, but the iron-willed Queen was adamant.

Alexandra arrived in England for her wedding two days in advance. A tumultuous reception awaited her. The people of England were in the mood for a joyous celebration. Since the time of George IV royalty had been either dowdy or strait-laced, usually both, and the arrival in the country of a princess known to be 'the ideal of youth and beauty' caused terrific excitement. There had been widespread disappointment that there was not to be a magnificent full-scale wedding in central London, for there is no spectacle the British people love more, and they were set on making up for this by a welcome that was unprecedented in its fervour.[3] When the ship bringing Alix and her family came into the Thames estuary every boat there – wherries, rowing boats, paddle steamers – was ablaze with bunting and people clambering up the masts, cheering for all they were worth and straining to get a glimpse of 'the fairy Princess'. Ashore it seemed that the whole local population had turned out, waving flags – both British and Danish – and yelling at the tops of their voices. For the royal party there was then a train journey from Gravesend to Southwark for which people had been waiting for hours, and every house, barn and haystack had been decorated. At Southwark there was a change into an open carriage and a drive through the City, where the crowds, in a state of exuberant intoxication, at one point threatened to overwhelm the procession, and it had to be rescued by the Life Guards with drawn sabres. Then it passed through the streets of London – some seven miles, lasting four hours, Alix bravely smiling, bowing and waving all the way. Finally it ended at Windsor Castle, after dark and in pouring rain, to be greeted by Queen Victoria, loving but doleful and with thoughts only of Albert. Through the long ordeal Alix had acquitted herself heroically, never faltering for a moment. An eye-witness (Lady Geraldine Somerset) was to write of 'the fascination she so really possesses combined of dignity, simplicity, grace and geniality'. An Eton schoolboy who had managed to get a close-up view put it. it more succinctly: 'She looked regular nailing.'

After the briefest of respites the nineteen-year-old from a European backwater was swept into the marriage service. The Queen's attempt to make this a low-key affair had not prevailed. The splendour was overwhelming. All the great and good were there in glittering array – robed, bemedalled and dripping with diamonds. Also in evidence were the heralds and trumpeters, the Yeomen of the Guard in medieval costume, the Knights of the Garter, as well as a battery of bishops and archbishops to conduct the ceremony. As was to be expected, all eyes were on Alexandra, and all agreed that she was perfect – dignified, unaffected and radiantly beautiful. Among the congregation was Charles Dickens, no royalist at heart but, for the time being, like everyone else, under Alix's spell: 'The Princess's face was very pale and full of a sort of awe and wonder. It was the face of no ordinary bride, not simply a timid, shrinking girl but one with a distinctive character of her own, prepared to act a part greatly.'

The only melancholy note in the proceedings was struck by a lone figure, hidden away in an alcove, distancing herself as much as possible from what was going on. As always, Queen Victoria's thoughts were fixed on her dead husband.

After the wedding came a week's honeymoon at Osborne, and then Bertie and Alix were plunged into the maelstrom of the London season with its round of balls, banquets, receptions and all kinds of entertainment.[4] Here they were welcomed with open arms by society, then at its richest, most aristocratic and most shamelessly hedonistic. It was a long time since it had been graced by royalty. Prince Albert had no time for it, and so Queen Victoria, too, had kept her distance. But Bertie, sociable and pleasure-loving, delighted in it, as also for a time did Alix. And once again she was a triumphant success – sought after everywhere, copied in all her ways and lavished with praise ('graceful, dignified, affable, fascinating, winning', etc.).

It was all too good to last. No one could ride as high as this for ever. Soon disparaging voices were heard, and one of the first was Queen Victoria's. The lifestyle of her son and daughter-in-law shocked her deeply. It was altogether too fast and loose. They were never still for a moment. 'A whirl of amusement,' she called it. It was not long before she was complaining in letters to her eldest daughter (the Crown Princess of Prussia) that Alix was looking 'ill, thin and unhappy . . . and was sadly gone off '. Alix was indeed feeling the strain. She had almost at once become pregnant, and the baby (a son) had been born prematurely and so unexpectedly that it had to be delivered into the pettycoats of Alix's lady-in-waiting, a circumstance which Queen Victoria ascribed entirely to her hectic lifestyle. And it was not only the pace of Bertie and Alix's life to which the Queen objected. She also took strong exception to the company they kept. Bertie did not confine himself to the old, respectable, well-established families; his tastes were more eclectic. New and unexpected people were admitted to his circle – rich Jewish financiers, racing buffs, actors and actresses, even Americans. Repeatedly his mother warned him against the dangers of such company and how in time they would become 'inconvenient' friends, but her warnings fell on deaf ears. Bertie and Alix always treated her with tact and deference, but then as often as not went their own ways. In ill temper the Queen would then write to her daughter that Alix had become 'haughty and frivolous' and that 'she never will or can be intimate'. However, when she was in Alix's company she always succumbed to her charm and was writing that 'she was a dear, excellent, right-minded soul'.

There were more serious matters over which the Queen and the Prince and Princess of Wales came to differ. In 1866 the long-standing dispute between

Denmark and Prussia over the provinces of Schleswig and Holstein came to a head and was settled when they were invaded by the Prussian army and annexed. Normally Alix was not politically minded, but on all matters relating to Denmark she felt passionately, and she was outraged by the Prussian action. Her fury knew no bounds, and she was quite ready openly to insult any Prussian with whom she came in contact, including the King and Queen. In this she was supported by her husband, who was in favour of intervention on Denmark's behalf by the British Navy. Queen Victoria, on the other hand, had strong ties with Prussia and other German states and was strongly opposed to any such idea. This disagreement caused much stress, and in a letter to her daughter the Queen wrote bitterly that Alix, 'good as she is, is not worth the price we have had to pay for her having such a family connection'. However, she relented in time, as she always did, and there was no danger of a permanent rift.

It was never likely that Bertie would remain a faithful husband for long. His restless character, immense energy and prodigious sexual appetite made such a thing impossible. He always had to be on the move. Quiet domestic evenings at home enjoying the simple pleasures of life were not for him. He could not abide being bored, so when Alix could not keep pace with him because of pregnancy or ill health he had no compunction in going off on his own. He loved the company of rich and successful men of the world and beautiful, sophisticated women. Nor was he always fastidious in his tastes. London at that time abounded in low haunts – opium dens, murky music halls with boxes for the well-to-do screened from public view, and 'night houses' which catered for every form of vice – and Bertie and his more raffish friends were probably not unacquainted with them. Certainly he lived dangerously and on occasions paid the penalty for it. Alix must have known from the beginning what Bertie was up to but decided that it was something she had to live with like many royal wives of the time. Indeed it might have been rather a relief as hers was not a sensual nature and, great beauty as she was, she was not so attractive sexually. She put on the best face possible, never becoming jealous or making angry scenes and never thinking of taking a lover of her own.

The first time Bertie's philanderings caught the public attention was when he visited Russia in 1866 (three years after his marriage) for the wedding of Alix's sister Dagmar to the Tsarevitch. Alix had been unable to go because of a pregnancy, and Bertie on his own attracted great attention.[5] Russian ladies, he found ,were both beautiful and willing, and he himself was not inaccessible. On his return to England (something of a conquering hero) he was dismayed to find Alix in serious ill health. Not only was she in the last stages of pregnancy but she was also suffering from rheumatic fever which was causing her great pain and misery. What followed showed Bertie at his worst. He should of course have been at her bedside, bringing her all the comfort he could; but instead he continued with a life of pleasure as if nothing were amiss – dining out, roistering with cronies and visiting Paris, where he was noticed in the company of female 'notorieties'. Alix's much loved lady-in-waiting, Lady Macclesfield, was horrified and noted, 'He really is a child about such things and will not listen to advice.'

In time Alix recovered from her illness, but it left its mark. She was a different person afterwards. One of her legs became permanently stiff and thereafter she always walked with a slight limp; and the vigorous exercise she so much enjoyed – riding, dancing, skating – had to be curtailed.[6] And there was a more serious matter: she had inherited from her mother an affliction which made her liable to deafness, and this gradually became worse, interfering with her social life. More and more she became tied to her home and family.

However, she continued to play a leading role in the social scene for some time yet. Soon after their marriage she and Bertie had moved into Marlborough House in the Mall which had been done up at considerable expense and which at once became the hub of London society, everyone with social ambitions striving to become a member of the 'Marlborough House Set'. Alix loved Marlborough House, but she became even more devoted to Sandringham, their country house in north Norfolk. This was surprising, as it was not beautiful and the surrounding countryside was somewhat desolate, with cold north winds blowing in strongly from the Wash. Queen Victoria on one of her rare visits there described it as 'wild-looking, flat, bleak country'. Yet Bertie, Alix and their family came to love it dearly. It provided Bertie with excellent shooting, and it reminded Alix of Denmark, and it also had the advantage of being a long way from Windsor and the brooding presence of the great Queen. The property had been bought by the Prince Consort at a bargain price, and he reckoned at the time that a large sum of money would be needed to make the house habitable; but Bertie in his enthusiasm soon exceeded that amount and then decided that it had to be rebuilt completely. When this had been done he and Alix entertained there magnificently. The railway line was extended from King's Lynn for the benefit of their guests, a new garden was created, and this unprepossessing East Anglian backwater became the focal point for the *beau monde*.

Entertainment there was not only princely but idiosyncratic. Visitors arriving would have to run the gauntlet of numerous dogs of all sorts running wild as well as none too orderly children. They might then find themselves among surprising company (as at Marlborough House drawn mainly from the business and racing community rather than the arts), and in due course they would be expected to join in all manner of games – billiards, bowls, charades, whist. There was liable to be some rough stuff, too, as both the Prince and the Princess had a strange liking for practical jokes – soda-water siphons let off, apple-pie beds made, whipped cream replaced by soap suds and mustard added to mince pies – anything went. It was all good fun and caused uproarious hilarity, but amidst it all the Prince and Princess somehow managed to retain their dignity. They were not squirted with soda-water siphons. But however disconcerted guests might be by these hazards they could not but be charmed by the warmth of their welcome. They were always carefully looked after and certainly did not go hungry, for Bertie's appetite for food was as great as for sex, and gargantuan meals were always being served. During the day a shoot might be organized when privileged guests staggered out after an immense breakfast accompanied by an army of loaders, beaters, spectators and attendants bearing a picnic, and this would not be just a packet of sandwiches and cheese and biscuits but a multi-course affair cooked on location. Then after the slaughter of innumerable birds they would return to the 'Big House' for an ample tea followed by a dinner of never less than ten courses. On other days there might be a fox hunt at which guests, however much they might dislike riding, were hustled on to horses and obliged to follow the hounds. The only day when there was some let-up from these frantic activities was Sunday, when the Prince put in a token appearance at church, arriving late and having previously impressed on the vicar that his sermon must on no account last longer than ten minutes. Guests might sometimes feel exhausted and overtaxed (and bilious), but they were always revived by Bertie's affability and Alix's charm. There were very few who did not long to be invited again.

In spite of their great love for Sandringham, Bertie and Alix spent only a few months of the year there; for the rest of the time they might be in Scotland (for the deer stalking), the Isle of Wight (for the Cowes regatta), on visits abroad and in London for the season where they were the centre of attraction and where Bertie continued to live dangerously.

It was always likely that one day trouble would come his way. The first time this happened was in 1869, when he was subpoenaed to appear as a witness in a divorce case – the first time this had happened to a Prince of Wales. The circumstances of the case were bizarre. A friend of Bertie's, Sir Claude Mordaunt, wanted to divorce his wife who had become insane and who had confessed to her husband that she had slept with a number of people including the Prince of Wales. In court this was firmly denied by Bertie, but it did transpire that he had once dallied with her and written her a number of foolish but innocent letters, which were published. During the trial both Queen Victoria and Princess Alexandra gave him their full support, and he emerged, if not whiter than white, at least with nothing proved against him. But the case had aroused widespread interest, and there were no doubt many strait-laced citizens tut-tutting over the newspaper reports and saying there was no smoke without fire. Certainly Queen Victoria was aware of this and wrote to the Lord Chancellor: 'Still, the fact of the Prince of Wales's intimate acquaintance with a young married woman being publicly proclaimed, will show an amount of imprudence which cannot but damage him in the eyes of the middle and lower classes.'

She was right. After the case Bertie's reputation, already low following his neglect of Alix during her illness, sank lower than ever and the once popular Prince who had been greeted with loud cheers whenever he appeared in public was now met either with a stony silence or hisses and boos. At the same time there was spreading across the country a conspicuous republican feeling owing in part to Bertie's behaviour and in part to the reclusiveness of Queen Victoria. The British people were disappointed in a monarch who shut herself away out of sight, leaving all public duties to others. No doubt she was hard at work, and her influence and private life were exemplary, but the public expected more; they wanted contact with the people and grand public occasions with all the pomp and pageantry of royalty which Queen Victoria dreaded. For a time the unpopularity of the Royal Family was pronounced; Alix, however, was always immune from it, for she was as popular as ever, and there were those who said that she alone – beautiful, pure and ill-used – was saving the throne for her husband.

Republican sentiment died down as quickly as it arose, and for an unexpected reason. In 1870, when he was twenty-nine, the Prince fell victim to the same disease (typhoid fever) as had killed his father, and for the same reason – the foul state of the drains in large stately homes. For a time his condition became so critical that there was serious concern for his life, and all his near family gathered round him at Sandringham to pay their last respects; but then, on the brink of the grave, he rallied and recovered, and throughout the country, even in some republican circles, there was a feeling of great relief and rejoicing. A service of thanksgiving in St Paul's was proclaimed by the government for which Queen Victoria, albeit reluctantly, was persuaded to drive with the Prince and Princess of Wales in an open carriage from Buckingham Palace. This, her first major public appearance since the death of Prince Albert, caused the wildest excitement. People poured into London from all over the country, and all the way the streets were lined by enthusiastic and emotional crowds. For the time being Bertie was back in popular favour. And for a time, too, while he was laid up and Alix had him to herself, the couple became as close as they were ever to be. Alix wrote: 'The quiet time we two have spent here together now has been the happiest days of my life. You would hardly know me now in my happiness. We are never apart and are enjoying our second honeymoon.'

As the Prince was approaching thirty the feeling was growing in some quarters that the time had come for him to play a larger part in government. Some responsibility, it was thought, would steady him down and give him invaluable experience for when he became king. He was well qualified: he had travelled widely, spoke three languages fluently and knew all the main European rulers, indeed he was related to most of them; and he himself was eager and willing. The case seemed unanswerable, but it met with implacable opposition from Queen Victoria who refused obdurately to consider him for any official post or even to allow him access to state papers. It seems that she had inherited the Hanoverian distrust of heirs apparent and was jealous of the least infringement of the royal prerogative. She also felt that Bertie's way of life and the company he kept made him unreliable. So when ministers produced schemes for possible employment she turned them down flat. This might have caused Bertie to become resentful and, as had happened in the reigns of the first three Georges, to set up a court of his own in opposition. But this he never thought of doing. In all his dealings with his mother he was endlessly good-tempered and patient and only ever raised the mildest of protests in the face of her relentless criticisms.

The exclusion of the Prince from all public affairs was certainly unfortunate, if only because he lapsed more and more into a life of pleasure and indulgence, entertaining and being entertained sumptuously and consorting with the great beauties of the time wherever he found them. In the year after his illness Alix gave birth to a sixth child, a weak, puny creature who only survived a few days, which caused both parents great distress, and it seems that Alix then decided that she would have no more children and that the physical side of her marriage was at an end. The consequence of this was that Bertie became more open in his association with other women and, like some of his Hanoverian forebears, designated one or the other of them as *maîtresse-en-titre* so that they were always keeping him company, and hostesses were expected to invite them together to their parties.

The first and perhaps the most renowned of these was Lillie Langtry, the 'Jersey Lily'. The daughter of a Jersey clergyman and the wife of a dim, complaisant Jersey businessman, she had taken London by storm. Such was her beauty and poise that people clambered on chairs to catch a glimpse of her passing by; and Bertie was far from the only one to be entranced. It might have been expected that Alix would have been strongly resentful of the Jersey Lily but not so. 'The most publicly wronged wife in Europe' she might be, but she was determined not to play that role. She seems to have accepted that Bertie's deviations, as with most European royalty, were part of his nature and could not be stemmed. Towards Mrs Langtry and her successors she felt no jealousy or malice, and she treated them with courtesy and in some cases even warmth. And in this she surely showed wisdom and magnanimity. She was not the featherbrain she is sometimes supposed to have been. It is true that she was no intellectual and in company sometimes seemed to be at sea, coming out with remarks of startling irrelevancy, but this was usually due to her deafness. There were those at the time who did not underestimate her intelligence. Lord Esher wrote of her: 'She has much of the force of character and a good deal of the sound sense of Queen Caroline. She says more original things and has more unexpected ideas than any of her family.'[7]

Although Bertie and Alix were increasingly going separate ways, their mutual respect and love remained intact. There was no bitterness between them. It was understood that Alix tolerated Bertie's infidelities while Bertie, for his part, was endlessly forbearing about Alix's foibles, notably her spendthrift ways and chronic unpunctuality. He also had no objection when Alix allowed one of his equerries to be her constant companion and enjoy a special relationship with her. In normal life Oliver Montagu was a somewhat roisterous Guards officer, ready to live it up with the best of them; but when with the Princess of Wales he became transformed into a chivalrous knight, idealistic and chaste. For twenty-five years he devoted his life to her. Usually this would have given rise to murmurings and gossip but not in this case. Such was Alix's reputation for purity, and so clearly was Oliver a starry-eyed romantic, that there was no breath of scandal and no one doubted, not even Queen Victoria, that their love was pure and noble. When Oliver died in 1893 at the age of forty-eight Alix mourned him deeply. In time she developed a similar relationship with another man but one of a very different ilk. The Marquis de Soveral was Portuguese (said to be of illegitimate royal birth), a friend of Bertie's, full of exuberant charm and worldly witticisms. Always exquisitely dressed, with twirling moustache and flamboyant buttonholes, he resembled no one so much as a villain in a Victorian melodrama. But he, too, in the presence of Alix became a discreet and devoted admirer.

As Bertie resumed his pleasure-seeking ways, Alix, partly because of deafness and partly because she had differing tastes, spent more and more time with her family. By the age of twenty-seven she had five surviving children, and there was nothing that gave her greater pleasure than to be with them – watching over them, playing with them and attending to their needs. Her ideas on the upbringing of children were permissive. Education, particularly of her daughters, she did not rate highly, and she was no disciplinarian. As a child she herself had been allowed the maximum of freedom, and she wanted her children to have the same. And to this Bertie had no objection. He had no great interest in small children, but when with them he was usually kindly and genial and determined that they should not have the severe, unbending upbringing he himself had had. At Sandringham, particularly, they were allowed to run wild – romping down the corridors, interrupting adult conversations and all too ready with some fiendish practical joke. Visitors were shocked by such behaviour, one remarking that they were 'past all management', and Queen Victoria was outraged. 'They are such ill-bred, ill-trained children I cannot fancy them at all,' she declared. Every now and then they might provoke a storm from their father, which could be terrifying, but never from their mother. After some prank (such as when they brought a pony into her sitting-room) she merely smiled and said that at their age she had been just as bad.

These free-and-easy ways, so different from previous royal families (and some later ones), may have brought about a blissfully happy childhood but may also have contributed to problems later on. Alix was a wonderful mother in many ways and her children adored her, but in time she became too possessive and her love too cloying. It seemed she did not want them to grow up but yearned for them to remain darling children for ever. She herself was always a child at heart and maybe (perhaps subconsciously) she wanted her children to be the same. She would have liked to keep them all permanently under her wing, but with her two sons this was impossible as they were in direct succession to the throne, and at the ages of thirteen and twelve Albert Victor (known in the family as Eddy) and George, marked for careers in the Navy, were sent off with a tutor on a long sea voyage. It had already become evident that Eddy had serious problems. He seemed slow and apathetic and uninterested in anything his tutor tried to teach him. The latter wrote in despairing terms to his parents, who were worried but convinced themselves that he was going through a phase and would in time grow out of it. But these hopes were not to be fulfilled, and the problem of Eddy was to become worse rather than better. His younger brother George was a more promising prospect – robust and reliable, although with limited interests and certainly not brilliant.

It was paradoxical that all the children of Bertie and Alix should have been unremarkable. None of them inherited their father's ebullience and panache or their mother's beauty and grace. The daughters were plain and somewhat gauche, known cruelly among their contemporaries as 'the hags'. And none of them was destined for great happiness.

Although their ways were diverging Bertie and Alix still spent much time together at Sandringham and Marlborough House and on state occasions where together they never failed to make a splendid impression. Alix was also always quick to come to Bertie's support when there was trouble. This became necessary in 1875 while Bertie was on a visit to India. With him at the time was an old friend, Lord Aylesford, who in the course of the tour received a letter from his wife informing him that she was about to leave him and elope with Lord Blandford, the eldest son of the Duke of Marlborough. This brought Lord Aylesford hurrying home bent on divorce, which alarmed the Marlborough family as it would bring them great social disgrace. In order to prevent it Blandford's younger brother, Lord Randolph Churchill (father of Winston), was prepared to use all means at his disposal, however unscrupulous. It happened that a few years earlier Bertie had had a minor flirtation with Lady Aylesford and had written her some mildly indiscreet letters which she had kept. These she now handed over to Lord Randolph, who threatened to publish them if Bertie did not prevent Lord Aylesford from suing for divorce. As Bertie at the time was in India, shooting tigers and elephants and hobnobbing with maharajahs, Lord Randolph, rashly and surely unforgivably, lodged the blackmail with Alix, who not unnaturally was overcome with confusion. An ugly and dangerous situation then arose, leading to Bertie challenging Lord Randolph to a duel, which was fortunately not practicable, since duels had long since been outlawed. Things calmed down to some extent when Lord Aylesford was persuaded to withdraw his application for divorce and Lord Randolph made some sort of apology; but this was not accepted by Bertie, who saw to it that for several years afterwards Lord Randolph and the Marlborough family were excluded from leading social occasions.

For some time after the Aylesford contretemps Bertie and Alix were free from serious trouble, but at the beginning of the 1890s misfortunes crowded in on them, of which the most prominent and most damaging was the Tranby Croft affair. Colonel Sir William Gordon-Cumming, a soldier with a fine record and a pillar of society, was accused of cheating at cards (baccarat, a game banned by law). The incident occurred at a house party attended by Bertie during a game in which he was playing and acting as banker. The cheating, which occurred several times, was witnessed by some of the guests; when confronted, Gordon-Cumming denied the charge, but in order to avoid a scandal he promised never to play cards again if the matter remained completely confidential. It did not, and the affair was soon a subject of clubland gossip, whereupon the colonel took his accusers to court for slander. The defendants did not include the Prince of Wales, but he was subpoenaed as a witness and had to admit that he was playing an illegal game in none too reputable company. Gordon-Cumming lost the case, but public opinion was strongly in his favour because it was believed that he had been victimized. Throughout the proceedings Bertie was strongly supported both by Alix and Queen Victoria, although the latter, with her usual perspicacity, was well aware of the harm that had been done. 'It is a fearful humiliation', she wrote, 'to see the future King of this country dragged (and for the second time) through the dirt just like anyone else in a Court of Justice.'

At the same time as this was going on Bertie had become entangled once again in a friend's matrimonial affairs. For some years after the lapse of his liaison with Lily Langtry he had dallied with a number of younger lovers (known irreverently as 'HRH's virgin band'), but then in 1889, when he was forty-eight, he became involved in the most passionate of all his romances. Daisy Brooke, later the Countess of Warwick, was a lady of outstanding beauty and personality. Elinor Glyn, the novelist, who had been around and during the course of her life met all manner of women from queens to film stars, wrote that she had never met anyone who was so completely fascinating. She was also extremely rich. At an early age she had married Charlie Brooke, heir to the Earl of Warwick, amiable, sporting, unintellectual and, as it later proved, infinitely complaisant. It was not long before they were going their separate ways and Daisy was casting around for diversions, chief among whom was Lord Charles Beresford, a gallant naval officer, Irish, hot-blooded and an irrepressible philanderer. Soon Daisy and Lord Charles were deeply in love, and they made no secret of the fact. How Bertie came to be involved in the affair is worthy of a play by Oscar Wilde. It began when Daisy discovered that Lord Charles's wife Minnie – ten years older than him and with fading charms – was expecting a baby which, in view of her age and repute for chastity, could only have been begotten by him. And she was outraged. She felt let down and humiliated and in her fury wrote Lord Charles a highly charged and indiscreet letter, accusing him of cruel infidelity and ordering him to leave Minnie at once. It happened that at the time Lord Charles was abroad on active service, and the letter was opened by Minnie herself. She was amazed and horrified by the insolence of it. How could Charles be accused of infidelity for sleeping with his wife? At the same time she realized astutely that the letter gave her the whip hand over Daisy, whom she had long resented, so she lodged it safely with a well-known London solicitor and then let Daisy know she was in possession of it. As expected, this threw Daisy into a state close to hysteria. Publication of the letter would bring disgrace and ridicule upon her. Somehow she had to get it back, and in her torment she turned for help to the Prince of Wales, with whom she was acquainted, although not as yet intimately. Such beauty in distress could not fail to make an impression on Bertie, and he agreed at once to do all he could to help – to the extent of calling on the London solicitor at his home in the middle of the night. But Minnie would not relent. She saw in the letter the means of avenging herself on the seducer of her husband, and she was not letting it go. By then Bertie was deeply in love with Daisy, and he was not giving up either. He had a potent weapon in his armoury: it was in his power to see that Minnie and her husband were excluded from society, and when Minnie proved intransigent he proceeded to wield his weapon. This brought down on his head the furious wrath of Lord Charles Beresford, maddened not only by Bertie's treatment of Minnie but also by jealousy at Bertie's appropriation of Daisy. Soon after his return from abroad he encountered Bertie by chance in Daisy's boudoir and a tempestuous scene ensued which only just stopped short of physical violence. In the end the matter was settled reasonably peace-fully and without public scandal following the tactful intervention of the Prime Minister Lord Salisbury.[8] The offending letter was restored, apologies of a sort were exchanged and Daisy began her nine-year reign as Bertie's *maîtresse-en-titre*. As Lord Esher was to remark: 'Lord Salisbury brought peace – whether with much honour or not may be questioned.'

At the time this episode was coming to the boil Alix was out of the country on one of her visits to Denmark. When she heard of it she was, it seems, unusu-ally upset and for once administered a semi-public rebuke: instead of returning to England to join in the celebrations for Bertie's fiftieth birthday she chose instead to go to Russia for the silver wedding anniversary of her sister Dagmar and the Tsar. In England this aroused comment, and there were those who wondered if she would return at all; but of course she did, indeed she came hurrying back earlier than intended when she heard that her younger son, George, had been struck down with typhoid fever which had killed his grand-father and nearly killed his father. For a time there was anxiety, but George proved resilient and recovered quickly.

Back at home Alix behaved with her usual grace and good humour and showed no ill will towards Bertie and Daisy. But there was another matter which weighed on her heavily. The position of her eldest son, Prince Eddy, was deteri-orating seriously. After his long sea voyage, from which he seemed to have gained nothing, it was decided to take him out of the Navy and send him to Cambridge, but here, too, he was found to be ineducable. As listless and uncomprehending as ever, he could not be stirred into any kind of intellectual activity. His father then decided he should go into the Army and be attached to a well-known regiment, but this, too, was a failure. The same mental inertia afflicted him, he became bored and was unable to carry out the simplest drills and manoeuvres. Worse still, he was led into bad habits, roaming the streets and keeping low company, and the voice of scandal was never silent. Once again his family had to consider what was to be done next. The Prince of Wales thought, as other fathers had thought before about the black sheep of their families, that he should be sent out to a far-distant colony. Queen Victoria opposed this plan, preferring that he spend time in Europe, learning foreign languages and becoming acquainted with foreign rulers; but his father felt this would bring him into too close contact with the fleshpots (although he was hardly in a position to adopt a high moral tone about these), while Alix was convinced he should stay at home where he would be kept on the rails by her love and tender care. On one point, however, there was general agreement – that he should marry as soon as possible; this was the one thing that might steady him. Prince Eddy himself was willing and immediately became engaged to the charming and beautiful Princess Hélène d'Orléans, daughter of the pretender to the French throne, the Comte de Paris. It seemed she would have made him an admirable wife, but there were problems: such a marriage might have caused difficulties with the leaders of the French Republic and, more importantly, she was a Roman Catholic and to comply with British law would have to become a Protestant, and this her father firmly forbade. It was therefore necessary to look elsewhere, and it so happened there was then available a princess with all the necessary qualifications – Protestant, a great-granddaughter of George III, virtuous, good-looking, intelligent and ready to take on the uncertain responsibilities of being married to Eddy. Princess Mary of Teck (known as May) seemed in every way ideal, and Eddy, who, whatever his other defects, was not unamenable, was willing to take her as his bride instead of Hélène. He proposed to her and was accepted, and everyone was delighted. But then fate struck a cruel blow. Seven weeks before his wedding day Eddy fell ill with influenza, not itself a very serious disease, but then it turned to pneumonia and within a week he was dead. For all the family this was a heartrending blow, but for Alix it was devastating.

He was her first born, and his weaknesses brought out all her maternal and protective instincts, and she loved him more than any other of her children. Eddy's death meant that his younger brother George became heir presumptive, and it was felt that he should now lose no time in getting married to provide heirs for the next generation. It seems as if he did have some ideas of his own as to whom he might marry, but when the great advantages of Princess May were pointed out to him he was ready to comply. This did not at first gladden the heart of Alix who dreaded the loss of a child to marriage. She looked on them always as children and for a long time continued to address George as 'Georgie boy' and her letters to him were always interlarded with baby talk.

This was not a happy time for Alix. Eddy's death was soon followed by those of Oliver Montagu and then her mother, to whom she was greatly devoted. And at the same time she had to accustom herself to a change of personnel in her husband's ménage. After nine years Daisy Brooke was being eased out. Her beauty and charm remained, but she had become passionately devoted to the relief of poverty as well as becoming an active and proselytising social- ist. Bertie was not blind to the horrendous poverty of the times, and after a visit incognito to the slums of St Pancras he had served for a time on a Royal Commission on the Housing of the Working Class. But he could hear too much of it and was not attracted by socialism, remarking sagely that societies grow and are not made. Daisy's place as *maîtresse-en-titre* was soon filled. In 1898, when he was fifty-seven, Bertie met Alice Keppel, half his age, attractive, sooth- ing and understanding, and he fell in love with her at once. She was married, but her husband was affable and tolerant, and soon she was Bertie's constant companion, and it became known that he expected her to be included in any party to which he was invited. She became adept at managing Bertie's moods and anticipating and preventing outbursts of anger. She was to remain *in situ* for the remaining twelve years of his life.

Another lady with whom Bertie had a relationship, although of a different kind, was Agnes Keyser, the daughter of a prosperous London stockbroker, who, following the example of Florence Nightingale, had forsworn society and set up a nursing home for wounded officers in her home near Buckingham Palace. Practical, forthright and a compelling personality, she was also a good listener, and Bertie loved to pour out his woes to her, so much so that he was even prepared to forgo his sumptuous meals in Buckingham Palace and be fed nursery food (Irish stew and rice pudding) for the sake of a long talk with her. A lasting result of their partnership was that, with financial help from Bertie's rich friends, one of London's most famous hospitals was founded, the King Edward VII or, as it is sometimes known, Sister Agnes. With this platonic friend- ship Alix could have little objection except, perhaps, the further realization that as a wife there were some roles she was unable to fulfil.

With the outbreak of the Boer War in 1899 Alix at once became involved in the care of the sick and wounded. She took part in the dispatch of a hospi- tal ship to South Africa and as well sent out twelve nursing sisters, chosen by her, who were to become the nucleus of the body later known as the Queen Alexandra Imperial Nursing Service, a large national organization. From then on she became increasingly concerned with hospitals in England, particu- larly the London Hospital in the East End which she visited frequently, showing no squeamishness about visiting the most gruesome wards and, as always, full of love and sympathy and ready to distribute largesse.

In 1901 an era came to an end with the death of Queen Victoria. She had been Queen for sixty-four years and Alix, like many others, was stunned and could not imagine life without her. In the course of their long relationship Alix had come in for much forthright criticism and advice, but underlying it all had been a deep love between them, and Alix had doubts as to how she would manage without her. She was, however, glad to discover a new freedom. Until then she had lived in the shadow of the great Queen, not always obeying her behests but always conscious of her strong prejudices and idiosyncrasies and aware that she was under close observation. Now at last she was free from these inhibiting influences and could lead a more independent life.

As Queen there was little doubt that Alix would be as great a success as ever. At fifty-six she was still wonderfully beautiful, her grace and charm as irresistible and her dress sense as infallible as ever. At the coronation all eyes were on her. An eyewitness later wrote: 'When the Queen appeared in the Abbey it was like a vision coming through the dark archway of the screen. I never saw anything more beautiful.' And Margot Asquith, the sharp-tongued wife of the Prime Minister, wrote at this time: 'The Queen, dazzlingly beautiful, whether in gold and silver by night or in violet velvet by day, succeeded in making every other woman look common beside her.' Her popularity in the country never lapsed. She showed that it was possible to be both glamorous and virtuous and was all the more loved because she was seen to be a wronged wife betrayed by a dissolute husband.

Yet Alix was no saint. Behind the glittering appearance there had always been flaws, and once she was Queen these became more apparent: her manner became more imperious, her temper more wayward and her determination to have her own way more steely. Her younger son George, who loved her devotedly, could yet write of her: 'Mama, as I have always said, is one of the most selfish people I know.' This selfishness manifested itself in various ways –insensitivity to the feelings of others, disregard of their convenience, unpunctuality and the assumption that what was best for her was best for everyone. This was particularly evident in her treatment of her three daughters, whom she bound closely to herself and for whom she made no special efforts to find husbands. She seems to have convinced herself that they did not want to marry and would be happy to remain for ever her companions and playfellows. This attitude did not meet with the approval of Queen Victoria, who believed strongly that for women the single state was 'unfortunate' and that sexual fulfilment was essential. Eventually the eldest, Louise, did marry a somewhat nondescript Scottish nobleman, the Earl of Fife (rewarded with a dukedom), eighteen years older than her, wealthy but hardly an exhilarating husband. For most of her marriage she was a nervous recluse, finding some comfort in salmon fishing at which she is said to have become very adept. The second daughter, Maud, was persuaded at the age of twenty-seven to marry a Danish cousin, Prince Charles, who later became King Haakon VII of Norway; but for her, too, marriage brought little joy, and she was endlessly homesick for Sandringham. The youngest daughter, Victoria, did not marry; it seems that she had been in love with several men, including Lord Rosebery, one of the richest and most talented (and unhappiest) men in the country; but marriage to a commoner was forbidden to her (in spite of the example of her eldest sister), so she remained a supernumerary lady-in-waiting to her mother, constantly in attendance, with little life of her own and sinking into hypochondria.

Even before Bertie became king it had become evident that he and Alix were growing apart, and this was to become more pronounced. They still had great respect and some warmth for each other, and on public occasions they were as splendid a combination as ever. But in private there was no intimacy. Bertie could not unburden himself to Alix in the way that he did to Mrs Keppel and Sister Agnes; while Alix did not feel at ease with him as she did with Oliver Montagu or the Marquis de Soveral. When Bertie came to the throne he embarked on his kingly duties with tremendous zest and energy. He had never worked so hard in his life. But from these activities Alix was almost entirely excluded. Unlike his mother, Edward did admit his heir apparent, Prince George, into the affairs of government and allowed him to have access to state papers, as he did, too, to Princess May; but not his wife. There were perhaps good reasons for this. Alix had few political views, but they were strong ones and were all based on family ties. Because her sister was the Dowager Empress she tended to be favourable to Russia, and she always gave unquestioning support to her brother George, King of Greece in all the troubles in which he so often became embroiled. And she was as bitterly hostile as ever towards Germany, and Kaiser Wilhelm II in particular, for the seizure of the Danish provinces of Schleswig-Holstein. Nor was she renowned for her tact and diplomacy. She spoke her mind and saw no need for discretion. So in view of the very delicate and dangerous political situation in Europe at that time, with a major war always imminent, the King felt that Alix should be kept at a distance, and on most of his trips abroad he went without her.[9] He also discouraged her from carrying out royal duties on her own, so for much of the time she remained alone at Sandringham or with her relations in Denmark. Very occasionally, for the sake of appearances, Edward would accompany her on these visits, but they were not a success; life at the Danish court bored him and he did not have enough to eat.

For most of the ten years he was on the throne Edward was much engaged in keeping the peace of Europe. In this he was a key figure: he was well acquainted with all the European rulers and related by family ties to nearly all the crowned heads – the Emperors of Germany and Russia and the Kings of Greece and Denmark were all his nephews. And no one was more aware than Edward of the fragility of European peace at that time. The large nations were squaring up against each other – Germany and the Austrian Empire against France and Russia, with Great Britain still lingering in so-called 'splendid isolation'. The

Sophia Dorothea of Celle, *c.* 1700
William Faithorne Junior; National Portrait Gallery

Left
Queen Charlotte of Mecklenburg-Strelitz, 1761
Sir Thomas Lawrence; National Portrait Gallery

Above
George III and Queen Charlotte and their six eldest children, *c.* 1770
Zoffany, Royal Collection 2005; Her Majesty Queen Elizabeth II

The marriage of George IV to Caroline of Brunswick, 1795
National Portrait Gallery

Caroline of Brunswick, *c.* 1800
Henry Meyer after Lonsdale; National Portrait Gallery

Above
Queen Adelaide of Saxe-Coburg, *c.* 1820
Thomas Lupton; National Portrait Gallery

Right
Queen Alexandra when Princess of Wales, 1863
W. and D. Downey; National Portrait Gallery

Above
Queen Alexandra when Princess of Wales, 1902
National Portrait Gallery

Left
Edward VII and Queen Alexandra with their eldest children, 1868
W. and D. Downey; National Portrait Gallery

George V and Queen Mary with their children, 1906
W. and D. Downey; National Portrait Gallery

Queen Mary, 1911
Bassano; National Portrait Gallery

Queen Mary inspecting the Green Cross Corps, 1919
National Portrait Gallery

The Duke and Duchess of Windsor, 1943
Dorothy Wilding; National Portrait Gallery

George VI and Queen Elizabeth inspecting
war damage at Buckingham Palace, 1940
Topfoto

George VI with Queen Elizabeth and their daughters Margaret (left)
and Elizabeth
Dorothy Wilding; National Portrait Gallery

Queen Elizabeth the Queen Mother fishing in the Waikato River, near Waiakei,
Auckland, New Zealand, 29 April 1966
© *Science & Society Picture Library/National Portrait Gallery, London*

main troublemaker was Edward's nephew, the Emperor of Germany, Kaiser Wilhelm II, whose behaviour and utterances sometimes verged on dementia. As he strutted the world stage, at times cooing like a dove and at others roaring like a lion, it was indeed frightening that such a man should have at his command the world's largest army. Unfortunately the relationship between uncle and nephew was strained. The two men put each other's back up. Wilhelm resented what he regarded as his uncle's patronizing manner, especially during the years when he was a crowned head and Edward only an heir apparent, and he was jealous of Edward's great reputation in Europe and later felt inferior when he became king and emperor of a much larger empire than his own. Edward for his part did not always conceal his opinion that his nephew was an aggressive and irresponsible braggart. If there had not been this strong personal antipathy the history of Europe might have been different. As it was Edward played a leading part in guiding Britain into the camp of France and Russia, especially after the Kaiser embarked on the building of a battle fleet to rival Britain's. Whether Edward was as great a peacemaker as he is sometimes represented or whether by taking the side of Germany's opponents he fomented German feelings of insecurity and aggression must remain in contention.

During her ten years as Queen of England Alix had mixed fortunes. Things started sadly in the first year with the death of Edward's eldest sister, Victoria, Dowager Empress of Germany. As a rule Alix hated everything German, but she made an exception of her sister-in-law, who was so essentially English and had been struggling valiantly but unavailingly to stem the tide of militarism that was sweeping Germany. It also upset Alix that in the first year George and May should embark on a long overseas tour to the colonies. She missed them sorely. To add to her woes there was another fire at Sandringham which did extensive damage and caused her to be hustled out of bed in the middle of the night to escape the danger. But perhaps her main sorrow was that Edward showed no sign of mending his ways with 'other women'. She had hoped that when he became king these women would become less prominent, but Mrs Keppel remained as much to the fore as ever. She seemed omnipresent, accompanying the King on most of his trips abroad, and for once Alix showed some irritation. But then the fates relented, and in 1903 she and Edward made a most successful tour of Ireland. In 1905 she went alone to Portugal, where she created the usual sensation. And in 1907 Edward at last took her with him to Paris where the French, deprived of their own glamorous royalty since the hurried exit of the Empress Eugenie in 1870, predictably went wild about her. 'Belle et magnifique' summed up the impression she made.

By then Edward's health was giving serious cause for concern. The eating of huge rich meals and the smoking of innumerable cigars were taking effect. He suffered from chronic bronchitis, had frequent bouts of indigestion and was apt to fall asleep at embarrassing moments. In 1909 he had serious difficulty getting through a state visit to Berlin. The strain of kingship was becoming too much for him: in Europe the danger of war was as great as ever, and at home a major political crisis had erupted over the Parliament Bill with a confrontation between Lords and Commons over the powers of the former. In the midst of this, with the basic question still unsettled, Edward died at Sandringham on 6 May 1910. To his deathbed Alix summoned Mrs Keppel to join the family for a last farewell.

Edward had been one of England's most splendid kings. He had more than a passing resemblance to Henry VIII, combining dignity with great bonhomie. His prestige and influence in Europe were exceptional, far greater than that of any foreign secretary. Certainly he lived life to the full – no man more so. In his private life he may have been grossly self-indulgent, but everything he did was on a majestic scale; there was nothing mean or paltry about him. As a husband he may have been flagrantly unfaithful, but otherwise he was kindly and considerate and did all he could to humour his wife and uphold her dignity. In spite of everything he never lost her love, and she could always comfort herself with the thought that 'he always loved me best'.

Alix did not take easily to widowhood. The death of Edward left her bereft: 'I feel as if I had been turned to stone,' she wrote, 'unable to cry, unable to grasp the meaning of it all.' George and Mary, the new King and Queen, were endlessly patient, but she did make difficulties about such matters as the ownership of jewellery and precedence on state occasions. She also dragged her heels about moving out of Buckingham Palace (into which she had moved so reluctantly ten years before); and there was no question of her moving out of 'the big house' at Sandringham, so George and Mary and their six children were left in cramped conditions in York Cottage on the estate.

For whatever reason Alix did not attend her son's coronation and for long periods would isolate herself at Sandringham feeling that her 'life was finished and there was nothing left for her'. Despite being surrounded by faithful and adoring attendants she felt great loneliness, and this was intensified when soon after the coronation George and Mary went off to India to be crowned at a Durbah. Alix missed them sorely but took comfort from their six young children who were left in her care. This was unalloyed joy, as she loved them dearly and especially the youngest, Prince John, then aged six, who suffered from epilepsy and whose brain would never develop normally; and, as always, Alix was drawn particularly towards the weakling of the family. The other children, too, had a welcome break while their parents were away, as in the upbringing of his children George had reverted to old Hanoverian methods of regimentation and discipline, while Mary, although a splendid wife, was ill at ease as a mother and could never manage a warm and easy relationship with her children. This, of course, was something at which their grandmother excelled, and while their parents were away they were spoiled outrageously. For much of the time they were allowed to run wild, and lessons, which had always been sacrosanct, were treated as of secondary importance.

Alix's foreboding that with Edward's death her life was finished and there was nothing left for her was soon dispelled. She was still the most widely known and best loved of the Royal Family, and her association with any charity never failed to give it a boost, and she was always generous with time and money.

When war was declared in August 1914 she was to the fore in the surge of patriotism that erupted, as well as in the outburst of vicious anti-German feeling. She readily believed all the stories of German atrocities in Belgium, and her general attitude was 'I told you so.' Ever since the invasion of Schleswig-Holstein more than fifty years before she had been convinced that Germany was out to dominate Europe, and she had not been backward in expressing her view that the sooner it was stopped by war the better. Her hatred of Germany was intensified when at the beginning of 1915 Zeppelins dropped bombs in the neighbourhood of Sandringham while she was in residence. This she regarded as a personal insult and wrote to her great friend and admirer Admiral Fisher, the First Sea Lord, asking for 'a supply of rockets with spikes and hooks to bring down a few of these rascals'.[10]

Although in 1914 Alix had reached her seventies, she undertook more work than ever. She was already actively engaged with, among other organizations, the Red Cross and the London Hospital, but she now took upon herself a heavy programme of visiting the wounded and the shell-shocked, a task she performed superbly: her warmth, charm and heartfelt grief at their sufferings made a deep impression and gave to many the will to survive. Her visits did, however, cause problems for the hospital authorities, as she was quite unable to adhere to any schedule, invariably arriving late and staying longer than expected as she insisted on talking to every patient, often at length. As an administrator plaintively remarked, 'It was easy enough to get the Queen into a ward but much harder to get her out.'

While Alexandra's war work was certainly of great value, it was to some extent offset by her adamant refusal to curb her lifestyle and adhere to wartime restrictions on food and fuel. While her son the King set an admirable example of Spartan living (even banning alcohol from royal meals), she refused to make any sacrifices and expected her way of life to be as it had always been. Rationing was not for her. More seriously, she made no attempt to rein in her unstinting expenditure, either for her personal needs or her lavish gifts to others. She had always been irresponsible about money, never counting the cost or relating expenditure to income. These were not her worries. Other people would take care of them, and previously they had, but now with heavy wartime taxation, to which she was liable, her income had been much reduced while she spent as freely as ever. When taxed with the matter she would dismiss it airily, saying that 'they' would pay, unaware that 'they' meant King George who, as in all things, treated his beloved 'mother dear' with the greatest generosity.

Queen Alexandra was more fortunate than most in not counting anyone very close to her among the casualties of the war. She had many relations on the battlefield, on both sides, but most of them survived. The most dreadful tragedy came in the last year of the war when, following the Bolshevik Revolution, the Russian Royal Family was murdered in cold blood. The Tsar, Nicholas, was her nephew, and the Tsarina, Alexandra, was her niece by marriage, and the blow was all the more shattering as it might have been avoided if George V had granted them asylum in England, but for fear of stirring up trouble among British revolutionaries he would not do so, and it must have always weighed heavily on him. When news of the killings reached England there was acute anxiety about the Dowager Tsarina, Alexandra's sister Dagmar, but here the King did intervene and a British cruiser was sent to the Crimea to rescue her and her entourage.

Queen Alexandra was not spared the afflictions of old age. By the end of the war she was stone deaf, and in 1920, when she was seventy-five, a blood vessel broke in her eye so that for a time she was almost totally blind. And there were signs that her mind was beginning to weaken; she became aware of loss of memory and described herself as 'feeling a perfect idiot'. There were fewer and fewer things she enjoyed doing and was able to do. Her annual visits to Denmark, which had been part of her life for so long, she could no longer manage, and all travel became irksome. Her sister Dagmar, with whom she had once been closer than anyone, visited her occasionally, but she had been unable to shed the ways of Tsarist Russia and was not an altogether easy companion. Until the end she was faithfully and devotedly attended: her daughter Victoria was nearly always with her and her lady-in-waiting Charlotte Knollys never left her side, and George V and Queen Mary were always loving and long-suffering.

In 1925, when she was eighty, Alexandra wrote: 'I feel completely collapsed. I shall soon go.' Nevertheless, at the same time a journalist who visited her at Sandringham could write of her 'exquisite fragility . . . her figure slender and willowy . . . and that wonderful smile which ravished all in the days when she came a girl-bride, remained with her in its undying beauty'. Soon afterwards she had a severe heart attack and on the following day, 20 November, she died.

7
MARY OF TECK
WIFE OF GEORGE V

No queen consort has given her husband and country such stoical and self-less service as Queen Mary of Teck. Lacking the beauty and charm of her mother-in-law, Queen Alexandra, and afflicted with a shyness she never overcame, she found some of the duties of a queen difficult and disagreeable, but she never held back or spared herself. At a time when all European thrones were in danger and many were disappearing she devoted herself totally to the cause of the British monarchy, and it was in no small measure due to her that it survived.

Mary was born in 1867 in Kensington Palace. She was a great-granddaughter of George III, her mother, Princess Mary Adelaide, being the daughter of his youngest son, the Duke of Cambridge. At the time of Mary's birth Queen Victoria, her mother's first cousin, was still in mourning for her husband, Prince Albert, and rarely appeared in public, but she came down at once to inspect the new baby whom she pronounced to be fine-looking and agreed to become her godmother. At her christening she was given the names Victoria Mary Augusta Louise Olga Pauline Claudia Agnes, but for the first part of her life she was known by none of these names but simply as May, the month in which she had been born.

Princess Mary Adelaide, the dominant influence in May's early life, was a striking character – high-spirited, big-hearted and enormously stout.[1] She was one of the best-known and most popular of royalty, but she had an irrespon-sible streak which laid her family open to many troubles. As the granddaughter of a king and at one time fifth in succession to the English throne she had been sought in marriage from an early age, but suitors had been put off partly by her eccentric ways and partly by her size. As the British Foreign Secretary, Lord Clarendon, irreverently remarked: 'No prince would venture on such a vast undertaking.' But this did not trouble Mary Adelaide, who had no great long-ing for marriage. In particular she dreaded spending the rest of her life in the dull, starchy court of a minor German princeling. She went her own way – laughing and joking, eating prodigiously and letting it be known that she was quite content to remain 'a jolly old maid'. But such a life could not continue indefinitely. The senior members of her family (her mother the Dowager Duchess, her brother George, the second Duke of Cambridge, and Queen Victoria herself) became alarmed at her behaviour, particularly her reckless extravagance, and decided that to settle her down and keep her in check a husband had to be found. In 1866, when she was thirty-three, someone was discovered who, it was thought, might adequately fit the bill. Prince Franz of Teck was four years younger than Mary Adelaide, good-looking, apparently even-tempered and not to be put off by her ever-swelling figure. However, there were drawbacks. In the first place he was almost totally impecunious, and secondly he was the offspring of a morganatic marriage and therefore not fully royal. His father, Duke Alexander of Württemburg, had married for love a beautiful Hungarian countess, Claudia Rhedy, well born but non-royal, and by so doing was barred from the throne of Württemburg, as were his heirs including Franz. In time Franz was given a minor title, that of Duke of Teck, but this carried with it only the prefix of His Serene Highness rather than His Royal Highness, and this was always a matter of great distress to him.

The marriage of Mary Adelaide and Franz, or Francis as he came to be called in England, was greeted with great popular enthusiasm, and at first all seemed to be going well. May was born a year later and was followed by three handsome and healthy brothers. They were provided with ample and impos-ing accommodation in Kensington Palace (where Queen Victoria and her mother had lived before she came to the throne) where they set out to enter-tain on almost the same scale as the Prince and Princess of Wales. To this residence was later added White Lodge in Richmond Park. Queen Victoria had been reluctant to give her consent to this as she knew that two establish-ments were beyond their means, but she had been persuaded partly on the grounds of the children's health – May having been seriously unwell as a result, so it was believed, of the effluvia emanating from the Round Pond in Kensington Gardens, then a virtual cesspit – and partly by the consideration that in the country Mary Adelaide would have less scope for spending money. But here the Queen was deceived, for Mary Adelaide lost no time in refurbishing White Lodge regardless of cost. For the time being the Tecks lived contentedly, but trouble was brewing.

It was not long before Francis became dissatisfied. He had had great hopes that once married to Mary Adelaide he would be created a duke with the prefix of His Royal Highness, but to this Queen Victoria would not agree on the grounds that there would be difficulties over precedence with other members of the Royal Family. So Francis, to his great chagrin, remained a mere His Serene Highness with the stigma of second-class royalty. He had also hoped that, in view of his service in the Austrian army, a high-ranking position would be found for him in the British army, especially as his brother-in-law, the Duke of Cambridge, was Commander-in-Chief. But this, too, was not forth-coming: it seems that his abilities were not highly rated; the only post to be found for him was that of honorary colonel of the Post Office Volunteers, rather a comedown after the Imperial Gendarmerie of Austria. At times other sugges-tions were made as to possible employment, including Viceroy of Ireland and

King of Bulgaria, but, perhaps fortunately, nothing came of these. He did, however, show ability in different fields – those of gardening and interior decorating – and Mary Adelaide was content to leave in his hands the refurbishment of White Lodge, which he carried out with skill and good taste. But of course this was not enough. He was all too aware that he was underemployed and unappreciated, and this affected his temper which he vented on his family, although not so much on May who was one of the few people who could have a soothing influence on him.

The main cause of the Teck family troubles, however, lay in Mary Adelaide's uncontrolled extravagance. She simply had no idea of making two ends meet; money was there to be spent, and if it wasn't there she spent it all the same. Financially she was not badly off with an income of some £6,000 a year (worth at least fifty times as much today), but it was not enough to support the lifestyle to which she aspired. It was reckoned that her expenditure was almost twice her income; and her debts grew ever larger.

It was in an atmosphere always loving but sometimes turbulent and almost always disorganized that May grew up. She could not be described as a pretty child. Queen Victoria, who had thought her such a fine baby, described her at the age of eight as 'very plain', but this was a phase which she soon outgrew. For most of her youth she was taller than average and apt to be gauche, wearing unflattering clothes and hairstyles. Virtuous she certainly was – taking her younger brothers under her wing and mothering them, soothing the irascibility of her father and assisting her mother in all her multifarious good works – and her own behaviour was always impeccable; there was never any sign of her 'kicking over the traces'. Life was not easy for her and was made harder by an obsessive shyness. Unlike her mother, who was always outgoing and self-assured, she was uneasy in the presence of strangers and hated to be the focus of attention, for she was in mortal terror of making a fool of herself; such things as doing a solo performance in a dancing class scared her rigid. Despite their differences there was a great bond of affection between mother and daughter, and for all her faults Mary Adelaide was not a bad mother. Unlike Princess Alexandra she did not overindulge her children; she saw to it that they were polite and obedient, and she did not neglect their education. From an early age, too, May was introduced into works of charity, accompanying her mother on visits to the poor to see at first hand the poverty and squalor of their lives. Although May was often tongue-tied on these occasions they made a deep impression on her, and the relief of poverty was always to be one of her main concerns.

By 1883, when May was sixteen, Mary Adelaide's financial troubles had come to a head; her debts were larger than ever, creditors were more and more pressing and no further help was forthcoming from her mother or brother or from Queen Victoria; she was told bluntly that the only course open to her was to move out of Kensington Palace, close down White Lodge for the time being and live quietly and economically abroad. This came very hard to her, but in the circumstances she and Francis had no option but to comply. On a September evening a despondent Teck family was seen off from Victoria Station to an enforced exile in Italy.

This was a great humiliation. Mary Adelaide was being publicly branded as irresponsible and feckless and Francis as a weak husband who could not control her. The effect of all this on May can only be guessed, as she never revealed her inner feelings either in letters or in her diary, but it must have been deeply disturbing. In the long run, however, notable benefits were to come from her time abroad, which was far from penitential. It had been decided that Mary Adelaide and Francis should travel incognito as Count and Countess Hohenstein, but this could not long be sustained; Mary Adelaide was all too recognizable, and almost at once there were welcoming deputations wherever they stopped, and within days of reaching Italy they were being dined by the King and Queen. After a brief stay in a villa, lent to them by a relative, the family moved into a hotel in Florence where for several months they occupied a whole floor – hardly, it would seem, a significant economy.

May did not immediately take to Florence. In one of her letters she said it was 'dull', the streets were too narrow and dirty and all Italians smelled of garlic. But she soon discovered the great artistic riches of the city and was writing home that she had been spending all her afternoons lately going to museums and how much nicer this was than going out to tea and gossip. Soon afterwards she was taking lessons in Italian and drawing and building up her knowledge of European art, which in time was to become unique among royalty.

Mary Adelaide, too, was not letting exile depress her. Resilient as ever, she was finding much to occupy her time, although not so much in the arts as in the social scene where, as the granddaughter of a king, she was much in demand. Certainly she seemed to be making no great efforts either to economize or to lose weight, and this resulted in several minor accidents which laid her low for a time.[2] Early in 1884 Francis suffered a paralytic stroke which for the time being incapacitated him. His wife's reaction to this was to assure everyone that it was no more than sunstroke which would soon clear up, and in the meanwhile she left most of the nursing to May who, only seventeen though she might be, shouldered the task uncomplainingly.

After their sojourn in Florence the Teck family borrowed a villa in the country where May led an idyllic life, painting, collecting wild flowers and practising her Italian. This was followed by a round of family visits to relatives in Germany which gave May first-hand experience of the court life of minor German royalty – strict protocol and benumbing etiquette combined with rough games and hearty jokes. She may have resolved then that this would not be the life for her and that get-togethers of what Queen Victoria called 'the royal mob' were, whenever possible, to be avoided.

The Tecks' exile lasted no more than two years. By then the Duke of

Cambridge, Mary Adelaide's brother, and her mother, the Dowager Duchess, had come to realize that it was proving no economy and they could exercise more control over her at home than when she was at large on the Continent. They were also concerned about the future of the children, particularly May who should at the age of eighteen be thinking about matrimony.

In the spring of 1885 the Teck family returned to England, where May found much to do, but before she could appear in public it was essential for her to 'come out', which meant being presented at Court, and this could not happen until she had been confirmed. Then everything was held up by the death of her paternal grandfather, the Duke of Württemburg, and it was necessary to go into mourning. Confirmation, however, did take place quite soon (described by May rather strangely as 'a very pretty service'), but she was not presented to Queen Victoria until March 1886 in time to take part in the London season, when she embarked on a hectic round of balls, fêtes, receptions and country-house parties. For May these were not unalloyed joy as she had still not overcome her shyness and tended to be stiff and silent with people she did not know. At some country-house parties, when among friends, she was able to relax somewhat and could be lively company, but there was always some reserve; she seldom allowed herself to laugh as she thought her laugh was ugly, and there were some country houses where she felt an outsider, notably Sandringham where she was ill-attuned to the fun and games of her Wales cousins; sliding downstairs on a tea tray and setting booby-traps were not for her, and she showed it and so came to be regarded by them as stuffy and heavy-going.

May's time was not occupied entirely by social events. She was kept very busy at home. Her father had made a remarkable recovery from his stroke, but his health and temper were still precarious and May was one of the few people who could comfort him. Her grandmother, the Dowager Duchess of Cambridge, also required constant attention. In her late eighties she had become a rather terrible invalid – bald and bent double – and May was expected to converse with her on her hands and knees, something she particularly dreaded. Later with typical understatement she wrote, 'An invalid rather frightens young people.'

However, the person who took up most of May's time was her mother. On her return to England Mary Adelaide, vital and voluminous, had plunged into a whirl of activity, partly social but mainly philanthropic. Her sympathy for all suffering was profound and genuine. She seldom refused appeals from charities for her patronage, and in giving assistance she did not confine herself to committee work but went visiting the poorest of homes and the most gruesome of hospitals, providing relief wherever she could. In these activities May was usually at her side, taking on the duties of secretary and lady-in-waiting – sorting papers, answering letters, making appeals for funds and coping with her mother's chronic unpunctuality and disorganized ways. Nor did she shirk the nitty-gritty. One charity, the Needlework Guild, brought into White Lodge at certain times of the year great piles of second-hand clothes, and May would be down on the floor sorting them out and then dispatching them to appropriate destinations. May inherited all her mother's care for the poor, and it remained with her always.

Although May was kept busy with good works, she was nevertheless determined to continue to expand her education. Her years in Italy had revealed to her the extent of her ignorance, and she was intent on making this good. Her efforts here were greatly stimulated by the arrival in the Teck household of a governess-companion, Hélène Bricka, a French lady of great intensity and erudition and the bluest of blue-stockings, who became one of May's closest confidantes. Together she and May drew up formidable reading lists comprising not only works of literature but also government Blue Books on social and industrial conditions. It was not always easy, but somehow May contrived to find five or six hours a day for serious reading, and under Madame Bricka's tutelage her interests expanded widely.[3] No other royalty was of her intellectual calibre.

During the six years following May's return to England there was one subject that was always being raised – that of marriage. Everyone had ideas about this, notably her Cambridge grandmother and Queen Victoria, both of whom were inveterate matchmakers. But there were difficulties here. Because of her father's morganatic birth which rendered both him and his descendants only demi-royalty, May would be ruled out as a suitable bride by most of the German principalities. Not that that worried her, as she had no wish to spend her life cooped up in a narrow, restrictive German court. She would rather remain single in England. There was the possibility of marrying a non-royal Englishman, but he would have to be rich as she was almost penniless. It seemed that she fell between two stools – not royal enough for some and too royal for others. These difficulties might have been swept away in face of a passionate love affair, but there was little likelihood of this. May was too staid and unemotional, and men tended to be put off by her reserve and overawed by her intellect. In 1894 she was twenty-four and apparently doomed to spinsterhood and a life of good works and serious study, when quite suddenly her prospects changed dramatically.

As mentioned in Chapter 6, Prince Albert Victor (known as Eddy), the eldest son of the Prince of Wales and heir presumptive to the English throne, had been giving his parents and grandmother cause for anxiety. Amiable enough and with a wistful charm, he had nevertheless failed in everything he had attempted to do and had fallen into bad habits. His family, who took differing views about his future, were agreed on one point: that what he needed as soon as possible was a wife of strong character and good sense, loving and ready to devote her life to him; and Queen Victoria had become convinced that May would be ideal. She attached no importance to morganatic marriages, and the more she saw of May the more she was impressed. The Prince and Princess of Wales, too, came to see that May was the right person to take Eddy in hand. The decision taken, it was assumed that there would be no opposition from the marriage partners themselves, and this proved to be the case. Eddy was compliant as ever, while May marvelled at the prospect and not only for worldly reasons; she was genuinely fond of Eddy and wanted to help him, perhaps because she found his very weaknesses appealing. Plans were set in motion to bring them together, but first it was necessary for May to go to Balmoral for a final inspection by Queen Victoria, which proved entirely satisfactory. 'So carefully brought up, so sensible and unfrivolous', the Queen later wrote. A suitable courtship was then arranged, beginning with a visit by both of them as guests to Luton Hoo, a stately home then occupied by the immensely rich Belgian ambassador, Monsieur de Falbe. This was intended only as a 'warm-up', and Eddy had been told not to propose on this occasion, but whatever his other failings Eddy was no laggard in love and, finding himself alone with May in Madame de Falbe's boudoir, full of exotic flowers and scented with the 'perfumes of Arabia', he was carried away and put the question; May, although taken by surprise, had no hesitation in accepting.

This was the supreme moment of her life. Suddenly from a modest life of good works and earnest study with Madame Bricka, patronized by relations as dull and not fully royal, she was to be transformed into the third lady in the land and the future Queen of England. This was a dazzling prospect indeed. At first all was euphoria. Congratulations poured in, led by Queen Victoria, who wrote to say: 'how much I rejoice at your becoming My Grandchild and how much confidence I have in you to fill worthily the important position to which you are called by your marriage with Eddy'. However, she added a characteristically sombre note to the effect that 'marriage was not all roses and the trials in life begin with marriage'. The Prince and Princess of Wales were also welcoming, although the Prince was somewhat heavy-handed and short tempered, impressing on May that she must keep Eddy 'up to the mark' and see to it that he did this and that, so much so that May wondered for a time if she had taken on more than she could manage. She confided these doubts to her mother but got short shrift from her. 'If I can put up with your father for twenty-five years,' she told her, 'you can handle the Heir Presumptive of Great Britain.'

May's dream lasted for no more than six weeks. At the beginning of January 1892 Eddy went shooting at Sandringham in vile weather and came down with flu. At first there was no great anxiety, but then pneumonia set in and a few days later he was dead. His last days were traumatic for May as he became delirious and his close relatives packed into his tiny bedroom. Most overcome of all was his mother who had doted on him and always been closest to him. Like Queen Victoria after the death of the Prince Consort, she ordered that everything in his room be left exactly as it was, with a fire burning day and night.

May's dream had ended in a nightmare. What was to become of her now?

Was she to return to White Lodge to wait in attendance on her mother, visiting ragged schools and hospitals and sorting out piles of old clothes? Fortunately Queen Victoria lost no time in deciding that May would make an equally good wife for Eddy's younger brother, George; and in these matters the old Queen (then aged seventy-four) usually had her way.

At the time Prince George was twenty-seven. He was a more robust and positive character than his elder brother and had had a successful career of fifteen years in the Royal Navy, reaching the rank of captain. But in 1892 he was in great need of support. He was still weak from an attack of typhoid fever, and the death of Eddy, to whom he was devoted, had upset him sorely. But what was really weighing on him was that he was now heir presumptive to the throne, something for which he had had no training and for which he had no inclination. He had to give up the Navy, assume the title of Duke of York and set about preparing himself for kingship. Just as much as Eddy he needed a strong, intelligent wife to support him, and once again May stood out above all others. At first the Prince and Princess of Wales were not happy about such a union, feeling that it would be an affront to the memory of Eddy, and besides the Princess could not bear the thought of her 'dear Georgie' marrying and being lost to the family circle. However, in the circumstances she saw that it had to be endured, and perhaps she felt, too, that May would be docile and unassuming as she had been in the past.

In most ways George and May were very different: May studious and bookish with a deep interest in music and the arts; George unintellectual and low-brow with few interests other than shooting, sailing and stamp collecting. But there were similarities: they were both unemotional and inarticulate, unable to speak of their deepest feelings, which meant that courtship was going to be difficult. Left together they became tongue-tied and ill at ease. Of honeyed words and tender embraces there were none. The only way they could tell of their love for each other was by letter. A month before their wedding May wrote in anguish:

> I am very sorry that I am still so shy with you. I tried not to be so the other day, but alas failed, I was angry with myself! It is so stupid to be so stiff together and really there is nothing I would not tell you except that I love you more than anybody in the world, and this I cannot tell you myself so I write it to relieve my feelings.

To which George replied:

> Thank God we both understand each other and I think it really unnecessary for me to tell you how deep my love for you my darling is and I feel it growing stronger and stronger every time I see you; although I may appear shy and cold.

George had not needed much persuasion that May was the right wife for him, but he had trodden warily as he had recently been rejected by his cousin, Marie, daughter of Queen Victoria's second son, Alfred, who had preferred the Crown Prince of Romania (surely a more precarious choice), and this had been a blow to George's self-confidence.

Generally George's and May's engagement met with approval in royal circles, but there were some who were less than delighted. Among George's aunts in particular there was marked displeasure, no doubt because they felt that their daughters should have had priority over the semi-royal May. The Princess Royal, now the Dowager Empress of Germany, wrote in uncharacteristically scathing terms that May was 'stiff and cold' and that 'many think her dull and superficial', and 'there is a mist of sadness and melancholy about their engagement'. Certainly May's assets did not include great joyousness and humour, but this was surely a harsh judgement, and the 'mist of sadness and melancholy' was not shared by the marriage partners themselves. On the eve of their wedding George wrote to May: 'I feel so happy that I don't know how to thank you enough for having made me so.'

The eight weeks of engagement put a heavy strain on May. There was so much to be done, and everyone seemed to be getting at her. 'We are all in a worried bustled state of mind,' she wrote to George. 'This is a simply horrid time we are going through.' And their apparent lack of warmth towards each other did not go unnoticed. An acerbic and unkindly disposed observer within the Court, Lady Geraldine Somerset, wrote that 'May is radiant at her position and abundantly satisfied but placid and cold as always and the Duke of York apparently nonchalant and indifferent.' But she could not have been more wrong.

When the wedding occurred in the Chapel Royal on 6 July 1893 London was *en fête*. Huge crowds lined the streets for their favourite spectacle, and the great and good from all over Europe were in attendance. In spite of her strong dislike of weddings Queen Victoria was in the procession, sharing the 'Glass Coach' with Mary Adelaide who, massive and smiling and waving vigorously to the crowds, rather overshadowed her.[4] When eventually all the ceremonies were over and George and May (or the Duke and Duchess of York, as they had now become) had appeared on the balcony of Buckingham Palace in front of massed crowds, they were able to get away by special train to Sandringham, and at the end of a day of unparalleled splendour and magnificence found themselves alone in York Cottage. From May's point of view a more unsuitable venue for a honeymoon could not be imagined. She may have been dreaming of an enchanting place in the sun surrounded by wild flowers and within easy reach of art treasures and places of historic interest, but what she got was an unattractive and inconvenient residence in the wilds of East Anglia.

Built originally as an annexe to 'the Big House' for male guests who could not be accommodated there, it had been given to Prince George by his father as a wedding present. It had then undergone alterations at the hands of an amateur architect so that with gables and turrets and varying styles of architecture it had come to resemble a monstrosity from suburbia. In the midst of rural Norfolk it was a prominent eyesore, and inside it was no better – all narrow corridors and undersized rooms. Of art and culture there were few signs, the prevailing ambience being sport and shooting, in which May had no interest. But George loved the place dearly, so May determined that she must do the same. She would have found this easier if she had been given a free hand in the matter of furnishing and decoration, but George, with the kindest of intentions – to save her trouble – had gone ahead and seen to these himself with the help of 'the man from Maples', and the result was not as May would have liked it.[5] Her mother had once said of May, thinking particularly of her years in Italy, that she could make herself happy wherever she was, but York Cottage tested her as never before. However, with that quiet determination which so many people had noticed, she set about the task of making it charming and convenient, and in this she was successful. It was to be her home for the next thirty-three years.

During that time she was able to make many changes for the better, but there was one problem she could not overcome – York Cottage's proximity to the 'Big House' and the pervasive presence of her in-laws. After she had spent only thirteen days alone with George the family arrived in force and lost no time in making their presence felt. Her mother-in-law, the Princess of Wales, was particularly intrusive. She was almost as close to George as she had been to Eddy, and his love for her was close to a fixation. With his marriage to May this fixation became relaxed; Alexandra was aware of this and was determined not to lose her hold on him. She would arrive at York Cottage at all hours, full of advice or sweeping George and May to the 'Big House' for some unwelcome entertainment. Her unmarried daughters also behaved with great insensitivity, treating York Cottage as their own and May as if she was not there. That there was not an open breach was entirely due to May's tact and patience. She put up with it all because she knew that for the sake of her husband she had to. The nearest she came to a complaint was in later years when she wrote with typical understatement: 'I sometimes think that just after we were married we were not left alone enough and had not the opportunity of learning to understand each other as quickly as we might otherwise have done.'

It was a considerable achievement that in these early days, in such unfavourable circumstances, the couple managed to lay the foundations of a happy and loving marriage. At first they were probably not deeply in love, and they still did not know each other well. But their love developed, as they were determined it should, so that in the end they became distraught if they were away from each other for even a short time.

It did not take May long to appreciate the truth of Queen Victoria's dictum that marriage was no bed of roses. Adapting to her husband's interests and way of life she could manage, as well as coming to terms with his ever-present relations. But her greatest affliction was child-bearing. Queen Victoria had warned her of this, describing starkly the pains and torments of pregnancy (although they did not stop her from having nine children). May's feelings were similar. It was a subject she found disagreeable and never wanted to talk about, and she found the publicity attendant on it totally abhorrent. Her first birth, a year after marriage, was a difficult one and was followed by post-natal depression so that after six weeks she had to leave the baby for a holiday abroad with her mother.[6] During the seven years between her marriage and the death of Queen Victoria three more children were to be born to her,[7] and she hoped and prayed these would be the last, but two more were still to come.[8]

May had other troubles, too, at this time. It may be imagined how her mother, Mary Adelaide, became completely lost without May to support her and manage her affairs. In her distress she took to dropping in at York House at all hours for prolonged visits which were not to the liking of Prince George who was fond of his mother-in-law but in small doses and was maddened by her unpunctuality and general disorganization.[9] Mary Adelaide was to survive just long enough to witness Queen Victoria's Diamond Jubilee in 1897. Her death was widely lamented as she had been the fount of great love and kindness, particularly by May who wrote that she had been 'the centre of all to us'.

By then the problem of May's father, the Duke of Teck, had become acute. His mind had become almost completely clouded, and he rarely made sense. Contact with members of his family seemed to upset him particularly, and he had to be consigned to the care of male nurses. He died in 1900.

May's years as Duchess of York, until the death of Queen Victoria, were not a time of great fulfilment for her. She had little scope to exercise her abilities. Queen Victoria allowed no sharing of her royal prerogatives, and all the members of her family were excluded from the workings of government; while at Sandringham May's mother-in-law, Princess Alexandra, kept everything under her control. But during this time May's relationship with her husband became ever warmer and more understanding. At times they went their separate ways. May was not expected to accompany George to the racing at Newmarket or regattas at Cowes, and George did not go with May on visits to museums or historic sites ('piles of old stones', as he had once described them). But when on official occasions or visits abroad George needed support May was always a tower of strength, and George was greatly appreciative of this. In the first year of their marriage he wrote to her, as he still could not bring himself to express his feelings face to face, 'I really think I should get ill if I had to be away from you for a long time.'

In the last years of her reign Queen Victoria became more and more drawn to May. They had much in common. Their sober, serious and low-key ways of life were similar, and both of them had a strong distaste for the so-called 'high life' – racing, gambling and pleasure-seeking – so zealously pursued by the

Prince of Wales and his set. In all her letters Queen Victoria sang her praises: 'so unaffected and sensible and so very distinguished and dignified in her manners'. In her last years, when she was deaf and blind and almost immobile, the Queen came to rely on May increasingly. She survived her Diamond Jubilee and lived to see in the twentieth century, but on 22 January 1901 the phenomenon that was Queen Victoria came to a close. That such a small, shy, reclusive old lady should have had such an influence and inspired such awe and respect in so many parts of the world was indeed phenomenal. Her appearance may have been unpretentious and homely, even dowdy, but strong men quailed in her presence. Her Court may have been sombre and dull, but there was about it a mystique lacking in more magnificent ones. Of course, being human, she had her quirks and aberrations, but these did not detract from her greatness. At her death people were benumbed. They could not believe it possible. 'The thought of England without the Queen is dreadful even to think of,' May wrote at the time. 'God help us all.' And many had even greater fears for the future – rightly, as it proved.

The death of Queen Victoria brought a new status to George and May. As heir apparent George at once inherited the title of Duke of Cornwall (along with the substantial revenues of that Duchy), and it was expected that he would also become Prince of Wales, but this was not automatic and for some reason his father delayed several months before bestowing the title on him.[10] Their new position created problems for the couple, of which the most immediate was a tour of the Empire (Canada, Australia, New Zealand, South Africa) which was due to start in March 1901 and would last for seven and a half months. In the circumstances neither was at all keen to go, and the King and Queen, too, wanted it put off. The King knew his health was shaky and did not want his heir out of the country for so long, and the Queen could not bear to be parted for long from her only remaining son. The government, however, was insistent, and they were made to feel that it was their duty, so they went.

In the event the tour proved a marvellous success. Not only did it engender great loyalty and goodwill but it was also of great benefit to George and May. Free from the constraining ambience of the King and Queen and other royalty breathing down their necks, both of them blossomed conspicuously. George, the bluff, plain-spoken sailor, always went down well, but the great star was May. In the frank and friendly atmosphere of Australia and New Zealand she became a different person. Gone were her shyness and timidity, and in their place came a new assurance. For the first time in her life she felt free to act on her own initiative, and this was greatly appreciated. She had read extensively about the countries to be visited, and her knowledge of them caused surprise and admiration as also did her grasp of social problems – a legacy of her mother – which was not expected of royalty. One of her ladies-in-waiting, Lady Lygon, wrote home at the time: 'HRH has quite got over her shyness abroad . . . Her smile is commented on in every paper and her charm of manner.

In fact she is having a *succès fou*.' And again later: 'Every state has successively fallen in love with her looks, her smile and her great charm of manner. She is at last coming out of her shell and will electrify them at home as she has everyone here.'[11]

Her husband was as delighted as anyone by May's success, and he expressed his gratitude fulsomely (still in writing): 'I take the first opportunity of writing to say how deeply I am indebted to you, darling, for the splendid way in which you supported and helped me during our long tour. It was you who made it a success.'

On their return to England at the end of 1901 George and May were at last created Prince and Princess of Wales and were immediately plunged into the arrangements that were under way for the coronation in the following year. Amid all the turmoil created when the ceremony had to be put off at the last minute and rearranged two months later. May won admiration for her calmness and quiet authority. When it was all over, however, the strain told on her; it had been made worse by her fifth pregnancy; and when George went yachting at Cowes while she withdrew with her children to their Scottish estate at Abergeldie, at the best of times an unexhilarating place and this time made worse by perpetual rain, she had one of her attacks of depression. This cleared, however, in 1903 when she was much occupied in moving from York House into Marlborough House, which her mother-in-law had been reluctant to leave. In 1904 she and George went on a grand state visit to the court of Franz Joseph, the elderly Emperor of Austria in Vienna, where her services as an interpreter (George speaking no foreign languages) and her knowledge of Austrian history and court etiquette proved invaluable. And in 1905 they went on a tour which made a deeper impression on May than any other, to India. The beauty and mystery of the sub-continent overwhelmed her. While George went off shooting tigers and rhinos she visited the Taj Mahal and other historic sites and was entranced by them.

Immediately after their return George and May set off for Madrid to attend the wedding of George's first cousin, Princess Ena, to King Alfonso of Spain. During the wedding service they were all but blown up by the bomb of an anarchist; and once again May was notable for her calmness and composure. Then, only a week later, they were setting sail for Norway to attend the coronation of George's sister, Princess Maud of Wales, and her husband, King Haakon VII, once Prince Charles of Denmark, a nephew of Queen Alexandra.

For the last years of King Edward's reign George and May did less travelling abroad, partly because George detested it and partly because the King, whose health was deteriorating, became more and more dependent on them.[12] Unlike his mother he was quite ready to initiate his heir into the workings of government and was willing to show official dispatches not only to him but also to May, although not to his wife as her tact and discretion were not to be relied on.

Besides giving support to her husband and father-in-law May was also concerned at this time with her children who, since the birth of Prince John in 1905, numbered six. Considering her strong antipathy to child-bearing she had indeed done her duty in this respect, but bringing up a family was not something she found easy. She did not have strong maternal instincts and, unlike her mother-in-law, contact with children did not come naturally to her. In no way was she a 'child at heart', and she tended to be unsympathetic to their needs and intolerant of their ways. She did her duty by them, read to them and joined in educational games, but there was too much constraint and admonition. She could not come down to their level; she could not even embrace them. There was always diffidence between them. Unfortunately, George, too, was an unenlightened parent. He did not have his father's bonhomie and tolerance. He was not basically an unkind person, as is shown by his angelic treatment of his wife and mother, but he seemed to think it necessary that his sons should be intimidated, and there was much reproof and repression.[13] In the claustrophobic atmosphere of York Cottage there was often tension and unease, and his eldest son, Edward (later King Edward VIII and Duke of Windsor), was to write in later life that this held back his natural development. He did, however, also record a debt of gratitude to his mother for providing in her boudoir an oasis of peace and calm; and her ministrations were not in vain for it was at her knee that his cultural interests began to evolve. May herself was confident that she had done the right thing by him. 'We have done our best for him,' she said at the time, 'and we can only hope and pray we may have succeeded and that he will ever uphold the honour and traditions of our house.'

For some time King Edward's health had been giving cause for alarm. Overeating and heavy smoking were taking their toll. He was grossly overweight and was subject to attacks of bronchitis and pleurisy. He had also had some unpleasant falls. But somehow he had survived. By 1910, however, even his immense constitution could take no more, and at the age of sixty-nine his health collapsed and he died suddenly. He was greatly mourned. His faults were manifest, but he was always genial and warm-hearted and, despite outbursts of temper, kindly and good-humoured; and on big ceremonial occasions he was magnificent. No other monarch in Europe was so admired, and his contribution to keeping the peace of Europe was unique.[14] May had not been close to him as their tastes and ways of life were entirely different, but she was genuinely shocked by his death. 'What a loss to the nation and to us all,' she wrote. 'God help us.' And George wrote movingly: 'I have lost my best friend and the best of fathers. I never had a word with him in my life. I am heartbroken and overwhelmed with grief but God will help me in my great responsibilities and darling May will be my comfort as she has always been.'

Thus did George – simple-minded, narrow and inexperienced – find himself, at the age of forty-five, King of Great Britain and Ireland and of the British Dominions beyond the Seas and Emperor of India. Few monarchs have come into such a troubled inheritance. At the time the country was in the throes of a vicious political crisis over the Parliament Bill, which would restrict the powers of the House of Lords, and the passing of this revolutionary measure depended on the willingness of the King to create enough new Liberal peers to see it through the House of Lords. This was a fearsome responsibility and one of which, not unnaturally, the new King stood in awe, but at the moment of crisis he did not waver.[15] There was also at that time great industrial unrest in the country, with strikes more widespread and more bitter than ever before. And overhanging all was the threat of a general European war, contributing to the feeling that the rulers of Europe were losing control of the situation. In the midst of all this George needed great support, and for this he depended mainly on May.

In addition to these momentous events May had personal problems of her own. One which was quickly settled was her designation. It was unsuitable that she should become Queen May, and the first of her baptismal names was Victoria, which was also inappropriate. Her second name of Mary was adopted and she became known henceforth as Queen Mary.

Other matters were less easily settled. It was necessary for her to move houses – from Marlborough House to Buckingham Palace, from Frogmore to Windsor and from Abergeldie to Balmoral. In this she encountered difficulties with her mother-in-law. Queen Alexandra had wondrous gifts: at sixty-six she was still radiantly beautiful, with great vivacity and charm, much beloved – and as always the most popular member of the Royal Family. But her gifts did not include unselfishness, and she did not step down graciously from being Queen to Queen Dowager. Prompted by her sister, the ex-Empress of Russia, she expected to have precedence over Queen Mary on formal occasions, and having made difficulties about moving into Buckingham Palace in 1901 she was then obstructive about moving out of it in 1910. She was also determined to remain in the big house at Sandringham. This she had the right to do as it had been left to her absolutely, but it might have occurred to her to make way for George and his family, who were crammed into York Cottage, but she had no such thoughts. May could not but be resentful of this, but George, as always, took his mother's side and continued uncomplainingly to live at close quarters in the cottage.

Queen Mary's main preoccupation at the beginning of her husband's reign was the preparations for the coronation. She was endlessly being consulted on such matters as the length of peeresses' trains and the number of their attendants. All this she found very tiresome. 'A great ordeal and we are dreading it,' she wrote to her aunt.[16] Yet when the coronation came on 22 June 1911 she found it a deeply moving and spiritual experience, as was evident in her demeanour. A nobleman present (the Master of Elibank) wrote later:

The Queen looked pale and strained. You felt she was a great lady, but not a queen. She was almost shrinking as she walked up the aisle, giving the impression that she would have liked to have made her way to her seat by some back entrance: the contrast on her 'return' – crowned – was magnetic, as if she had undergone some marvellous transformation. Instead of the shy creature for whom one had felt pity, one saw her emerge from the ceremony with a bearing and dignity, and a quiet confidence, signifying that she really felt that she was Queen of this great Empire, and that she derived strength and legitimate pride from the knowledge of it.[17]

After the coronation there arose the matter of the Durbah in India, a great ceremonial gathering to pay homage to the new King Emperor. No previous king had attended this, but George was determined to go, and Mary was equally determined to go with him. Difficulties were put in their way, but these were swept aside. On 11 November 1911 George and Mary left on the specially chartered liner SS *Medina*, designed to carry 650 passengers but on this occasion no more than twenty-four. As always for Mary, the voyage did not start well. Every luxury had been provided, but these did nothing for her seasickness, and in the rough waters of the Bay of Biscay she suffered acutely. She was always to have a loathing of the sea. In India a vast array of tents awaited them outside Delhi – some 40,000 in number, covering an area of forty-five square miles and providing for some 300,000 people. Such splendour had never been seen before and has not been equalled since.[18] George in uncharacteristically eulogistic language described it as 'the most beautiful and wonderful sight he had ever seen'. When it was all over he proceeded to something he probably enjoyed even more, indulging for six weeks in what one of his ministers described as 'his unholy fascination for killing animals' (a bag of thirty-one tigers, fourteen rhinos and four bears). Of course Mary did not accompany him on this slaughter but went instead on a visit to the Taj Mahal and other historic sites; on one of her trips her host was misguided enough to organize a tiger shoot during which the Queen took more interest in her knitting than in the wild animals. George and Mary took a sad farewell of India, both knowing in their hearts that they would never see the country again. The visit had made a profound impression on them, giving them greater self-confidence and deeply impressing on them the magnitude of Britain's imperial responsibilities.

On their arrival back in England the King and Queen found much to cause them concern. The Parliament Act had been passed, but the intention of the Liberal government to grant home rule to Ireland was raising the prospect of civil war in that country. Industrial unrest, too, had intensified, with widespread strikes in docks, coal mines and railways. There was also mounting trouble from the Suffragettes. Queen Mary did not have great sympathy for their movement, and such as she might have had was drained away by their militant tactics – breaking windows, arson and assaulting prominent politicians. To her orderly mind and equable temperament these were outrages, and she expressed her horror of them. As for the industrial unrest in the country at large, she had mixed views. On the one hand, she blamed Liberal politicians strongly for their intemperate language during the passage of the Parliament Bill, 'putting class against class . . . encouraging socialism . . . and pandering to the Labour Party'. But, on the other, she was always interested in practical schemes for the relief of poverty and the improvement of working conditions. That she really cared about these was shown in 1912 and 1913 when she and the King went on tours of some of the worst-hit mining and industrial areas. These were the first royal 'walkabouts' in which the sovereign came into direct contact with the working classes. They went to pitheads in colliery buses and greeted miners as they emerged from underground. They also visited miners' cottages, where Mary was not satisfied with being given a cup of tea in the best parlour but penetrated into the kitchen and got down to practical domestic matters with the wives, something she knew much more about (thanks to her early experiences with her mother) than anyone expected. It was typical of the King and Queen's behaviour on these tours that after one long day they arrived at the house where they were staying to be told of a disaster in a local pit in which a number of miners had been killed; although exhausted, they insisted in setting out at once to console the bereaved. It was the same when Queen Mary visited hospitals and institutions for the poor. She might not be very good at social chit-chat or pouring out sympathy, but in noticing practical defects and suggesting improvements she had few equals. Margaret Bondfield, a Labour politician, once said of her that she would have made an excellent factory inspector.

During the early years of her husband's reign, among other troubles, Mary became the victim of malicious and mendacious gossip. In certain quarters it was considered smart to make a mockery of her. The fast, rich set patronized by her father-in-law looked on her with condescension and scorn. She was not one of them. She did not go racing or yachting, and she was clearly uninterested in shooting or other sports. She was regarded as staid and dull and was an easy target for worldly wits. George, too, came in for some venom, being regarded as equally dull, and his quiet, retiring ways were contrasted unfavourably with the ebullience and brio of his father. It is unlikely that George and Mary were greatly troubled by this tittle-tattle, but it was another matter when totally false fabrications were put abroad – that George because of his somewhat mottled complexion was a habitual drunkard and that Mary went in mortal terror of him – and the ludicrous old *canard* that he had been married in his youth to an admiral's daughter in Malta was resurrected, resulting in a journalist being taken to court and sentenced to imprisonment.

War, which had been hovering over Europe for so long, finally broke out at the end of July 1914. It began with the assassination of an Austrian archduke and his wife in the Balkans. It seems incredible that this quite minor incident should have led to the most ghastly war in history, but that was what happened. War began between the Austrian Empire and the independent state of Servia (Serbia), and the situation spiralled out of control as one European power after another felt impelled to join in. Following the German invasion of Belgium, Britain declared war on 4 August, and that night large crowds surged outside Buckingham Palace, cheering and singing in the wildest excitement. They little knew what they were in for. As so often the voice of sanity was Queen Mary's: 'To have to go to war on account of tiresome Servia beggars belief,' she wrote at the time.

Within days of the declaration of war Mary was setting up an organization for the provision of comforts and clothing for British servicemen. She had seen how during the Boer War well-meaning women had sent in what they thought fit, much of which proved to be unsuitable, while what was needed was overlooked. She was determined that this should not happen again, so she adapted her Needlework Guild to act as a central body to give appropriate advice and encouragement. Soon many thousands of willing hands were at work knitting scarves and gloves and sewing shirts.[19] However, their enthusiastic efforts were to have unfortunate consequences. Numerous women in the garment industry, already earning pitiable wages, were put out of work by the influx of amateur products, and they were soon facing starvation. When the plight of these women became known to the Queen she saw at once that something must be done for them and summoned to Buckingham Palace the secretary of the Women's Trade Union League, Mary Macarthur, a fiery Glaswegian with not much time for royalty; but her meeting with the Queen was an eye-opener. Expecting to find a high and mighty lady talking graciously but irrelevantly, she found instead a serious, practical woman with a knowledge of social problems and determined to be of help. 'The point is the Queen does understand and grasp the whole situation from the trades union point of view,' she told a colleague. Working together the Queen and Mary Macarthur set up an organization which was able to do much to find employment for women during the war years.

There were many other matters which occupied the Queen's attention at this time. The one she found most gruelling was visiting the wounded from the battlefields. With her horror of pain and suffering she was appalled at the sight of men who had lost limbs, been gassed and blinded and reduced to nervous wrecks by shell shock. Unlike her mother-in-law, Queen Alexandra, who on these occasions was full of sympathy and talked freely, she was struck dumb and could only utter a few banal words of comfort. Her husband was similarly affected. He was not a man given to overstatement, but in later years he was reported as saying: 'You can't conceive what I suffered going round the hospitals in the war.' But much as they detested it they did not flinch from it.

As the Germans stepped up their U-boat campaign, food and fuel became in short supply in the country, and the King and Queen at once set an example of austere living. Rigid rationing was introduced into Buckingham Palace, few rooms were heated and those only partially, and the King allowed himself only one hot bath a week. Later in the war perhaps an even greater sacrifice was required of them when the Prime Minister, Lloyd George, became convinced that heavy drinking was affecting industrial production and clamped down on the hours in which alcohol was available. To boost his anti-drinking campaign he asked the King to set an example, and as always he responded. So in the darkest days of the war, when stiff drinks were often badly needed, all that was available at Buckingham Palace was mineral water and ginger beer.

Throughout the war the Queen lost no opportunity to do her bit. At Sandringham she lent a hand in planting potatoes and in gathering conkers which were said to be of use in the manufacture of explosives. But her most vital task, as always, was giving support to the King – and he was in desperate need of it. At times the strain became almost unbearable as he took on an ever-increasing workload.[20] Matters got worse when in 1915 he had a serious accident. On a visit to France his horse took fright, reared and fell over backwards, crushing the King underneath it. This resulted in cracked ribs, a fractured pelvis and great pain. Although he was not out of action for long George never made a complete recovery; his physical and, more particularly, his nervous strength were not the same again. Still he did not spare himself. In the last part of the war, when there was industrial unrest in northern districts, the government asked him to go on an extended tour, which he did, with the Queen by his side, and they both had to take an interest in such things as blast furnaces and riveting machines. But they also made an important discovery – that, like Queen Victoria, they found it easier to establish rapport with the working classes than with the higher ranks of society.

In the end their devotion to duty was rewarded. When at last, after heavy defeats and immense losses, the war was eventually won and peace declared, it was to Buckingham Palace that the people came streaming. The wildly cheering crowds were not only celebrating victory, they were also paying tribute to the selfless and valiant part played in it by George and Mary.

It was indeed a triumph that the British monarchy was so firmly entrenched in 1918. In Europe crowns and thrones were toppling; the Russian, German and Austrian emperors had all been dethroned, as had all the minor German royalty. Republicanism was rife. The King and Queen were aware of this and determined to resist it, and there was only one way they knew how – by devotion to duty and an example of impeccable family life.

The times ahead were to be hard. 'The land fit for heroes', promised by Lloyd George, proved an illusion. Strikes, hunger marches and massive unemployment pervaded the inter-war years. And there was great social change. The lifestyle of the Victorians – decorous, respectable and conventional – was passing. People were becoming less formal, clothes more casual and morals less compelling. As might be imagined, none of this was to the liking of

George V and Queen Mary. The King abhorred all change, and his constant endeavour was to keep things as they were.[21] This was unavailing, of course, and he could only look on aghast as women shortened their skirts, drank cocktails, smoked and applied lipstick. However, life at Court reverted from the exuberance and panache of his father to the rigidity and parsimony of his grandmother. Everything ran like clockwork; punctuality was all-important, and nothing must be out of place. This narrow life must have been a great trial to Queen Mary. Left to herself she would have liked to make concessions to modernity, but if she ever did – trying out a new style of hat, raising the hemline of her dresses by a few inches or attempting the steps of a new dance – the King would vent his disapproval. It added to the strain of life that entertainment was kept to a minimum. This meant that the King and Queen usually dined by themselves, and as neither was a ready conversationalist and the King wanted to talk only about shooting and the Queen about furniture and works of art, meals tended to be solemn occasions. Some queens in the past might have been tempted to break loose from such a life but not Mary. Her commitment to the British monarchy was total: to soothe and comfort the King, to protect him from unnecessary irritations and to conform wherever possible to his idiosyncratic ways were to her sacred duties, and she never flinched from them.

It must not be supposed, however, that her life was a misery. Far from it. Although he might occasionally bark at her and lose his cool, George was at heart a kindly, considerate and totally faithful husband and always deeply appreciative of how much he owed to her and how dependent he was on her. Perhaps the most touching example of this occurred when he was preparing a speech at the time of his Silver Jubilee and he told his secretary to put his tribute to his wife at the very end as it would certainly bring tears to his eyes.

After the war Mary's support continued to be as necessary as ever, as on the political front George was having a rough ride. Serious trouble broke out in Ireland, leading to long and embittered negotiations, a civil war and finally the establishment of the Irish Free State. Soon afterwards George watched apprehensively as the first Labour government came into office, including among its members a one-time engine driver, foundry worker and mill hand. But he need not have worried: he had no difficulty in establishing cordial relations with most of them, notably with the Prime Minister, Ramsay MacDonald, and more particularity with J.H. Thomas, the most palpably working-class minister whose bluff manner and ribald humour he much appreciated.[22] The King saw it as his duty to make everything as easy as possible for them, even making concessions on a matter close to his heart, that of wearing correct Court dress (including knee breeches) on ceremonial occasions.

The Labour government lasted no more than nine months, and soon afterwards George became seriously ill with bronchial catarrh, the disease that had killed his father. Much against his will he was sent on a Mediterranean cruise, which cured him. Soon afterwards, however, the country became embroiled in the General Strike of 1926 in which, as always, he played a moderating role. Two years later he was struck down by a critically serious illness – septicaemia – during which for six weeks he was close to death and even the Queen was not allowed to be with him. And still his troubles were not over, for in 1931 the country was struck by the Great Depression, facing the stark danger of national bankruptcy. In this crisis the King played a crucial, if controversial, role. He was convinced that salvation lay in the formation of a National Government under Ramsay MacDonald, for whom he had come to have a great admiration, once describing him as his best Prime Minister. This was done, and in time the crisis passed; it was notable that the King kept his head admirably throughout, and people marvelled that a man who could be sent into a frenzy by a fault in dress, or lateness at meals, was cool and decisive when confronted by a major crisis.

For the remaining five years of his life the political scene at home was relatively quiet, but abroad there were sinister developments with the rise of the Fascist dictators.

At nearly all state functions and on official visits Mary was at her husband's side, but there was one remission for which she was thankful: she was not expected to accompany him on his sporting ventures. While he was occupied with these, Mary pursued her own interests. For a long time she had been fascinated by antiques and *objets d'art* and on becoming Queen had set about sorting and arranging the numerous works of art in Buckingham Palace and the other royal residences. This was no mean undertaking as for years they had been neglected by monarchs who had had little interest in them; but in time Mary had them listed and labelled with relevant annotations. She also started collecting on her own account, and in this she received much help from the Finnish art historian Tancred Borenius, Professor of Art History at London University, who was invited to Buckingham Palace regularly to give advice and to answer the Queen's numerous questions. Her particular interest was in miniature pieces with royal connections, and for these she scoured antique shops and auction rooms. On visits to private houses she could be very alert, even somewhat grasping. If anything took her fancy she made it clear and was ready to press the point so that her hosts felt an obligation to make her a gift of it. In time this propensity became well known, so people hid away their finest treasures before the Queen's arrival. Mary's knowledge of antiques was extensive, but her tastes were narrow. It was noted that she never bought an important picture or gave encouragement to modern artists.

One felicitous outcome of Mary's love for the miniature was the creation of a splendid doll's house. This imaginative idea came from Princess Marie Louise and was intended as a tribute to the Queen for her work on the Royal Collection and the arts in general.[23] Never can so many distinguished people have contributed to the construction of a doll's house. Sir Edwin Lutyens took time off from building New Delhi to design a four-storey Georgian house which would show how royalty lived in the twentieth century. Everything was to the scale of one inch to a foot. Leading artists and craftsmen were invited to make the furniture and paint the pictures, and every detail was attended to: the dining-room was laid for dinner with gold plate with exact replicas of china and cutlery, there was specially woven linen for the bedrooms, water flowed freely in the baths and lavatories, there was a well-stocked wine cellar and a library with two hundred volumes, the size of postage stamps, to which nearly all leading contemporary writers had contributed.[24] All that was missing was any sign of a royal personage; the only human beings to be seen were a pipe major and five guardsmen. Mary watched progress eagerly and arranged the pictures and furniture herself as she thought fit. The house was the star attraction at the British Empire Exhibition of 1924 before coming to rest in Windsor Castle.

In the inter-war years there was much strife, but it was not all gloom and crisis. There were heart-warming occasions, too, most notably the Silver Jubilee of 1935 when there was a tremendous outpouring of loyalty and affection, particularly from poorer districts, which surprised no one more than the King. 'I had no idea they felt like that about me,' he said. 'I am beginning to think they must really like me for myself.' And indeed they did. In spite of his limitations and peppery temper he had become greatly beloved; and this affection was much enhanced by the broadcasts he made to the nation and empire on Christmas Day and at the time of the Jubilee. He had needed much persuasion to undertake these, but the sincerity and warmth with which he delivered beautifully simple and brief messages went straight to people's hearts.[25]

During the inter-war years the King and Queen experienced a mixture of joy and sorrow from their family. In 1919 they had had to bear the loss of their youngest son, Prince John. An epileptic and mentally handicapped, he had lived apart from the rest of the family, but he was certainly not ignored or rejected. His death at the age of thirteen could be looked on as a merciful release, but the death of a child, however handicapped, can be an agonizing experience. What Mary felt one cannot know, as her deepest feelings were always hidden. The marriage in 1921 of their only daughter, Princess Mary, gave the King and Queen much pleasure. The groom, the Earl of Harewood, who was fifteen years older than the Princess, shared both the King's addiction to shooting and the Queen's to works of art. Besides, he was very rich. They were delighted, too, when in 1923 their second son, Albert (later King George VI), married Lady Elizabeth Bowes-Lyon, daughter of the Earl of Strathmore. George was utterly charmed by his daughter-in-law and lavished kindness on her as on few others. Lapses in punctuality, which in others might have caused a storm, were overlooked. He was equally delighted when in 1926 a daughter was born (the future Queen Elizabeth II). Perhaps no one brought such light into his last years. Two of his other sons also made happy marriages: Prince George, Duke of Kent, in 1934 to Princess Marina, granddaughter of

King George II of Greece (brother of Queen Alexandra), and Henry, Duke of Gloucester, to Lady Alice Montagu-Douglas-Scott, daughter of the Duke of Buccleuth. All the King's children were then married except for David (as the family called the future King Edward VIII), the eldest, who was now over forty, and about him there was considerable anxiety.

By 1935 George V and the Prince of Wales had grown far apart. They saw little of each other. The Prince found the atmosphere in Buckingham Palace intolerably oppressive, and when he went there it was usually to be snubbed or upbraided. At the end of his life the King complained: 'I hardly ever see him and don't know what he is doing.' But he did know that for years he had been consorting with married women and in recent years had been much in the company of a Mrs Simpson – American, twice married and once divorced – and this weighed heavily on him. 'After I'm dead,' he said, 'the boy will ruin himself in two months.'

The Jubilee celebrations had been a wonderful experience for the King, showing how greatly he was loved and appreciated; but they had taxed his strength severely, and soon afterwards his health began to fail. At Sandringham that Christmas he was very frail and kept to his room for most of the time. It became clear that his life was ebbing away, and he died peacefully on 20 January 1936.

The story of the Abdication belongs to a later chapter of this book. Here we are concerned only with the part played in it by Queen Mary. Edward had been associating with Mrs Simpson since 1934; his mother had become aware of this and, while disapproving strongly, had said nothing as she hoped it was a liaison that would soon pass. It might be thought that she ought to have broached the subject with her son and made clear her own view and that of his father and impressed on him where his duty lay, but this she felt unable to do. Much as she doted on David and rejoiced in his glittering successes as Prince of Wales, relations between them were uneasy and reserved. There was no plain speaking. For a time the British press kept silence on the subject of Edward's relations with Mrs Simpson, but this could not last long after he became king, and matters came to a head on 16 November 1936 when Edward told first the Prime Minister, Stanley Baldwin, and then his mother that he intended to marry Mrs Simpson whatever the consequences – even, if necessary, abdication. The Queen, of course, was devastated by this. The idea of a twice-divorced American adventuress (as she regarded her) marrying her eldest son and becoming Queen of England and Empress of India was unthinkable. So, too, was abdication. To Mary the English monarchy was sacred; it was her religion; and to walk away from it for any reason was a shameful abrogation of duty and a betrayal of all that she and George V had been striving to achieve. She tried to impress this on her son but, as she feared, found him intractable. He was hopelessly besotted and nothing could move him. He begged his mother to meet Wallis Simpson, as he was convinced that she would then see what an exceptional woman she was, but this Mary had promised her husband she would never do. Abdication was formally announced on 10 December.

Although this was a crushing blow to Queen Mary, she knew that at this moment of crisis she must not falter. So much depended on her. Only she could hold the Royal Family together and ensure that the crown passed smoothly from one brother to the other. Albert, Duke of York and now King George VI, had dreaded coming to the throne. He was of a retiring, nervous disposition with an impediment in his speech and was completely unprepared for king-ship.[26] The prospect brought him near to a nervous breakdown, and his mother saw that it was up to her to prop him up and see him through his ordeal. She also considered that she had to set an example of dignity and calmness, so she made a point of making frequent public appearances to show that she was unbowed. The Anglo-American diarist Chips Channon, who saw her at this time, described her as 'magnificent, mute, immovable and very royal'.

The year 1936 had certainly been an *annus horribilis* for Mary, the Queen Dowager as she had now become. It had started with the death of her husband and then in the midst of the tiresome and poignant business of moving out of Buckingham Palace back into Marlborough House had come the realization that her eldest son was becoming increasingly beguiled by the wiles of an 'adven-turess'. And then there was the heart-rending business of the Abdication, with one son in agony because he was renouncing the throne and another in even greater agony at the thought of acceding to it.

The following year dawned more brightly. Mary's fears that the Abdication would be a death blow to the monarchy were not realized. The British people took at once to their new King with his charming, smiling wife and two small daughters. The change-over had gone more smoothly than anyone had dared to hope, and for this Queen Mary was largely responsible. As long as she was there, apparently unruffled, people felt that nothing essential could be wrong with the Royal Family. The image she and her husband had been at such pains to establish of a monarchy – hard-working, caring and of impeccable probity – had stood up to the crisis and come through triumphantly. For some time yet she would be vitally necessary to the new King and Queen; with her experience and know-how she was in a unique position to guide them. And she continued to show a brave face in public: going on an extended round of visits and attend-ing all state functions including the Coronation,[27] where she was described by Chips Channon as being ablaze (with diamonds), regal and overpowering.[28]

During the following years George VI and Queen Elizabeth continued to gather strength, helped on their way by two highly successful tours abroad – to France and America. While they were away on the latter Queen Mary was involved in a most unpleasant accident when the car in which she was travel-ling collided with a lorry, and she and the other passengers were piled up on the floor. However, with the help of a ladder she emerged safely with her dignity intact, apparently suffering no harm other than a broken umbrella and a snapped hat pin. Later, however, it was found that she was badly bruised and shocked, but, as might be expected, she made light of it and allowed herself only a brief respite from her duties.

Soon after George VI's return from his American visit the long-expected war with Hitler's Germany broke out. Thought had already been given as to where in that event Queen Mary should be housed. Sandringham was considered too dangerous because of air raids and possible attempts by German parachutists to abduct her. In the end the King decided that she would be safest with her niece, the Duchess of Beaufort, in Badminton House in Gloucestershire.[29] This plan was not altogether to the Queen's liking, but she felt she must acquiesce, and a few days after the declaration of war she arrived there, somewhat to the Duchess's consternation, with a retinue of over fifty.

At first Mary was ill at ease. Her surroundings were completely different from anything she had known before – deeply rural, with agriculture, fox hunting and horse shows predominant, in none of which she had a great interest. Besides, she felt isolated, far away from friends and family and out of touch with what was going on at the centre of affairs. Under the circumstances she might have given way to depression, complaints and self-pity, but this was not in her nature. All through her life she had shown herself ready to adapt to any situation, and this she did again at Badminton with great success. As long as she was occupied she was content. Her great wish was to be of use, and at Badminton she sought out little tasks that she thought needed doing. In particular she felt a strong aversion to ivy, which she thought was doing great damage to trees and stonework; and with the help of ladies-in-waiting, equerries and dispatch riders she saw to it that quite large areas were cleared.[30] She also joined enthusiastically in the government's campaign for salvage, and while being driven in her Daimler would stop and gather up bottles, tins and sundry ironwork that caught her eye.[21] Much as she might join in rural activities, however, no one would ever have mistaken the Queen for a countrywoman. Rural pursuits did not come naturally to her, and her dress remained the same as ever.

In time she found work of a different sort, visiting local factories, army camps and hospitals, and after a heavy air raid on Bristol she lost no time in going to the city to comfort the victims. In 1942 she herself suffered a heart-rending blow when her youngest son, George, Duke of Kent, was killed in an air crash. Of all her sons he was the one to whom she was closest, and at his funeral she needed all her fortitude and stoicism to maintain her composure.

By the end of the war Queen Mary had come to love the life at Badminton, and when the time came for her to leave there were tears in her eyes. Not for a long time had she known such freedom and informality, and by her kindness and sympathetic interest in people's lives she had become greatly loved. 'I have been very happy here,' she said just before she left. 'Here I have been anybody and everybody and back in London I shall have to begin being Queen Mary over again.'

It was to a bomb-blasted Marlborough House that Queen Mary returned in the summer of 1945. The windows were all boarded up, the glass having been shattered; doors had been blown off their hinges and walls and ceilings were crumbling. But at seventy-eight she set about restoring it into some sort of order and putting in place the furniture and *objets d'art* which had been sent away into safety during the war.

Gradually she resumed her former routine, although at a slower, gentler pace, visiting art galleries and antique shops, receiving most important visitors to London and attending family occasions. During the eight years of life that were left to her there was much that gave her pleasure, notably a reunion after nine years with the Duke of Windsor, unaccompanied by the Duchess. She kept her promise to George V never to receive her. In 1947 she was delighted by the engagement of Princess Elizabeth to Prince Philip of Greece, and a year later she took great pride in the birth of Prince Charles and in becoming a great-grandmother.

At that time the country was in the throes of a dire economic crisis; nearly everything was rationed and in short supply, mainly on account of a scarcity of dollars. In this matter the Queen had no mean success when a carpet on which she had been working for some years was put on view in North America and drew large crowds; it was sold for $100,000, all of which the Queen handed over to the Exchequer.

But the fates had a further blow in store for her. The health of George VI had never been robust, and in 1949 it took a turn for the worse when he developed a thrombosis and had to undergo an operation which was not entirely successful. He seemed to be recovering, but then in 1951 cancer of the lung was discovered, and on 6 February 1952 he died in his sleep. Queen Mary never recovered from the shock of this. She lived for one more year, but it was evident her life was ebbing away. She died on 24 March 1953, two months before the date fixed for her granddaughter's coronation. One of her last commands was that on no account was this to be put off in the event of her death.

No Queen Consort has been so greatly admired as Queen Mary. By the end of her life she had become a magnificent institution from another age. She had made few concessions to modernity: her style of dress never varied, she had never made use of an aeroplane or a telephone, and for such things as cocktails and cosmetics she had no time. But her record of sacrifice and public service was unsurpassed, her influence immeasurable.

8
WALLIS SIMPSON
Wife of Edward VIII

Few women have been so reviled and at the centre of so much controversy as the Duchess of Windsor. Her story attracts endless attention. This is not surprising, as it defies belief. How did it happen that a woman approaching forty with no great beauty, no intellectual pretensions, of dubious sexuality and with two husbands living could so beguile the world's most idolized bachelor that for her sake he was prepared to give up his throne?

The many mysteries surrounding the Duchess of Windsor began with her birth, which took place in circumstances of peculiar secrecy. Even the date is uncertain, although 1896 is most often accepted. Both her parents – Teackle Wallis Warfield and Alice Montague – came from well-to-do Maryland families with ancestry stretching far back into English history, and in the normal course of events the birth of a daughter would have been a notable event; instead, everything was done to hush the matter up. Shortly before the baby was due the parents were sent off to a health resort in a remote country area, ostensibly because of Teackle's tuberculosis, but primarily, it would seem, so that the birth of the baby would attract the minimum of attention. For some time afterwards a veil was drawn over the matter: there was no public announcement, her birth was not registered and she was not baptized. The most likely explanation is that the child was conceived and born out of wedlock. There had been strong opposition to her parents' marriage because of Teackle's tuberculosis, which was severe, but they were deeply in love and a pregnancy ensued. Soon after the birth of the baby they were married but very unobtrusively, in the house of the local minister with few family present, no wedding party and no honeymoon. A few months later Teackle Warfield died, and Alice was left to cope as best she could, virtually penniless, with a baby daughter who for some reason had been given her father's name of Wallis.

Throughout her childhood Wallis and her mother were dependent financially on Warfield relations, principally Teackle's elder brother Solomon (known as Uncle Sol) who was a wealthy banker and railroad proprietor. He was a curmudgeonly character and tight-fisted, but he did see to it that Wallis went to the best schools and had a proper 'coming out' as a débutante. Wallis was not a pretty child, nor a particularly intelligent one, but she had great vivacity and personality and was always able to make herself attractive to the opposite sex. She later claimed to have had a happy childhood, but she did feel a sense of shame at being a poor relation and was fiercely determined that one day she would be the richest of her clan. Money became an obsession, and for this marriage was essential.

Wallis's first marriage was a disaster. In 1916 when she was twenty-one she was introduced to a young airman in the US Navy – Earl Winfield Spencer – outwardly all charm and bravura but beneath the surface an alcoholic and bisexual. The marriage ran into trouble from the beginning. Winfield was subject to sulks and rages which he made little effort to control. These were possibly inflamed by Wallis's inability or unwillingness to have children and also by the comparative failure of his naval career; because of his alcoholism he was not sent abroad into the fighting when America came into the First World War, and this caused him great bitterness which he took out on Wallis. In time his behaviour became intolerable and they were separated. Wallis's thoughts turned to divorce, but here she met implacable opposition from her family, particularly from Uncle Sol who regarded divorce as the greatest of all disgraces. For the time being, then, Wallis lived apart from Winfield in Washington, consoling herself with various lovers including the Italian ambassador, Prince Gelasio Caetani (the first of several Italian liaisons), and an Argentinian diplomat, Felipe Espil (perhaps her most passionate love).

In 1922 Winfield was appointed to the command of a gunboat in the South China Seas, and he begged Wallis to come and join him in China to try to make a go of their marriage. Wallis agreed, and after a horrendous voyage in the most primitive of troopships she reached Hong Kong in 1924. Their reunion did not last long. He soon reverted to his old ways and they separated again, but not before he had taken her round some of Hong Kong's seedier spots including the high-class brothels he frequented known as 'singing houses' where, so rumour had it, Wallis learned of arcane sexual practices which she was later to employ on the King of England.

After leaving Winfield, Wallis lingered in China for two years and during that time all manner of slanderous stories about her were recounted. She was known to be a courier for American intelligence, but she was also suspected of being a double agent, spying for some foreign power, possibly Russia whose Communist government was very active in China at that time. Among the naval wives there was much gossip about her love affairs, and although these were no doubt exaggerated it seems certain that her life then was promiscuous. Later she admitted in her memoirs that there was 'a dashing British military officer and a gallant Italian naval officer who brisked briefly in and out of my life'. This was an understatement; her affair with Alberto de Zara, Italian naval attaché in Peking, was more than a brief whirl. He seems to have made a deep impression and imbued her with sympathy for Fascism which she retained and later passed on to King Edward VIII. She was also reputed to have had a liaison with Count Galeazzo Ciano, son-in-law of Mussolini and a future Italian Foreign Minister, resulting in an abortion that went wrong and which prevented her from ever having children.

In later years, when some people in England were doing all they could to blacken her name, it was believed that a 'Chinese Dossier' was compiled containing all her nefarious activities. Such a catalogue was never discovered, but if it had been it might also have included a report emanating from the Gender Reassignment Clinic that Wallis was a case of androgen insensitivity syndrome, which meant in effect that she was male rather than female. Positive evidence of this is non-existent, but it is not without some credibility: her general demeanour was not particularly feminine and some of her ways were distinctly masculine; she also had large unladylike hands. But that is all there is to support such a theory, and at the end of her life a French doctor who examined her was quoted as saying that she was in no way physically sexually abnormal.

After two years Wallis felt it was time for her to leave China, which she did with some sadness. In spite of the turbulence in the country resulting from civil war, plague and famine, and in spite of the danger she had experienced from bandits and marauding soldiers, she had come to love China and wrote of it later: 'without doubt the most delightful, the most carefree, the most lyrical interval of my youth – the nearest thing to a lotus-eater's dream that a young woman brought up in the "right" way could expect to know'.

Back in America Wallis made it her main objective to obtain a divorce, which, with some collusion from Winfield, she managed to do in 1927 at the age of thirty-two. She had already been casting around for another husband and thought she had found one who might suit her well. Ernest Simpson was the antithesis of Winfield Spencer – quiet, self-effacing, conventional and with a deep and genuine interest in the arts. He was born of a British father and took great pride in his British roots, having served for a time during the First World War with the Coldstream Guards and thereafter in America behaving and dressing like an ex-Guards officer (bowler hat, rolled umbrella and regimental tie).[1] He was hardly an exciting character, and it is doubtful if Wallis was ever seriously in love with him, but he could give her what she most wanted at that time – stability, respectability and a comfortable income. The only difficulty was that he was already married with a young daughter, but to Wallis this was not an insuperable barrier. When she met him his marriage had begun to break up, and she helped it on its way. As it happened his divorce came through at the same time as Wallis's, and soon afterwards his business (that of shipbroker) required him to relocate in London where he and Wallis were married, somewhat unromantically, in Chelsea Register Office.

Once settled, Wallis set about making her way into London society, which at that time was fast and frenetic. In the industrial areas there may have been poverty, but in London, especially during the season, money was lavished freely on flamboyant parties and endless chasing of 'the good time'. At first Wallis was at a disadvantage as she knew few English people, but in time her American connections proved more than adequate. In particular she became friendly with Thelma Lady Furness who was not only rich but also, because of her intimacy with the Prince of Wales, influential, and under her auspices Wallis and Ernest were accepted into social life at a high level. In 1931, when she was thirty-five, came the realization of her most cherished dream when she was introduced to the Prince. The meeting had been set up by Thelma in a country house in Leicestershire, and Wallis was in a fever of excitement, having spent most of the previous day at the hairdresser, and during the train journey from London she practised her curtsy; but the Prince was too preoccupied with horses and hunting to take much notice of her. Wallis, however, was determined that this should not be the last he saw of her. He had long been her idol. Along with millions of others his rare charm and good looks – youthful and wistful as of one with a secret sorrow – had haunted her. At thirty-seven he was still the most popular member of the Royal Family, and he was still single, although not unattached.

Since coming of age the Prince's love life had not run smoothly. All might have been well if he had been able to marry his first serious love, Rosemary Leveson-Gower, daughter of the fourth Duke of Sutherland. She herself was eminently suited to be Princess of Wales and later Queen, but there were skeletons in the family cupboard. Since the death of her father, her mother in the course of five years had divorced two husbands, not without dishonour; and her uncle, the Earl of Rosslyn, was a notorious roué who had also been twice divorced, had gambled away a large fortune and was usually so drunk that he could not be relied on to comport himself with dignity on public occasions. King George V had therefore opposed the match (which later he must have much regretted), and Rosemary, learning of this, backed out and married someone else. Thereafter the Prince became involved only with married women, of whom the most devoted and long-lasting was Freda Dudley Ward whom he first met in 1918 when they were both taking cover from an air raid in Belgrave Square.[2] Freda, who was not of noble birth and who was unhappily married to a much older man, became the Prince's *maîtresse-en-titre* for the next fifteen years. During that time she was always a good influence, restraining his drinking and other excesses and keeping him on track while at the same time being quite firm that marriage between them was impossible as it was out of the question for the heir to the throne to marry a divorcée. Freda's reign was jeopardized but not ended when in 1929 the Prince became enamoured of Thelma Furness, a famous American beauty who at the age of sixteen had eloped with a rich man twice her age and then, after a divorce, had landed the British shipping magnate, Viscount Furness, even older and with whom she had little in common and who generally let her go her own way. Thelma's association with the Prince was less beneficial than Freda's. She made no effort to curb his vulgar, populist tendencies, even encouraged them, and it was during her ascendancy that the character of the Prince began to decline. The Prince Charming of yesteryear who had performed his royal duties with such diligence and *élan* was beginning to turn into an irritable, self-centred middle-aged man, increasingly putting pleasure before duty.

Although she may not have realized it, in aiding and abetting this change Thelma was paving the way for Mrs Simpson. Not that she had any idea Wallis might displace her in the Prince's favour, for she continued to arrange meetings between them, seemingly unaware of her increasing hold over him. In the year after their first meeting the Prince was to be found dining at the Simpsons' flat and inviting them to stay at his country house of Fort Belvedere.[3] The crunch came in 1934 when Thelma went on a trip to California, bidding Wallis look after the 'little man', as she called him, while she was away – a task she performed all too well. It was then that the Prince fell under her spell, so much so that he submitted himself to her completely and could not bear to be away from her. The reason for this infatuation has given rise to much speculation. Was it sorcery? Or hypnotism? Or was she able, with techniques learned in the Orient, to overcome his sexual difficulties? Wallis was not inexperienced in the arts of seduction, and she soon realized the essential truth about Edward – that he did not want flattery and deference, he wanted a commanding, motherly figure who would dominate and even humiliate him.

When Thelma returned from America she was soon made aware, none too kindly, that she had been displaced and felt compelled to console herself with the not inconsiderable charms of the Aly Khan.[4] Freda Dudley Ward was treated even more peremptorily. When she telephoned Fort Belvedere about a family matter she was told by the telephone operator that she had instructions not to put through any calls coming from her. Such treatment of a loyal and devoted friend was further proof of the deterioration of Edward's character.

In 1935 the Prince's attachment to Mrs Simpson became more publicly apparent. She was seen dining alone with him, and she was included in his parties abroad without Ernest, who was increasingly relegated to the background. In the circumstance it was to be expected that the matter would have caught the attention of the British press, but no publicity was given to it; there was an agreement among newspaper proprietors that for the time being there should be no mention of it. Foreign newspapers were not so inhibited, however, notably in republican France and America where they trumpeted every detail they could lay their hands on, and these found their way into Britain where there were more and more people in the know. Gossip about Mrs Simpson was rife, and diarists of the time recorded their impressions of her, some surprisingly erroneous. Chips Channon wrote of her after an early meeting that she was 'a jolly, plain, intelligent, quiet, unpretentious and unprepossessing little woman', which seems to be wrong on every count; and a few years later he changed his tune and wrote that she had 'charm, sense, balance and great wit with dignity and taste'. Harold Nicolson was even further off the mark, writing not long before the Abdication that she was 'a perfectly harmless type of American'. One person who never changed her tune was Elizabeth, Duchess of York (the future Queen Mother). They first met in 1934 and took a spontaneous dislike to each other. Between them there was to be deadly discord. To Wallis, Elizabeth was 'the dowdy duchess', and she was heard to make other sarcastic comments about her appearance and 'her justly famous charm being highly evident'. To Elizabeth, Wallis was 'that woman', and although she rarely spoke of her she was inveterately hostile, although in later years she insisted that she never hated her, as that would be demeaning herself.

By the end of the reign of George V there were many who were seriously concerned about the Prince's relations with Mrs Simpson. It was conceded that in some ways she had been a good influence, tidying him up and steadying him, and it was noticeable how his general morale had improved since his association with her; he was looking less sorry for himself. But there was dismay about other matters – the amount of money and jewellery he was giving her and the way she was taking over the management of his household, dismissing some servants and reducing the wages of others. Worst of all was the influence she was believed to be bringing to bear on him in the country's foreign policy. Perhaps because of her Italian paramours she had a liking for the Fascist dictator Mussolini, as did Edward, and she encouraged this in him so that when Italian troops invaded Abyssinia in 1935 he was strongly opposed to taking any action, even the imposition of sanctions. Towards Hitler, too, he and Wallis were favourably disposed, and they expressed open admiration for his so-called 'economic miracle' in overcoming unemployment.

On the death of George V in January 1936 and Edward's accession to the throne there was much speculation about his marriage plans. It was still hoped that his passion for Mrs Simpson would subside as others had done before, but there were no signs of it. He was still totally in thrall to her, and although he did not make his intentions clear it seemed that he wanted to marry her and make her Queen and Empress. Wallis's intentions were even less clear. It is doubtful if she was ever deeply in love with Edward, and she often showed signs of finding his cloying devotion tiresome, but she did not want to lose her influence over him, or indeed the great rewards that came her way because of it. She would probably have been content to be the King's *maîtresse-en-titre*, wielding the same power as before but unencumbered with the duties of Queen. But Edward would have none of this: he wanted a strong, supportive wife on whom he could depend and who would be by his side at his coronation and crowned with him.

In the months following his accession Edward's relationship with Mrs Simpson became more and more overt, causing great concern particularly to his senior courtiers whose job it was to keep him on track and guard his image. And there were other matters that worried them. Edward was taking his duties as king all too lightly: official papers remained unread and were sometimes left lying about for all to see; visitors were kept waiting and engagements cancelled, often for no better reason than that he was dallying with Wallis. There was more. It had long been settled that a constitutional monarch accepted the policies of his ministers, but during his brief reign Edward was often engaged in undermining them, particularly in foreign affairs where his stance was becoming increasingly sympathetic to Germany and Italy which he regarded as the bulwarks against Communism. In word and deed he was often indiscreet, and Wallis was even more so, to the point that she came under suspicion by the Secret Service of being a Nazi agent. However, no evidence for this has been found, nor is there proof that she had an affair with the German Ambassador and later Foreign Minister, von Ribbentrop, but there were those who believed it.

It is remarkable that for the first nine months of Edward's reign the British press maintained its silence about his relations with Mrs Simpson, but the foreign press was becoming ever more insistent. In the summer of 1936 Edward chartered a yacht and with Mrs Simpson and a party of friends cruised in the Mediterranean down the Dalmatian coast; wherever they landed they were greeted by hordes of reporters, as well as by a rapturous local population who looked on them as the great lovers of the age. It seems, however, that the cruise was not the romantic idyll it was supposed to have been. Lady Diana Duff Cooper, who was one of the guests, later wrote that Wallis often showed signs of irritability and boredom. It was to become evident later that she was beset with doubts about marrying Edward and becoming Queen of England. When the cruise was over she wrote to him from Paris, where she had gone alone, that she would not marry him and wanted to stay put with Ernest. But she was to find that she was no longer in control of her destiny. Edward replied that in that case he would cut his throat. Ernest, too, proved recalcitrant. No one could have been a more patient and long-suffering husband than he, but there were limits even to his complaisance. In the American press he had been held up to ridicule as the cuckold of all times, and he was longing to fade out of the limelight and settle down with another wife.[5, 6] In order to do this he was willing to be divorced as the guilty party, going through the ritual of spending a night with a professional co-respondent (known as Buttercup Kennedy) at the Hotel de Paris in Bray. The divorce petition was heard in Ipswich at the end of October and, although it bore all the hallmarks of collusion (not least the venue of Ipswich where neither party had ever been), Wallis was granted a decree nisi. This event was noted by the British press, but they still made no mention of her relationship with the King. Abroad it was hot news. An American newspaper proclaimed: KING'S MOLL RENO'D IN WOLSEY'S HOME TOWN.[7]

Soon afterwards, on 16 November, the British Prime Minister, Stanley Baldwin, felt he could ignore the affair no longer and in an interview with Edward asked him to make his relationship with Mrs Simpson less conspicuous and at the same time to persuade her to withdraw her divorce petition; but his plea fell on deaf ears, and to Baldwin's horror the King told him that he intended to marry Mrs Simpson even if it meant abdication. At the time he was still hoping that Mrs Simpson would become Queen, and although Baldwin warned him that the country and the empire would not tolerate a Queen with two ex-husbands still living, he reckoned that his popularity, which was still widespread, would carry him through.

The King saw Baldwin again ten days later, and this time the idea was mooted of a morganatic marriage. This would mean that Mrs Simpson would not become Queen but a figure in the background with some suitable title but with no rights of inheritance either for herself or for any children she might have. Such an arrangement had not been uncommon on the Continent, notably in the case of Queen Mary's grandfather, but it had never been considered in England. Edward favoured the idea and Baldwin agreed to consider it, and he put it to the Cabinet and the governments of the Dominions, all of whom proved to be strongly opposed to it.

By then Wallis was in torment. She had always prided herself on being decisive and in command of her fate, and she now found herself a pawn in a hard-fought power struggle to which there seemed no satisfactory outcome. She had little freedom of action. Since the intervention of Baldwin it was no longer open to her to become Queen. She could remain *in situ*, unmarried, as the King's mistress, but Edward would have none of this. He insisted on marriage, which could only happen if he abdicated, and this Wallis was desperate he should not do. Another option might have been for her to disappear, perhaps in the depths of South America as she once suggested. But Edward was definite that wherever she went he would follow, and he would abdicate in any case; if she did not marry him he would have done so in vain. So in the end it had to be abdication and marriage.

A week later, on 3 December, the British press could be contained no longer and broke silence on the relations between the King and Mrs Simpson as well as on an impending constitutional crisis, for Baldwin had made it clear that if the King went ahead with his marriage the government would resign and there would be a General Election which would divide the country bitterly and do untold harm to the monarchy. From then on Wallis's position in England became intolerable: abusive letters, threats of violence even of assassination were raining down on her, and her house was beset by noisy, aggressive crowds. As public feeling against her intensified she felt she must get out of the country and arranged to take refuge with friends from China days, Herman and Katherine Rogers, in their villa of Lou Viei near Cannes. Edward agreed to this and at the dead of night she set out by car accompanied by a close friend of the King, Lord Brownlow (a brave and kindly person but no great map-reader), to catch the Newhaven ferry. Three days later, after a nightmarish journey through France in foul weather during which they several times lost their way and were harried remorselessly by swarms of press reporters, they reached the Rogers's villa with Wallis on the car floor covered by a rug.

Meanwhile in England Edward had communicated his decision to abdicate to Baldwin and the Royal Family, who were aghast at the idea, but he was not to be dissuaded. Wallis, too, was saddened by the announcement. She had always hoped that it could be avoided, and she issued a statement to the press that she was ready 'to withdraw forthwith from a situation which had been rendered both unhappy and untenable'. This was greeted with cynicism by some, notably Baldwin and the Royal Family, who thought she did not really mean it and was trying to escape the blame for the Abdication. But the likelihood is that she was genuinely upset, especially by Edward's farewell broadcast in which he declared: 'You must believe me when I tell you that I have found it impossible to carry the heavy burden of responsibility and to discharge my duty as King as I would wish to do, without the help and support of the woman I love.' Later she was to write of this as 'the dregs of my cup of failure'.

After abdication it was necessary for Edward, or the Duke of Windsor as he had become, to live apart from Wallis for four months until her divorce became absolute. To have any contact with her while it was pending would have given rise to suspicion of collusion, in which case the divorce petition might be rejected. During this time he was housed in a Rothschild mansion in Austria, Schloss Enzesfeld, in great comfort but restless and on edge and counting the days until he could be with Wallis again; she remained at Villa Lou Viei, lonely and unhappy and desperately worried that her divorce might go wrong.

As soon as it was possible the Duke rejoined Wallis, who by then had moved to a French castle, the Château de Candé, owned by an American millionaire, Charles Bedaux – generous and outgoing but with strong Fascist leanings which caused concern in England as it was already known that Edward and Wallis had similar inclinations.[8] By then relations with the Royal Family had become even more strained: there were disputes about money, a subject on which Edward was obsessive and not always straightforward.[9] Even more bitterly argued was the question of Wallis's status. After her marriage she could not be denied the title of Duchess of Windsor, but in an unusual move George VI issued a Letter Patent conferring on Edward the title of His Royal Highness but withholding it from the Duchess. This was unorthodox and of doubtful legality. It had always been the custom for a wife to have the same rank and title as her husband. Wallis was being discriminated against.[10] This was an insult which Edward felt keenly and never ceased to rail against; he let it be known wherever he went that he expected the Duchess to be addressed as Her Royal Highness and to be curtsied to, which caused great difficulties to ladies meeting her as Buckingham Palace had expressly forbidden it. In other ways, too, Wallis was shown disfavour: she was not to be received at Court or in any way made part of the family. As far as possible she was to be treated as if she did not exist.

A month after their reunion Edward and Wallis were married in an improvised chapel in the Château de Candé. There had been some difficulty about finding an Anglican priest to conduct the service as the hierarchy of the Anglican Church had forbidden all its ministers to do so, but at the last moment an errant clergyman from the North of England volunteered his services, which were gratefully accepted. There were no members of the Royal Family at the ceremony and only very few close friends.

In the months that followed the Duke and Duchess caused increasing concern by their outspoken Fascist sympathies, and this came to a head in the late summer of 1937 when it was announced that they would be visiting Nazi Germany 'for the purpose of studying houses and working conditions'. The dismay this caused was due partly to the unpopularity of the Nazi regime and partly because it was a clear indication that the Duke was not going to be content with a quiet life out of the limelight but was intent on an active political role, possibly with a view, as some of his more indiscreet remarks seemed to indicate, to returning one day to England at the head of a Fascist-inspired party. In Germany the Windsors were given a royal reception. Everything was laid on for them, and Wallis was given special treatment, being addressed as Your Royal Highness and curtsied to everywhere. Under the aegis of Dr Robert Ley, one of the more unattractive of the Nazi thugs, they were shown round carefully selected German factories where bright-eyed workers came forward to speak in glowing terms of their way of life. On such occasions Edward was at his best – charming, forthcoming and chatting easily in fluent German – and he made a great impression on all he met. Wallis, too, was much admired, not least by Hitler whom they met at the end of their visit. She would have made a good queen, he told his interpreter. The Duke's and Duchess's predilection for Nazism was woefully misguided, but it should be remembered that at that time there were other eminent English people (including David Lloyd George) who held similar views. The full horrors of Nazism had not then been revealed; although concentration camps had begun to appear there were as yet no programmes of mass genocide.

In 1938, as they continued to be unwelcome in England, the Windsors decided to live for the time being in France and acquired two houses – a luxurious villa in Cap d'Antibes and an elegant house in Paris on the Boulevard Suchet, both of which they furnished and decorated lavishly, and their lifestyle was far from retiring. In that year Hitler's armies invaded Austria and Czechoslovakia, but this did not seem to shake their Nazi sympathies; they were always the strongest supporters of appeasement.

The outbreak of the Second World War in September 1939 put the Duke in a difficult position. He disapproved of the war and thought it unnecessary but felt obliged to return to England to offer his services, although he was unwilling to do so without an assurance that he and the Duchess would be accorded their full rights as members of the Royal Family; but this was not forthcoming. They went back all the same on a destroyer provided for them, but no member of the family or the government was waiting to receive them and no offer was made of accommodation in a royal residence. They were left to fend for themselves. Their presence in England was clearly causing great embarrassment. The Duke did, however, have an interview with his younger brother, the King, without ladies present to talk about a suitable job for him, which was proving difficult. By then Wallis had come to be regarded by the British Secret Service as a security risk; there were even those who suspected her of being a German agent. This she surely was not, but she chattered freely to all manner of people, including Nazi sympathizers, and could not be entrusted with secret information; and as the Duke told her everything, nor could he. The King was also anxious that his brother should not have an appointment in England. The prospect of his presence in the country, with his famous charm and still great popularity, perhaps giving voice to subversive thoughts, filled him with alarm. In the end he was found an innocuous job as a liaison officer with a British military mission in France with access to French units but not to British. That this was a fabricated post of little importance was widely recognized, but such as it was the Duke carried it out with reasonable diligence, while the Duchess returned to Paris where she took on duties with the French Red Cross and where she continued to be under surveillance by the Secret Service.

On 10 May 1940 the so-called Phoney War came to an end with the German invasion of Holland and Belgium. Hitler's armies soon broke through the French lines of defence and cut off the British Expeditionary Force at Dunkirk. With the permission of his commanding officer (granted not unwillingly) the Duke took leave of absence to get the Duchess out of France into neutral Spain. This proved difficult and dangerous, but after a car journey of four days they arrived in Madrid on 23 June (nine days after the Germans entered Paris). Here they were provided for by the British Ambassador, Sir Samuel Hoare, who found their presence irksome, as the Spanish dictator, General Franco, had strong leanings towards Germany and Italy and might come into the war at any moment.[11] The Windsors stayed in Madrid for a week, during which time the Duke acted with great indiscretion, associating with Nazi sympathizers and making no secret of his view that the war was lost and that the best course open to Britain was to sue for a negotiated peace; and when ordered by the British government to return to England via Portugal he demurred, raising again the matter of his wife's status and insisting on future employment for himself. However, he did feel obliged to leave for the comparative safety of Portugal, where he found a stern letter from Churchill reminding him that he was in the army and that disobedience of orders could result in a court-martial. The Duke's behaviour at this, his country's greatest moment of peril aroused fury in England: Churchill's secretary, Jock Colville, described him as 'maddening and cantankerous', while the King's secretary, Sir Alexander Hardinge, put the main blame on the Duchess: 'This is not the first time that this lady has come under suspicion for her anti-British activities and as long as we never forget the power she has exerted over the Duke in her efforts to avenge herself on this country we shall be all right.'

The King and Prime Minister, brooding painfully over the Duke's future, finally decided that, in view of his still frigid relations with the Royal Family and his indiscretions in Spain and Portugal, he should not be brought back to England but sent direct to some far-away place with a post of some dignity and little responsibility where, it was hoped, he would be out of harm's way; suitable for this purpose seemed to be the governorship of the Bahamas, a small British colony in the Caribbean off the coast of Florida. As might be expected, the Duke had little enthusiasm for this idea and was well aware that he was being pushed aside. German sympathizers in Portugal tried to dissuade him from accepting, for the German Foreign Minister, von Ribbentrop, had given orders that everything should be done to keep the Duke in Europe, if possible lured back into Spain, where he would be kept in readiness for peace talks, which the Germans were confidently expecting, and ultimately perhaps to become a puppet king of a German-dominated Britain. It was urged on him that he might soon have an important role to play in Europe and that in the Bahamas he was being exiled and liable to assassination. However, the Duke would not listen to this. He gave no thought to secret negotiations with the enemy and realized that in the circumstances he had no alternative but to accept the British proposal. On 1 August he, the Duchess and a fair-sized entourage set sail first for Bermuda and then on to the Bahamas.

It was never likely that the Windsors would love the Bahamas – a group of twenty-nine islands whose total area was half that of Wales with a population of 70,000, most of whom were black, living in the direst poverty, unemployed and scratching a living as best they could from fishing and smallholdings. There was little organized agriculture or industry and the economy of the islands depended, unreliably, on tourism.

The Windsors arrived there in the middle of summer when the heat was stifling, and although they were given a warm welcome they were appalled when they were taken to Government House, which it seemed to them was almost derelict – damp crumbling walls, fading decorations, riddled with termites and full of large ugly furniture. It did not take them long to decide that it was uninhabitable, and while extensive refurbishments were carried out they moved into a house lent to them by the Bahamas' chief citizen, Sir Harry Oakes, who had made a fortune prospecting for gold in Canada and had since become involved in various other activities, not all of them above board.[12]

The prospect of living in the Bahamas for five years, which was their term of office, appalled Wallis and she was soon pouring out her woes in letters to her Aunt Bessie: 'I hate this place more each day . . . the locals are petty-minded, the visitors common and uninteresting . . . This moron paradise.' She was clearly out of her element. She found Nassau, the capital where more than half the population was clustered, claustrophobic and provincial and longed to be out of it. However, she determined to make the best of a bad job and set about turning Government House into a reasonable home or, as she put it to Aunt

Bessie, 'dish this shack up so that at least one isn't ashamed of asking the local horrors here'. This she did with her customary skill. She also became involved in public works, joining the Red Cross, visiting hospitals and orphanages and doing what she could to relieve the worst of the poverty.

The Duke also took his job seriously. It was expected that he would be no more than an amiable figurehead, but he aspired to be more than that, attempting to tackle unemployment and to build up a more stable economy. Unfortunately, however, he did not renounce his defeatist talk and half-hearted attitude to the war. He continued to associate with German sympathizers and to tell people that Hitler should have been 'managed' and left to fight it out with Communism, which was a greater evil than Fascism. He was also quoted as saying that America should stay out of the war, which brought an angry rebuke from Churchill, the crux of whose policy was to bring America in. Because of his views the British government was unwilling to allow him to visit America, which both he and the Duchess longed to do, as he might have given encouragement there to the Isolationists. They did, however, make visits later on and were always greeted enthusiastically. To many Americans the Abdication would always be the love story of the century and Edward and Wallis the heroes of romance. There were, however, some dissident voices who found their lifestyle too luxurious and too far removed from the austerity of wartime Britain. Wallis was too beautifully dressed, and it appeared she could not travel anywhere without numerous staff and as many as fifty pieces of luggage.

The Duke resigned the governorship of the Bahamas on 30 April 1945, the day Hitler shot himself in his Berlin bunker. The question then arose again: What next for the Windsors? He longed for a job which would keep him fully occupied and give him scope to exercise his abilities. He had his eyes on the governor-generalship of Canada or the viceroyalty of India, but he was aiming too high; and even lesser jobs could not be found. It was not easy to place an ex-king; his wartime indiscretions told against him, and he was not retreating from the opinions he had expressed. In spite of the horrors uncovered in the German death camps he was still maintaining that terms should have been made with Hitler and the war avoided; and documents were now coming to light from German sources which cast a shadow over his conduct in Spain and Portugal in 1940. His plea for a job fell on deaf ears. His brother, George VI, was opposed to the idea, and even Churchill, who in spite of Edward's misdeeds still had a soft spot for him, was hesitant; and his successor, the Labour leader Clement Attlee, was definite. Even a place of residence was proving difficult to find. It was made plain to them that they would not be welcome in England where there was still no question of Wallis being received at Court and where they would be expected to pay income tax – always a telling point with them. America was considered, but it would be too expensive for the high lifestyle they required. It looked as though they would have to settle for France, where they still had two houses and where they could live tax-free. But even here there were reservations: the French government was wary of their pre-war associates, some of whom were being charged with collaborating with the Germans; and the Duke, who had no great love for France, thought that the political situation there was unstable and might result in a Communist takeover. However, in time these difficulties diminished and the Windsors decided that for the time being France would be their main base, although they intended to do much travelling.

The year 1946 was a bad year for the Windsors. In England there was only frustration – no work, no remission from income tax, and they were still cold-shouldered by the Royal Family. In the following year the chasm between them became even greater: they were not invited to Queen Mary's eightieth birthday celebrations or to the wedding of Princess Elizabeth and Prince Philip. This ostracism was deeply wounding, and the Windsors responded by falling into an affluent and hedonistic lifestyle – endlessly partying and flitting around the pleasure resorts of Europe and America, often in dubious company.

This aimless existence deeply shocked King George and Queen Elizabeth, who might have realized that the only way to prevent it was by providing the Duke and Duchess with worthwhile work, but this could not be done. They fell into ever more prodigal ways, which became especially conspicuous towards the end of the 1940s when a particularly notorious character erupted into their lives. Jimmy Donahue – drug addict, bisexual and heir to an enormous Woolworth fortune – had been involved in every sort of scandal and was always ready for more. Eighteen years younger than the Duchess (then aged fifty-three), he fascinated her with his boyish charm and outlandish ways, and for nearly four years she could not long be parted from him. Inevitably this set tongues wagging that the most famous marriage of the century was breaking up. However, there was no danger of this. Until his death the Duke remained in thrall to the Duchess, pandering to her every whim and never looking at another woman, and while the Duchess might have had occasional diversions these never went far and she always knew that her life was irretrievably bound up with her husband. This did not, however, stop her from rounding on him viciously, often in public, but he seemed unworried by such treatment, indeed he seemed rather to relish it. And he was untroubled by the Donahue affair. 'Oh, she's quite safe with him,' he told a friend, and no doubt sexually she was, but the man was taking up more and more of her time. The Duke's complaisance inevitably gave rise to comment and scandalous rumours about his own relations with Donahue. It was not the first time he had been suspected of homoerotic tendencies. There is no positive evidence of these, and he was always outwardly homophobic, but perspicacious and openly avowed homosexuals like Noel Coward had little doubt of his inclinations. In time Wallis's attachment to Jimmy ran its course, ending suddenly and even violently.[13] Jimmy died six years later at the age of fifty-one from acute alcoholic and barbiturate intoxication.

As if the Jimmy Donahue affair was not provocation enough, further offence was caused to the Royal Family by the announcement in 1947 that the Duke was intending to write his autobiography, including a personal account of the Abdication under the title 'A King's Story'. Nothing could have been more upsetting than this to the King and Queen and to Queen Mary, to whom it was an inviolable rule that royalty did not appear in print. No wonder that the Windsors were further isolated, being excluded from George's silver wedding celebrations in 1948 and from a party at the British Embassy in Paris in honour of Princess Elizabeth and Prince Philip. Owing to Edward's lack of application his book took several years to complete, even with the help of an experienced American journalist. It was unfortunate that it began to appear in serial form in 1950 when King George's health was taking a serious turn for the worse, and it roused him to furious anger. In the following year his left lung had to be removed following a diagnosis of cancer, and from then on his life hung on by a thread. When he died on 6 February 1952 the Duke came at once from New York for the funeral but without the Duchess who, he knew, would not be welcome.

The Windsors were hopeful that the new Queen would be more sympathetic to them than her father. At the time of the Abdication she had been only ten and she did not have the same bitter feelings as her parents. Left to herself she might perhaps have been lenient, but under the influence of her mother and grandmother she would not yield an inch, and the Duke obtained none of the things he wanted – a suitable job, a welcome to come and live in England tax-free and the granting of the title of Her Royal Highness to the Duchess. On the subject of the title the Queen and her advisers were especially adamant, for the title once granted would be Wallis's for life and if the Duke predeceased her and she were to marry again, perhaps to some questionable character, there could be even further embarrassment. Besides, it would have meant revoking the Letter Patent of 1937 issued by George VI, implying that he had been wrong, which would have been an intolerable insult to his memory.

There was also no invitation to his niece's coronation. A few weeks before this occurred Queen Mary died, leaving strict instructions that there should be no interference with the ceremony. The Duke loved his mother but could never forgive her for her intransigent attitude towards his wife. At the time of her funeral he wrote to the Duchess, who had remained in New York: 'I somehow feel that the fluids in her veins must always have been as icy as they now are in death.' Any hope that her death would lead to a more flexible attitude was soon dispelled as the Queen Mother was as implacable as ever in her hostility. The antagonism of the two sisters-in-law now reached its peak. The Duchess openly mocked the Queen's clothes and figure while the Queen Mother referred bitterly to the Duchess as 'the woman who killed my husband'.

The Windsors had to make the most of life in France. They had recently acquired a millhouse outside Paris (Le Moulin de la Tuileries) – very attractive but needing a lot doing to it, which was a challenge to the Duke who liked nothing better than creating a garden, while the Duchess saw to the rehabilitation of the buildings. Wallis may have had a limited range of interests – she read little and was no intellectual – and had no taste for outdoor activities such as gardening or any form of sport; but there were certain things she did supremely well. She was an excellent hostess – her parties were always of the highest order – and her dress sense was unmatched – she was regularly voted one of the best-dressed women in the world. But perhaps her greatest gift was for interior decoration where her touch was unfailing and she could soon transform the most unpromising of rooms into a place of dazzling charm and comfort. Later these gifts were again called into play when the French government with great generosity offered the Windsors at a nominal rent an imposing mansion in two acres of land in the Bois de Boulogne which they gratefully accepted and which was to be their main home for the rest of their lives. Here the Duchess, presiding over a staff of thirty including liveried footmen and a chef of national repute, ran the house on a magnificent scale. After a visit there in connection with his life of Queen Mary the author James Pope-Hennessy wrote: 'Every conceivable luxury and creature comfort is conscripted to produce a perfection of sybaritic living. It is, of course, intensely American. The Queen Mother by comparison at Clarence House led a lodging house existence.' Certainly the Windsors lived in great style and were much in demand, but theirs was still an empty life. So much pleasure soon palled. They were aware that the Duke's talents were being wasted and longed for him to have a more significant role. His autobiography had earned him over a million dollars, and in 1954 the Duchess began work on hers, published two years later with the somewhat novelettish title *The Heart Has Its Reasons*. With professional help it was smoothly written but, as might be expected, slanted and with much left out; but like her husband's it became a bestseller.

With the coming of the 1960s and the so-called 'Permissive Society' the rigid attitude of royalty towards divorce came under strain. A more liberal attitude was abroad, and besides the Royal Family was experiencing divorce close to home. In 1953 Princess Margaret had fallen in love with Group Captain Peter Townsend, a Battle of Britain fighter ace and a member of the royal household. He returned her love and they wanted to marry, but the Group Captain had been married before. He had been the innocent party in a divorce, so the Princess was confronted with the same situation as her uncle: it was made clear to her that she could either marry her lover, in which case she would lose her royal status (and income), or she could relinquish him and remain as she was. Unlike her uncle, after long hesitation, she bowed to the precepts of the Church of England and chose the latter course. Four years later she married Anthony Armstrong-Jones, the son of divorced parents. Later both the sons of the Princess Royal were to go through the divorce courts, as also eventually did Princess Margaret herself. There was then less reason for the stigma attached to Wallis for being a divorcée, especially as by then her marriage to the Duke had lasted for more than twenty years and was still intact.

By the mid-1960s the Queen and perhaps even the Queen Mother were becoming aware of a groundswell of popular opinion in favour of the Windsors. This had been voiced movingly by the Queen's cousin, the Earl of Harewood:

> All of us knew that he [the Duke] was condemned for putting private life above duty. But it was hard for the younger amongst us not to stand in amazement at the moral contradiction between the elevation of a code of duty on the one hand, and on the other the denial of central Christian virtues – forgiveness, understanding, family tenderness.

To others, too, it seemed petty-minded that the Duke should still be treated as an outcast. In spite of his misdeeds (of which there was mounting evidence) his popularity was undimmed; his charm and sad, apologetic look still had great appeal, whenever he appeared in public in England he drew enthusiastic crowds, and his television interviews always had top ratings.

The first sign of a royal thaw came in 1964 when the Duke underwent an abdominal operation in Houston, Texas, and the Queen sent him flowers. In the following year came another breakthrough when he had an operation on his eyes in the London Clinic, and the Queen came to visit him and for the first time met the Duchess. It was also the first time he made a request to the Queen which was granted – that he and Wallis should be buried side by side in the family graveyard at Frogmore. Two years later came a further act of reconciliation when both the Duke and the Duchess were invited to attend the unveiling of a plaque in memory of Queen Mary. This would bring face to face the Duchess and her great antagonist the Queen Mother, and there was some curiosity as to the outcome of this. As it happened they seemed to talk together quite amiably, although Wallis, markedly, did not curtsy as protocol required.[14]

During the last three years of the Duke's life, when his health was deteriorating rapidly, he and Wallis became more devoted than ever. In a television interview in 1970 the Duchess stressed how happy they had been together in spite of some hard times. And later in the year at a dinner in their honour at the White House the Duke gave a moving reply to the toast: 'I have had the good fortune to have had a wonderful American girl consent to marry me and have thirty years of loving care and devotion and companionship – something I have cherished above all else.'

In 1971 a biopsy revealed that the Duke was suffering from a cancerous tumour in the throat. No operation was possible, so he had to endure the horrors of cobalt treatment. He also had to undergo an operation for a double hernia. On 18 May 1972 he was visited by the Queen and Duke of Edinburgh, who were on a state visit to Paris. By then he was desperately weak and being fed intravenously so that his face was a mass of tubes, but he insisted on these being removed and being fully dressed to receive his visitors. Eleven days later he was dead.

Arrangements were in place for his death, and his coffin was flown in an RAF plane to England and taken to St George's Chapel in Windsor for a public lying-in-state and to which around a thousand people came to pay their respects. The Duchess, worn down by the ordeal of the last weeks, did not accompany the coffin but came to England two days later where at last she was invited to stay in Buckingham Palace. Here she was looked after with care, but she clearly found the funeral a great strain. At times she seemed to be overwhelmed and her mind to be wandering, asking where her husband was.[15] In her confusion she was taken in hand and comforted by the Queen Mother who told her: 'I know how you feel. I've been through it myself.'

Back in Paris the Windsors' house in the Bois de Boulogne was as splendid as ever, but for Wallis it had become dead without the Duke. 'He was my entire life,' she said, 'and I can't begin to think what I'll do without him.' Fourteen years of widowhood stretched in front of her – years of misery, pain and physical and mental decay. At first she made faltering attempts to resume a social life, but her health was not up to it. Soon after the Duke's death she had a fall which resulted in a broken hip and in the following year (1973) she had another which left her with five broken ribs. Both of these required her to spend time in hospital, where she was a restless and wilful patient. Her mental instability became more pronounced: her understanding was blurred and she was subject to hallucinations – one in particular that she was in danger of being kidnapped and held to ransom. She also became agitated about her finances, which was unnecessary as the Duke had left her everything and altogether she was worth several million pounds; and the French government was continuing to allow her to live in her Paris house at a peppercorn rent and free of tax. She also had fears – and these were not wholly without foundation – that she was beset by people who were after her money and treasures. Lord Mountbatten in particular showed a keen interest in the disposal of her fortune, and he paid her several visits urging her to return to England certain royal insignia and to set up a charitable trust in which he would have a leading role. From this she was extricated by her French lawyer, Maître Suzanne Blum, a tough and belligerent woman who had in her day successfully represented such prestigious clients as Walt Disney, Charlie Chaplin and Metro-Goldwyn-Mayer. As Wallis's condition weakened and her fears increased Blum established herself as her guardian, watching over her interests and reputation and every aspect of her life.

Not long after the death of the Duke it became apparent that Wallis's reconciliation with the Royal Family would be short-lived. Partly because of the continued ambiguity about her status and partly, perhaps, because of her increasingly strange and unpredictable behaviour, she was once again kept at a distance: she was not invited to Princess Anne's wedding in 1973 or to the funeral of her brother-in-law, the Duke of Gloucester, in 1974. And still there was no sign of any concession on the title of Royal Highness. In 1978 all justi-fication for withholding this title disappeared when her nephew Prince Michael of Kent married a divorced lady of aristocratic Czech origins who was per-mitted the title. But by then Wallis was past caring; a series of falls and abdominal operations had laid her so low that she was hardly conscious. This was a mercy as she was not fully aware of the controversy which was stirred up by the publi-cation of a life of Edward VIII by Frances Donaldson for which, it was clear, the author had had help from the Royal Family and which was markedly unfavourable to the Windsors. Although Wallis was unable to read the book or comment on it, Maître Blum took up the cudgels on her behalf, especially when Thames Television announced the making of a seven-part programme based on the book. Blum at once demanded (unsuccessfully) to see the script of the programme and later described the series as 'a wave of calumnies' and 'largely and essentially a fable based on incorrect or distorted interpretations of the facts'. It was also criticized by people who knew Wallis well for portray-ing her as soft and innocent and 'an *ingénue*' which, as she was over forty at the time of the Abdication and twice married, she certainly was not. Lady Diana Duff Cooper, a close friend, said that she was 'hard, hard, *hard*'.

If Wallis was unaware of the hostile opinions being voiced about her it is to be hoped that she was aware of one welcome development – the ending by the Queen Mother of the feud between them. In 1976 she came on an official visit to Paris and let it be known that she would like to visit her sister-in-law. A time was arranged, but at the last moment a message was received that 'owing to the Duchess's continuing ill health it would not now be possible for Her Royal Highness to receive Her Majesty that afternoon'. By some such a message would have been considered provocative, but the Queen Mother knew that it was genuine and instead of taking offence sent her a large bouquet of roses with a card attached on which was written 'In friendship, Elizabeth'.

By 1980, when she was eighty-four, Wallis was paralysed from the waist down, she had lost the power of speech and her mind was a blank.[16] For another six years some form of life remained in her. During this time she remained in her Paris house, which by then had become a grim fortress surrounded by a high-security fence and bristling with burglar alarms. The garden was untended and most of the house shut up. She was looked after by a devoted butler and a team of nurses under the authority of Maître Blum, whose regime had become a ruthless tyranny. Maître Blum may have been a world-famous advocate but she was also unbalanced and in her relations with Wallis obsessive to the point of dementia. She seems to have fallen under her spell in the same way as Edward VIII had once done and regarded her as a supreme being to be protected and exalted at all cost. To this end, armed with a power of attorney, she took control of Wallis's life in every detail – what she should eat and drink, when she should go into hospital, and how her property should be disposed of. She also took it upon herself to ban all visitors, even Wallis's oldest friends. Incredibly she was able to persuade herself and tried to persuade others that the life of the Duchess (and the Duke) had always been pure and virtuous, devoted to the poor and underprivileged. All stories of their profligate lifestyle and Fascist sympathies were lies and '*ordure*'.

The Duchess finally died on 24 April 1986. Her coffin, escorted by the Lord Chamberlain, was flown to England where after a brief funeral service in St George's Chapel, Windsor, attended by 175 people including the leading members of the Royal Family, she was buried by the side of her husband.[17]

Controversy still surrounds the Duchess. Was she, as some thought, a scheming adventuress out for what she could get? Or was she, as friends maintained, a comparative innocent, kind and generous, who found she had stirred up forces she could not control, a woman who would have liked to withdraw but because of the magnitude of the sacrifice made on her behalf felt obliged to accept the situation and do the best she could for the man who was so enthralled by her? And a paradox remains. It is unfortunate that those who decry her and blame her for the Abdication do not recognize a debt of gratitude to her. Edward VIII would have been a dangerous and inadequate monarch, and it was Wallis, albeit unwittingly, who was the cause of his departure, opening the way for the infinitely preferable George VI and Elizabeth II.

9
ELIZABETH OF GLAMIS
WIFE OF GEORGE VI

Elizabeth Bowes-Lyon was the first commoner to be Queen of England for four hundred years. At the age of twenty-three she had had to adapt to a royal way of life when she married Prince Albert, second in line of succession to the throne. At the time she could hardly have known what was in store for her. Thirteen years later she found herself suddenly Queen on the abdication of her brother-in-law, Edward VIII. Soon afterwards the Second World War broke out, and in this she took on herself a crucial and often harrowing role. Then after the death of her husband in 1952 she created a new life for herself during nearly fifty years of widowhood as Queen Mother – vital, prominent and intensely active. She became a well-loved national institution until she died at the age of 101.

Elizabeth came from the heights of the aristocracy. Her father, the fourteenth Earl of Strathmore, was descended from Robert II, King of Scotland in the fourteenth century; and his ancestors had taken a prominent, often turbulent, part in Scottish history, at times on the winning side when they lorded it over vast areas, at others defeated and in hiding.

The fourteenth Earl was of a retiring disposition but public spirited, a conscientious landlord and deeply religious. His wife came from an English aristocratic family, the Cavendish-Bendincks, one of whose members, a Duke of Portland, had been Prime Minister briefly during the reign of George III. Although wealthy, the Strathmores did not live extravagantly, keeping their distance from smart society and not associating closely with royalty. They devoted themselves mainly to raising a large family (altogether ten) and the management of their estates, which were extensive. Principal of these was Glamis Castle, one of the largest and most historic in Scotland, abounding in ghosts, legends and dark deeds – men killed in duels and tortured on the rack and a woman burned as a witch. There was also the mystery of 'the monster of Glamis', a deformed child who in the early nineteenth century had been immured in the recesses of the castle, out of sight and as far as possible out of mind. The family estate also included another castle in the north-east of England, Streatlam (since demolished), a mansion in Hertfordshire, St Paul's Walden Bury, and a house in London in St James's Square.

Elizabeth was born in 1900, the ninth child of her parents and something of an afterthought, seven years having elapsed since the birth of their previous child. But two years later a son, David, was born, and 'the two Benjamins', as they were called, became close companions. Their childhood together was idyllically happy whether in the lovely rolling countryside of Hertfordshire or in the wilder setting of the Grampians. Both places offered endless scope for enjoyment and excitement – riding, exploring secret homes, waging imaginary wars – and for Elizabeth (but not for David) only a light application of formal education, imparted for the most part by her mother.

When the First World War broke out Glamis Castle was converted into a convalescent hospital for the wounded, and although Elizabeth was only fourteen she at once took an active part in the running of it, ministering to the needs of the patients – writing letters and shopping for them and doing what she could to cheer them up, which was not easy at times as she herself had to confront personal tragedy when one brother was killed and another wounded and taken prisoner.

With the coming of peace it was time for Elizabeth to 'come out' and enter the social scene in London. Here she was an immediate success. Her vitality, charm and good looks brought her many suitors, prominent among whom was Prince Albert, the second son of George V, who came to realize almost at once that Elizabeth was the only girl he could ever marry.

Unlike Elizabeth, Albert (or Bertie, as he was known) had not had a happy childhood. He was not a robust child, and constant hectoring from his father and maltreatment from a sadistic nurse had affected his nervous system; he was afflicted with a speech impediment that dogged him all his life. Ill health had caused him to be invalided out of the Navy (although not before he had fought in the Battle of Jutland), and he had grown up diffident and highly strung. He had also had to endure being constantly compared unfavourably to his brilliant and outgoing elder brother David. But Bertie was unbowed. He went his way quietly and purposefully, developing a mind of his own as well as characteristics lacking in his elder brother, notably balance and self-discipline. In his early twenties he had little idea of the cataclysm that was to overtake him in middle age; he seemed set on a quiet, useful life out of the glare of the footlights. However, on one point he was certain: he must have a strong-minded and supportive wife; and he wanted her soon. He was finding life with his parents tedious and oppressive. His father, although kindly at heart, still found it necessary to be gruff and censorious with his sons, while his mother, also kindly, was unbending and unsympathetic. Life at Buckingham Palace, and indeed all the royal residences, was undeniably dull and unvarying, the least suggestion of change being testily suppressed by the King. No wonder Bertie longed for an establishment of his own. So he lost no time in proposing to Elizabeth Bowes-Lyon, who was everything he could wish – beautiful, understanding, reliable. He could not wish for a more perfect helpmate. But she was not to be easily won. She had doubts about marrying into the Royal Family and at first held back, but Bertie was not to be put off. With quiet determination he persisted until she finally succumbed.

The news of Albert and Elizabeth's engagement was greeted in the country with great enthusiasm. Not since the time of the Tudors and Henry VIII's eclectic choice of wives had a royal prince so near to the throne chosen a British commoner as his wife. The change from dim, often unprepossessing foreign royalty was acclaimed by everyone, even, indeed especially, the King and Queen. George V was enraptured by his new daughter-in-law, so different from what he had been dreading – a 'modern woman' with bobbed hair and short skirts, heavily made up and knocking back cocktails. For her he was ready to make every allowance, even unpunctuality at meals – and their relationship was to be a special one. Later, on his death, Elizabeth wrote: 'I miss him dreadfully. Unlike his own children I was never afraid of him, and in all the twelve years of having me as a daughter-in-law he never spoke one unkind or abrupt word to me, and was always ready to listen and give advice on one's own silly little affairs. He was so kind and dependable.'

Albert and Elizabeth's wedding on 26 April 1923 was a royal spectacular. To the dismay of republicans, crowds poured into London and camped for hours on cold pavements to get a glimpse of the bride and bridegroom. Elizabeth did not disappoint them. She already showed a near genius for responding to cheering crowds – just the right blend of royalty and the common touch, and her smile was irresistible.

Soon after the wedding Albert, now Duke of York, had further proof of his wife's ability to handle public occasions – a christening and a wedding in the Balkans. This might have been difficult, as they were packed into an uncomfortable, overcrowded palace full of foreign royalty with their various idiosyncrasies, but Elizabeth charmed them all and even made it an enjoyable occasion for Bertie.

Back in England the Duke and Duchess settled down to an unpretentious lifestyle. The Duke enjoyed hunting and shooting (pleasures not shared by the Duchess), but they kept clear of the hectic social life surrounding the Prince of Wales. They rarely went to nightclubs and travelled abroad only when duty called. An exception to this was when they went on safari in East Africa, where the Duchess showed great physical prowess – wading through floods, battered by storms, enduring acute physical discomfort and occasionally taking a rather half-hearted shot at big game.

During the first years of their marriage the Yorks were handicapped by having no suitable residence. It so happened that all the grace-and-favour houses in London were then occupied by elderly royal relatives who could not be persuaded to move; and the only place available for them was White Lodge in Richmond Park. This had once been an attractive country house, but over the years it had become encompassed by suburbia and had long been unoccupied and was in a sorry state of disrepair. For four years the Yorks struggled with inadequate heating, precarious electricity and primitive drains. The location, too, was inconvenient and lacking in privacy; there was little protection from the crowds who were always gathering to get a peep inside. It was not until 1926 that a suitable house was found for them in central London at 145 Piccadilly near Hyde Park Corner.

Shortly before this the Duchess had given birth to her first child, the future Queen Elizabeth II, and she and the Duke were looking forward to spending as much time as possible with her while at the same time supervising the restoration of their new home. But then they were required by the King to go on a royal tour to New Zealand and Australia where the Duke would formally open the new parliament building in Canberra. For both of them, but the Duchess in particular, this was a painful wrench. It would mean being away from her baby for six months, and she minded this dreadfully; but it did not occur to her or her husband not to obey the summons.

On 6 January 1927 they set out on the battle cruiser HMS *Renown* on a round-the-world voyage. In Australasia there had been some reservations about the choice of the Yorks for the occasion. People remembered the wildly successful tour of the Prince of Wales seven years before and were hoping for a return visit from him. They were kindly disposed towards the Yorks but wondered whether the Duke with his stammer and unsound health would prove capable of such a tour. They need not have worried. From the moment the Duke and Duchess arrived in New Zealand on 2 February everything went superbly. Their modesty, charm and artlessness won all hearts. They had a different kind of appeal from the Prince of Wales's, but it was no less effective. There was a moment of anxiety halfway through the New Zealand visit when the Duchess was confined to bed with tonsillitis and the Duke wondered whether there would be so much enthusiasm for him on his own, but this did not diminish. Everywhere crowds were as large and eager as ever, which not only surprised him but did wonders for his self-confidence.

After an emotional farewell from New Zealand the Duke and Duchess arrived to a tumultuous welcome in Australia. Here the exuberance and uninhibited friendliness overwhelmed them. Any shyness they may have felt was swept away. In the course of their visit it fell to the Duke to make a number of speeches, particularly at the opening of the parliament building, and there was anxiety that on this occasion he might be overcome by his stammer, but this did not happen. It seemed that as long as the Duchess was beside him, confident and radiant, all went well. At the end of the tour there were paeans of praise from all sides. The Governor General of New Zealand wrote to George V: 'It is quite unnecessary to say that they both made themselves adored by everyone. The visit has done untold good.' And the Governor General of Australia wrote: 'The Duchess leaves us with responsibility of having a continent in love with her.' These warm feelings were reciprocated by the Duke and Duchess. Their success had done much for their morale and had given them a new understanding of their potential. Twenty-six years earlier, King George V and Queen Mary (when they were Duke and Duchess of York) had had the same experience when they visited Australasia. They had arrived shy and buttoned up but soon thawed from the warmth of their reception. Back home there was widespread praise for what they had achieved, although from the Palace this was somewhat muted. The King had watched their progress with an eagle eye for the least irregularity of detail which he had been quick to point out. Surprisingly the Yorks were not required to go on another royal tour during the remaining nine years of George V's reign.

They returned to the way of life that suited them best – unostentatious and unfashionable – dividing their time between public duties (mostly rather mundane) and family. Another daughter, Princess Margaret, had been born in 1930. Few royal families, before or since, have been able to create such a happy and relaxed family atmosphere. This was partly due to the Duke, who was determined that his children should not have to endure the taut upbringing he had had, as well as to the Duchess with her brisk good-natured common sense and love of the simple things of life – party games, jigsaw puzzles and popular dancing. It was to be expected that such domestic delights would attract ridicule and condescension from smart society. 'Such a sweet little couple,' wrote Duff Cooper, 'and so fond of each other.'[1] Even more patronizing was the novelist Virginia Woolf, who wrote of Elizabeth: 'a simple, chattery, sweet-hearted, little round-faced young woman in pink'. How wrong she was! Few people who knew her well were unaware of a vein of steel underneath the smiling, benign exterior.

The Yorks wanted no change in their ordered way of life, but from 1930 onwards clouds began to gather, for in that year the Prince of Wales first met Wallis Simpson, and his slavish devotion to her and his increasingly raffish lifestyle were causing serious concern. Could he really become king?

Such thoughts were for the most part as yet unspoken, and Albert put them right out of his mind for the idea that he himself might become King was a nightmare. In spite of his great success in Australia and New Zealand he still dreaded big public occasions. He had not overcome his natural shyness, and his speech impediment, although much improved, still plagued him whenever he had to speak in public. So it was with growing dismay that he witnessed his brother's infatuation with Mrs Simpson. He hoped and prayed it would be temporary and that, like previous affairs, it would run its course and then subside, but there was no sign of this; rather, it seemed to be intensifying. Great as was Bertie's antipathy to Mrs Simpson, Elizabeth liked her even less. From their first meeting she took against her, having no doubt she was an unscrupulous adventuress out for what she could get. Smart, fashionable, wisecracking – Elizabeth saw in her everything she most despised, and she tended to show it. For her part Wallis had an open contempt for Elizabeth, regarding her as frumpish and too sweet by half.

On the death of George V in January 1936 and Edward's assumption of the throne, his relationship with Mrs Simpson became ever more blatant. Not only was she his constant companion but she was also beginning to give herself the airs of a future queen. When she stayed at Balmoral in the autumn of 1936 she seemed to be acting as hostess, and her condescending manner infuriated Elizabeth who responded by behaving as if she was not there. As the prospect of Edward's abdication grew, no one was more appalled than Albert, who saw the crown closing in on him, and his ordeal was made worse by his brother's neglect. Edward made no attempt to contact him and take him into his confidence, so he was kept in the dark about developments. As Elizabeth exclaimed bitterly at one point: 'We know nothing, *nothing*.' By then Albert's state of mind was becoming desperate, and his agony increased when Elizabeth went down with flu and could not be at his side in the final stages. But his mother was there, steadfast as ever, and it was on her shoulder that he once gave way and wept for over an hour. However, his courage returned. 'You can rest assured', he said at the time, 'that I will do my best to clear up the inevitable mess, if the whole fabric does not crumble under the shock and strain of it.' He realized full well that the future of the British monarchy depended on him, but with Elizabeth once again in support he could face up to this.

In the next months the burden on both them was heavy indeed. There was the usual round of public duties including the state opening of Parliament and the speech from the throne, which caused the King special anxiety. There was also the move from their well-loved house in Piccadilly into the gaunt discomfort of Buckingham Palace; and for George there was the daunting task of ploughing through the ever-accumulating red boxes filled with official documents that had to be read carefully and mastered, a task of which he had had no previous experience. Then there were all the arrangements for the coronation. Normally this occurs eighteen months after a monarch's accession, but as preparations were already under way for the coronation of Edward VIII on 11 May 1937 it was decided to stick to that date. The King and Queen had only five months to be decked out in all their finery, learn their roles in the ceremony and be ready to entertain the thousands of guests who would be pouring in.

On the great day everything went as smoothly and splendidly as could be hoped.[2] In front of a congregation of over seven thousand (including crowned heads, maharajahs, sultans and all the grandest of the aristocracy) George and Elizabeth played their parts impeccably, and those who had been whispering doubts about the King's ability to get through the service because of his stammer and highly strung nerves were silenced. But it was the Queen who stole the show. It was she more than anyone else who saw her husband through his ordeal, and her bearing and poise were beyond praise. 'Nothing', wrote Harold Nicolson, 'could exceed the charm and dignity which she displayed, and I cannot help feeling what a mess poor Mrs Simpson would have made of such a situation.' This was an opinion with which all Mrs Simpson's supporters (including Winston Churchill) could not but agree.

The coronation behind them, there was little respite for the King and Queen.

The situation in Europe was becoming ever more critical as the Fascist dictators became more aggressive. The British government was anxious to strengthen relations with the country's principal ally in Europe, France; and it was felt that this could not be done more potently than by a royal visit to Paris. One was accordingly arranged for the end of June 1938, but a week before it was due to start Elizabeth's mother, the Countess of Strathmore, died, and the visit had to be postponed for three weeks, a period not only for Elizabeth to come to terms with the loss of a dearly loved parent but also to make drastic changes in her wardrobe. It was felt that for a visit in these circumstances the bright colours that had been chosen were unsuitable, but so, too, was funereal black; it was decided that as a compromise the Queen should be dressed in white, and somehow in the time available a new set of clothes was turned out by her dressmaker, Norman Hartnell. The Queen had not before been noted for *haute couture* and had never felt bound by the dictates of fashion – not for her the flattened chest and wasp waist. Rather she had gone for a style of her own, free flowing and comfortable with plenty of chiffon and tulle. Such clothes suited her figure admirably, but there were doubts as to how in virgin white they would be received in the centre of world fashion; but they proved a wild success and were eagerly copied. The combination of the King's diffidence and friendliness and the Queen's charm and ever-winning smile took Paris by storm. Everywhere they went Parisians turned out *en masse* to catch a glimpse of them, and there were scenes of wild enthusiasm hardly witnessed since the famous visit of the King's grandfather thirty years before. Summing up the general view a newspaper wrote: 'France had become a monarchy again.' And surveying the scene from a distance in Berlin, Adolf Hitler, contemplating his next aggression, was heard to remark that Elizabeth was 'the most dangerous woman in Europe'.

The success of the King's and Queen's visit to Paris was important for several reasons. Not only did it cement Anglo-French relations but it was also a unifying force in France; at that time there were bitter divisions in the country, but nearly all parties could come together in admiration of the King and Queen. And, of course, it did much for them, too: their reputation at home was greatly enhanced and there was less talk now of 'a substitute king' who was not up to the job. Britain was coming to appreciate how fortunate the change of monarchs had been.

Such was the acclamation of the Paris visit that the government was soon urging the King and Queen to make another tour, this time to Canada where there were murmurings of discontent and threats of neutrality in the event of war. When this was agreed President Roosevelt invited them to extend their visit to the United States, and this, too, was agreed. It was to be a historic tour – the first time a reigning British monarch had set foot in a Dominion or in the United States. It was attended by some danger as there had been threats from Irish extremists and American Nazis, so security was tight. Danger threatened even before the royal couple arrived when the liner on which they were travelling was caught in a dense mist amid icebergs, and, bearing in mind the fate of the *Titanic* twenty five years before, progress for three and a half days was of the slowest.

Once safely in Canada everything went superbly. The warmth of their reception exceeded all expectations, and once again the response of the King and Queen was perfect. The Governor General of Canada at the time, Lord Tweedsmuir (the author John Buchan), was overcome with admiration and wrote of them with great perceptiveness: 'The King was a mixture of shrewdness, kindliness and humour', while 'the Queen had a perfect genius for impulsive gesture . . . and the small unscheduled things that count most'. The Canadian tour was an exceptionally arduous one since the King and Queen had to travel many thousands of miles and meet all sorts of people, not only officials but also Great War veterans, lumberjacks and Native American chieftains (complete with elk teeth and bear claws). At the end it was generally agreed that they had worked wonders, not only in binding Canada more closely into the Commonwealth but in bringing together the different ethnic strains of which Canada was made up.

Just as successful, if not more so, was their visit to the United States. In the broiling summer heat of Washington thousands of people lined the streets to watch them go by, and they were delighted by what they saw. The expectation in some quarters had been that the King would be shy and at a loss and the Queen plump and ill-dressed. On the contrary, the King had been well primed and took a genuine interest in American politics. He established at once a close rapport with President Roosevelt, who formed a high opinion of him, and they talked deep into the night on the international situation and the impending war in Europe. The Queen, too, was universally admired, notably by Mrs Roosevelt, a dispassionate critic not easily bowled over by royalty, who admired her graciousness and her apparent ability to smile at a hundred people at once; but she also remarked that she was perhaps 'a little self-consciously regal'.

When, only a few months after the end of the tour, the Second World War broke out American sympathy and support became vital, and no one had done more to foster it than the King and Queen, certainly far more than any contemporary politician could have done. On their return home another tumultuous welcome awaited them. The British people had followed their progress with avid interest and were enthusiastic about what they had achieved. Doubts about their suitability had now vanished. 'It was the American tour that made us,' the Queen said later.

Great as had been the successes of the King and Queen in France and America, their finest hour was yet to come. During the Second World War their courage, sense of duty and insistence on sharing to the full the hazards and hardships of wartime brought the throne, in the words of Winston Churchill, 'more closely together with the people than ever before was recorded and Your Majesties are more beloved by all classes than any of the Princes of the past'.

During the first seven months of the war, the so-called 'Phoney War', the Queen spent much time visiting London's air defences – the gun emplacements, barrage balloon sites and air-raid shelters. She always gave a great impetus to everyone's efforts, yet surprisingly little was done at first to introduce proper air-raid precautions at Buckingham Palace, with near-fatal results later.

The character of the war changed abruptly on 9 April 1940 when German armies overran Denmark and Norway and then a month later Holland, Belgium and France. Within six weeks all these countries had capitulated and Britain was left alone, most of her army rescued miraculously from the beaches of Dunkirk but with arms and equipment all abandoned. There was little with which to resist a German invasion. At this time of mortal danger there was talk of the Princesses being evacuated to Canada, but the idea was quickly scotched. 'The children couldn't go without me,' the Queen declared. 'I could not possibly leave the King, and the King never would go. I should die if I had to leave.' The Royal Family stayed put, ready to fight it out to the last. Indeed it might well have come to this. Rumours were rife that German parachutists might attempt to abduct the King and Queen and hold them to ransom. Something similar had been attempted in Continental Europe. In preparation for such a contingency the Queen took lessons in the use of firearms and a shooting range was set up in the garden of Buckingham Palace.

In the ensuing months a German invasion was held off by the victory of British fighter pilots over the Luftwaffe in the Battle of Britain, but in September of 1940 the aerial bombardment of British cities began. It was then that the King and Queen came into their own, losing no time in visiting the hardest-hit areas, particularly the East End of London. There scenes of agony awaited them – bombed-out families, loved ones killed or buried in debris and their homes and worldly possessions shattered. This was a gruelling ordeal for both of them; they felt deep anguish for the sufferers, and although they were sometimes near to breaking point they never shied away and were charming, smiling and sympathetic at all times – something which required tremendous courage and determination. That their visits did good is widely attested. People were greatly touched by their concern; it made them feel they were not being neglected and left to their fate. Herbert Morrison, Minister of Home Security and a Labour stalwart, said later: 'The example of the King and Queen did more to keep up the spirits of the people than any other single factor.' And one Cockney bomb victim said of the Queen: 'She was a great old girl. We always felt she was one of us.'

As it happened Buckingham Palace was one of the first victims of the Blitz: on 13 September a lone German raider suddenly emerged from the clouds and, flying low down the Mall, dropped a stick of six bombs on the Palace. The King and Queen were in residence at the time and narrowly escaped death; they were unhurt but shaken, and the reaction of the Queen was typical: 'I am glad. It makes me to feel I can look the East End in the face.' Altogether there were nine occasions when bombs fell on the Palace.

As well as bomb damage there were other hardships to be endured at Buckingham Palace during the war. The King and Queen were at great pains to show that they were not exempt from wartime austerity. Food rationing was rigidly enforced. Such delicacies as reconstituted egg, sausages of dubious content and fish croquettes were included in the royal menu, made only slightly more palatable by being served on silver plates. Fuel, too, was severely restricted. Large, cheerless rooms were heated by only the smallest of electric fires, and people taking a hot bath were reminded that it had to be a shallow one by a painted line above which water should not be allowed to go. And there were more substantial privations: Sandringham and Balmoral were closed down and their lawns and golf courses dug up to grow vegetables.

Much more serious than these physical hardships was the stress caused by the fluctuating fortunes of British arms. In the first three years of the war there were all too many calamities, and the King was fully informed of these and knew how desperately critical the plight of the country often was. At first his relations with Churchill had been uneasy, as the latter had been an outspoken supporter of Edward VIII at the time of the Abdication. But in time they drew closely together and came to trust each other completely and to buoy each other up. In their weekly meetings Churchill confided more fully and freely in the King than in anyone else, and it was a great relief to him to be able to unburden himself in this way to someone wise, dispassionate, free of political tensions and jealousies. No one did more than the King to ease Churchill's awesome responsibilities. But the strain of this and the King's many other activities took their toll. He was not physically strong and his nervous system was unsound, and he, too, needed support; fortunately he had this in full measure from the Queen.

As the war dragged on into its sixth year the King and Queen, like many others, were near to exhaustion, but when it ended in the summer of 1945 they had their reward. The wildly enthusiastic crowds outside Buckingham Palace on VE Day told their own story. People realized instinctively how much they owed to them. They had been no mere figureheads. They had been in the thick of it – alongside bombed-out families amid the ruins of their homes, with troops about to go into battle and liable to be killed, and in factories, dockyards and mines where, however great the national crisis, they always put on a brave, smiling face. They had played their part to the full and with the coming of peace they were the focal point of the nation's rejoicing.

Amid all the jubilation surrounding VE Day, and two months later VJ Day when the Japanese capitulated, the King and Queen had their anxieties – as also to an even greater degree did Winston Churchill. The British people, war-worn and weary, were looking for a quick return to peacetime conditions – to the end of rationing, shortages, drab clothes and utility furniture. Above all, they wanted adequate housing. But by the end of the war Britain was nearly bankrupt, barely able to afford the basic necessities of life. Lean and hungry years still lay ahead. Moreover, the threat of Nazism had been replaced by the hardly less dreadful spectre of totalitarian Communism. Amid this encircling gloom the King and Queen did what they could to bring some light, undertaking more duties, meeting more people and setting an example of good cheer. It had been a worry to them at first when in the General Election after VE Day the Labour Party had been swept into office with a large majority. They did not know quite what to expect. But they were soon reassured. The new Prime Minister, Clement Attlee, was hardly in the mould of Lenin or Trotsky, and although radical measures were introduced nothing threatened the constitution; and the royal couple soon came to trust him and help him all they could.

They also tried to bring some cheer into the lives of their two daughters, who had had little enjoyment at Windsor during the war, and when on the night of VJ Day they disappeared into the crowd outside Buckingham Palace to join in the revelry and the Queen became concerned the King said, 'Poor darlings. They've never had any fun', and did not attempt to recall them.[3] The Queen also arranged dances for them at Windsor and Balmoral where she was invariably the life and soul of the party, dancing indefatigably through the night – not only dignified waltzes and highland reels but more uninhibited numbers such as the hokey-cokey and even bumps-a-daisy.[4] Her influence was paramount in maintaining a tight, happy family circle, although there were signs that it might soon be depleted, for Princess Elizabeth, aged twenty in 1946, had fallen in love with a handsome naval officer.

Prince Philip of Greece and Denmark was a grandson of King George I of Greece and a great-great-grandson of Queen Victoria. As a baby he had been smuggled hurriedly out of Greece in a makeshift cot at a time of revolution and brought to England where, as his father was of a roving disposition and his mother had withdrawn into a convent, he had been cared for by his uncle, Lord Louis Mountbatten, who had always marked him out as the future husband of Princess Elizabeth. He had served with distinction during the war and seemed highly suitable, but the King had doubts and stipulated that they could not become officially engaged until Elizabeth was twenty-one.

Not altogether willingly, Elizabeth accompanied her family on a tour of South Africa in the winter of 1947 – the first and last tour they carried out as a family. As always it was a resounding success, although the King was nagged by thoughts that he ought to be back in England where the most severe winter in living memory had set in – long freeze-ups followed by widespread floods, made worse by desperate shortages of food and fuel and massive unemployment. During the war the King and Queen had always made a point of sharing the country's hardships, and they felt they should still be doing so. They even contemplated breaking off the tour.

When they did return to England three months later they found that Prince

Philip had renounced his titles and become a British citizen as Lieutenant Mountbatten RN. Soon afterwards his engagement to Princess Elizabeth was officially announced, and four months later, in November 1947, they were married. If there had been any ideas of a quiet, low-key wedding they were soon dispelled. The overwhelming wish of the people was for a grand spectacle to lighten the austerity of their lives, and they had it in full and delighted in it.

Five months later the King and Queen celebrated their Silver Wedding anniversary, and seven months after that there was further cause for rejoicing when Princess Elizabeth gave birth to her first child, Prince Charles. However, the marked deterioration in the King's health caused mounting anxiety in the following years. There had been worrying signs in South Africa, where it was noted that he became easily tired and his nerves were more on edge, resulting in outbursts of temper, sharp and short-lived and usually about something trivial. He had always been susceptible to these 'gnashes', as they were called, but they were becoming more frequent.[5] More alarming were the cramps he was having in his legs. A few days before the birth of Prince Charles he was diagnosed as having arteriosclerosis, which might lead to gangrene and a leg amputation, and to prevent this a major operation was necessary. This was the beginning of a period of intense worry and activity for Queen Elizabeth: not only did she have to comfort her husband on his sickbed but she would have to care for her grandchildren when their parents were out of the country; and she also made a point of continuing to perform all her own public duties as well as some of the King's, which he was unable to carry out.[6] The operation took place in March 1949 in Buckingham Palace and was successful up to a point; the danger of amputation was removed and the King gained greater mobility, but he was warned that he must take life easier and that prolonged rest was necessary. For a time he was able to carry out modified duties, including, in the summer of 1951, the opening of the Festival of Britain – a brave attempt to stir up enthusiasm for British achievements. But then in the autumn of that year an ominous bulletin was issued, signed by nine doctors, stating that after a series of examinations it had been found that 'structural changes had developed in the lung'. The word cancer was not used, but that was what it was – a malignant growth. An operation was performed to remove the lung, but the surgeons knew, although they did not reveal it, that his condition was terminal. He lived for another five months, during which time many of his duties were performed by Counsellors of State, of whom the Queen was the head and on whom the brunt of the work fell. On 5 February 1952 the King had a happy day out shooting at Sandringham and was in good spirits, but that night he died peacefully in his sleep.

Although she behaved with all her customary courage and poise, Elizabeth was profoundly shocked by the King's death. It was generally supposed, with some reason, that it was she who kept him going, but no one had realized how much he kept her going. During their twenty-nine-year marriage he had grown greatly in stature and become in a quiet, unassuming way a strong and compelling figure heeded with respect by all who came in contact with him, including such giants as Churchill and Roosevelt. Over the years he had become the dominant partner and she had come to lean on him more and more, and when his support was removed she was at a loss and for a time in despair. Beside facing up to this great void in her life she also had to come to terms with her new situation. She was no longer the first lady of the land. She had been replaced by her daughter. Of course she was still treated with great respect and deference and was greatly loved by all her family, but her position was different. She was no longer the central figure.

The Queen Mother's widowhood lasted for nearly fifty years, ten years longer than that of Queen Victoria, but she spent it in a very different way. The 'widow of Windsor', beside herself with grief and self-pity, was never out of widow's weeds and for twelve years went into seclusion. The Queen Mother, on the other hand, soon decided that the greatest assuagement of her sorrow lay in activity. If she had ever had thoughts of retiring into the shadows she soon put them aside. Churchill warned her against them, telling her how much she was needed, not least by her young and inexperienced elder daughter. Her graciousness and ability to cope with all sorts of people and all sorts of situations were assets that could not be lost. So within three months of her husband's death she was attending public functions in this country, and after a year she was making tours abroad. At the same time her social life was reviving, and she was kept busy moving out of Buckingham Palace into Clarence House and from Balmoral into Birkhall. At her daughter's coronation she was a magnificent presence, and it was noted how she played the second lead in the ceremony as beautifully as she had played the first seventeen years before.

In adjusting to her new life the Queen Mother was much helped by a visit she paid to the United States in 1954. Its object was to receive a large sum of money which had been raised as a memorial to George VI to provide scholarships for students from the Commonwealth in American universities. She had been apprehensive about going as she remembered the rip-roaring success of her state visit with the King in 1939 and was afraid it would be a very different matter going on her own, 'the middle-aged widow of a king', as one newspaper unkindly put it. But she need have had no fears. She was received rapturously and mobbed wherever she went, and in a moving ceremony at Columbia University, where an honorary doctorate of law was bestowed on her, she was hailed as 'a noble queen whose quiet and constant courage in times of great stress sustained a nation and inspired a world'. The visit did much to boost her self-confidence and help her on her way to a new life.

She arrived home from her American visit to a painful and potentially damaging family crisis. Her younger daughter, Princess Margaret, had fallen in love with a royal courtier sixteen years older than herself and recently divorced. Group Captain Peter Townsend was a war hero, an outstandingly successful fighter pilot who had shot down many German planes and shown great qualities of leadership. In 1944 the King appointed him to the royal household as an equerry where he had made a very favourable impression, particularly on the tour of South Africa, and on the King's death he had been appointed Controller of the Queen Mother's household in Clarence House. By the time of the coronation he and Margaret had fallen in love and wanted to marry, but there were difficulties. In the 1950s, although some eyebrows might have been raised, it would not have been impossible for the Princess to marry a commoner of non-aristocratic descent with modest means and much older than herself, but his divorce was an insuperable barrier. By the Royal Marriages Act of 1772 it was necessary for the Princess, until she was twenty-five, to have the Queen's consent to marry, and this the Queen as Supreme Governor of the Church of England could not give to someone who had been divorced, innocent party though he might be, for the doctrines of the Church were definite that Christian marriage was indissoluble. It would therefore be necessary for Margaret to wait until she was twenty-five (in 1955), but even then there would be objections from certain quarters, notably from High Church courtiers and government ministers. Rather strangely, one person who did not take a strong stance at the time was the Queen Mother, although, as already noted, at the time of Edward's abdication her views on the sanctity of marriage were rigid. For whatever reasons – maybe because she was still in a state of shock after her husband's death, or perhaps she thought this was a temporary infatuation that would blow over – she decided to hold back. Others, however, were less reticent. When Peter Townsend told the Queen's secretary, Sir Alan Lascelles, that he wanted to marry the Princess, the latter exploded with rage and told him he must be either mad or bad, and when the Princess and her mother were out of the country he arranged for Townsend to be transferred to the post of Air Attaché to the British Embassy in Brussels, a nebulous post which put an end to his career both at Court and in the Royal Air Force. When Margaret became twenty-five a final decision had to be taken, and it was made clear to her that if she did marry she would have to forgo her royal status, including her income from the Civil List. By then their love affair had become public knowledge and there was keen speculation over what would happen. The Queen Mother was in favour of saying nothing and letting the matter fade away, but Margaret insisted on issuing a statement that in deference to the teachings of the Church there would be no marriage. Peter Townsend disappeared from the scene. Later he was to speak warmly of the Queen Mother: 'She was always wonderful, always there being kind . . . with exquisite tact.'

By the mid-1950s the Queen Mother was in full swing. 'Work is the rent you pay for life,' she once declared, and she paid it to the full, forever taking on new responsibilities and accepting engagements of every kind – Chancellor of London University, Master of the Bench of the Middle Temple, colonel-in-chief of eight regiments and patron of innumerable charities. It was not uncommon for her to have four engagements in one day, often far apart. Her energy in fulfilling these tasks was phenomenal, as was her enjoyment of them, and it was this more than anything that made them so successful. People responded to her and she had the gift of bringing out the best in them.[7] No Queen Dowager in history had played such a prominent role, and none, not even Queen Alexandra, was so greatly loved.

In between all these activities the Queen Mother saw no need for a frugal lifestyle. At Clarence House, attended by a staff of fifty, she indulged her pleasures in life. Some of these were of a simple nature – party games, charades and singsongs round the piano, always helped along with quite strong libations. Some people were surprised by the size of these, and the Duke of Edinburgh was said to have been rather shocked, so that his mother-in-law would sometimes hide them behind the flowers when he came to visit. Others were more sophisticated. Lavish lunch parties were given, and these were often sparkling occasions. Queen Elizabeth liked to have around her men (preferably single) who were articulate, sharp-witted, well informed and somewhat offbeat; she engaged them in animated conversation on all sorts of topics (except sex and religion) and enjoyed probing them for inside information and the latest gossip. She loved to listen to them, and they were invariably enchanted by her. Noel Coward, the playwright and entertainer, was completely bowled over. 'I am at her feet,' he once wrote. 'She has infinite grace of mind, charm, humour and deep-down kindness. In addition to which she looks enchanting.' Roy Strong, waspish director of the Victoria and Albert Museum, wrote that 'her *joie de vivre* was an inspiration . . . leaving one in a haze of happiness'. Always favoured on these occasions were figures from the world of horse-racing, for this was Queen Elizabeth's great love.[8]

She acquired her first racehorse in 1949, but she soon added many more and became a leading owner and devotee of the sport, studying form closely, examining pedigrees and with her own views on which horses to run where and when. She had many successes as well as disappointments, but perhaps her greatest moment came in the face of disaster. In 1956 her horse Devon Loch seemed all set to win the Grand National and was galloping home way ahead of the field when for some reason he suddenly collapsed. This was a huge disappointment, but the Queen Mother's thoughts were only for the jockey and the stable lads and she went at once to console them, at the same time gracefully congratulating the winning owner. The Duke of Devonshire, who was there at the time, described it as the most perfect display of dignity he had ever witnessed.

In the matter of residences the Queen Mother was well supplied. In addition to Clarence House, where she spent most of her time, there was also the Royal Lodge in Windsor Great Park where she went for country air at the weekends and which was especially dear to her, as it was where she and her family had spent blissfully happy days in the first years of her marriage. For holidays there was Birkhall on Deeside, eight miles from Balmoral, where there was scope for another of her favourite occupations, that of salmon fishing; she was no mean hand at this and would spend hours knee-deep in cold and sometimes turbulent water to land a catch. There was a further, somewhat audacious, addition to her homes soon after the death of George VI. While on a visit to the north of Scotland she came across an ancient castle standing on a lonely crag, storm-battered, almost in ruins and about to be pulled down. On an impulse she decided that she must save it, and she bought it. It seemed the wildest of follies – on the northernmost tip of Scotland, accessible only with great difficulty and far from habitable – but she fell in love with it, restored it and made it fit to live in, which brought her great satisfaction and helped her through difficult years. Of all her homes the Castle of Mey was the one where she found most peace of mind – away from the pressures of life, on the rugged Caithness coastline in the teeth of rampaging waves and hurricane-force winds.

In 1960, when she was thirty, Princess Margaret became engaged to Antony Armstrong-Jones, a professional photographer and son of the Earl of Rosse, who was divorced from Tony's mother and had subsequently married a former actress and then an air hostess. It can hardly have been the marriage the Queen Mother had hoped for her daughter, but she was desperate for her happiness and welcomed Tony into the family and got on well with him, more easily than with her other son-in-law, Prince Philip. For a time all went swimmingly. Tony introduced Margaret into chic bohemian circles and they did unconventional things together. But it did not last. Both were difficult partners, and after three years the marriage began to fall apart. Tony could not adjust to royal routine. In 1978 they were divorced, which predictably caused the Queen Mother great distress. An elderly courtier, Sir Arthur Penn, reported that it was the only time he had ever seen her in tears. Soon afterwards she was further saddened when Margaret was seen openly consorting with Roddy Llewellyn, a man fifteen years her junior. But strongly as she may have disapproved she did not make an issue of it. Perhaps she knew it would make no difference and only cause bad blood. So, as with the Townsend affair, she appeared to see nothing.

In 1981 Prince Charles married Lady Diana Spencer, the granddaughter of a close friend of the Queen Mother, Ruth Lady Fermoy. With her youth, dazzling beauty and irresistible popular appeal it seemed, as the Archbishop of Canterbury said at their wedding, to 'be the stuff of which fairytales are made'. However, it proved to be no fairytale, rather the prelude to fifteen years of torment and strife. Diana had had a disturbed childhood and was suffering from the affliction of bulimia which often made life a misery. She was highly strung, wilful and unable to come to terms with royal protocol. Besides, she knew that Charles loved another whom he was unwilling to put out his life.

Camilla Parker-Bowles was the antithesis of Diana – sturdy, down to earth, resilient, somewhat boisterous. One could see at a glance that she came from rural England; there was about her an aura (and sometimes an aroma) of stables and kennels. She was totally without shyness and her self-introduction to Charles was typical: 'My great-grandmother [Alice Keppel] had it off with your great-great-grandfather [Edward VII], so how about it?' Charles, a diffident unconfident twenty-two-year-old, was greatly struck by this brazen approach and fell for her at once. At the time, however, Camilla, eighteen months his senior, did not fall for him. She was in love with a dashing cavalry officer, Major Andrew Parker-Bowles, and married him while Charles was away on service in the Navy. This was a blow to Charles, perhaps more severe than he realized at the time. If he had married Camilla then, his life would probably have been passed on an altogether more even keel. The country would not have had its most brilliant princess, but Charles would have been spared the agonies of a desperately unhappy marriage. Camilla would not, perhaps, have been an ideal Princess of Wales, but she was sensible and warm-hearted, so she could probably have been tidied up and brought into line. After her marriage it might have been expected that she would fade out of Charles's life, but this did not happen; his love persisted and became as compulsive as that of his great-uncle, Edward VIII, for Mrs Simpson. Camilla's marriage to Parker-Bowles was affectionate but loosely knit; at times they went their separate ways, and Camilla's way was back to Prince Charles. By the time he was into his thirties they had become secret lovers, although not so secret that many people did not know about it, including, fatefully, Diana Spencer.

Charles was not, of course, the first Prince of Wales to have a mistress; his great-great-grandfather, Edward VII, had had several which his wife, Queen Alexandra, had accepted philosophically. But this Diana was unable to do. She became enraged and obsessed by the continued intrusion of Camilla, and her marriage to Charles became a battleground in which one was always driving the other to distraction. They also sought to outshine each other in the public eye. This proved an unequal contest. No one could outshine Diana. When they appeared together she always stole the show, and people were far more enthralled by pictures of her cradling crippled babies and embracing AIDS sufferers than they were of Charles at work on his worthy but more prosaic charities for urban renewal and finding work for the disadvantaged.[9]

In this conflict, despite his occasional follies and indiscretions, the Queen Mother's sympathies lay with Charles. There had always been a deep bond between them: in his miserably unhappy schooldays she had been a great comfort and always much closer to him than either of his parents. She was, of course, aware of his peccadilloes, but as far as possible she overlooked them and did not reproach him; she suffered in silence when a particularly sleazy telephone conversation between him and Camilla was made public and when, to her dismay, he made a public confession of adultery on television. Any sympathy she might have felt for Diana vanished after she made a suicide attempt and gave a tell-all television interview. She knew well how hard it was for an outsider to adapt to the life of royalty. She had had to do it herself and thought that Diana ought to have tried harder and been more ready to make sacrifices. But in this she was surely less than fair: her situation had been quite different; she was supported by a loving and totally loyal husband and a doting father and mother-in-law who did all they could to make life easy for her, whereas Diana was often confronted by formality and coolness. Diana later wrote: 'The Queen Mother was meant to help me, to teach me, but she did not do anything at all.' She also said that she was 'tough and interfering'.

The woes of Charles's marriage was not the only family sadness the Queen Mother had to bear at this time. The marriage of Prince Andrew also fell apart. In 1986 he had married Sarah Ferguson, an attractive, racy lady from a somewhat loose-living family who could in no way adapt to a royal way of life and caused her in-laws great distress by her flamboyant behaviour.[10] Four years earlier Princess Anne's marriage to Mark Phillips had also come to an end. With her strong views on the sanctity of marriage the Queen Mother must have been deeply distressed by all these divorces, but she did not let them affect her relationship with her grandchildren, which remained as close and loving as ever.

Like everyone else the Queen Mother was stunned by Diana's sudden death in 1997, and she was also taken aback by the outpouring of grief which it engendered, the like of which had not been seen in the country before. At the age of ninety-seven she could hardly be expected to realize the tremendous impact of Diana's life and death on the country as a whole, as well as on the nature of the monarchy, which was not to be the same again.

Although there was much to sadden her in her last years the Queen Mother was not bowed down and continued to maintain an extraordinary momentum, fulfilling engagements which would have exhausted a much younger person; and this in spite of bouts of ill health – the removal of her appendix at the age of sixty-four and a more serious abdominal operation two years later and in her mid-nineties two hip-replacement operations. There was no stopping her. She withstood all efforts to cut down her activities. There are worse things, she said, than being overworked and exhausted.

Her eightieth, ninetieth and then one hundredth birthdays were celebrated with widespread and heartfelt enthusiasm. Just before she died in her hundred and second year the fates dealt her a final blow. Princess Margaret's health had been breaking down, and following a series of strokes she died at the beginning of 2002. Her mother was extremely frail at the time but insisted on making the journey from Sandringham to Windsor to attend the funeral. She herself died seven weeks later on 30 March.

Outwardly the Queen Mother seemed to be an uncomplicated person – benevolent, gracious and smiling. Most people would agree with Prince Charles that 'she belongs to that priceless brand of human beings whose greatest gift is to enhance life for others through her own effervescent enthusiasm for life'. But there was another side to her. She was not all sweetness and soft soap. 'I am not as nice as you think I am,' she once said. Those who knew her well were aware of a strong will and a hard streak under the surface. Lord Charteris, secretary to her daughter and a great admirer, said she could be 'tough and resourceful'. Others were more outspoken. In his book *The Queen and I* the Labour MP Willie Hamilton, a strong anti-royalist, wrote: 'If a personal public image is the thing to cultivate today, then the Queen Mother is among the best of gardeners.' And he quotes 'a very prominent, right wing, ex-Labour Cabinet Minister' who once described her as 'the most reactionary member of the Royal Family. She makes no speeches of any consequence. She gets through her public relations by pleasing facial exercises, or by purposely chatting to "the lads in the back row" and taking a drop of the hard stuff, her native Scotch whisky. Yet behind the matey tipple and the ever-ready smile, there lurks the mind of a shrewd businesswoman.' This is a harsh judgement but not perhaps without a grain of truth.

The duality in her character is reflected in some of her portraits. Pietro Annigoni had no doubts, however. 'One of my best pictures is the one I did of the Queen Mother. And I'll tell you why this is so. It's because she has such an inner beauty. It is all very well to look glamorous on the surface, but without that personal quality your subject is nothing but a dummy. The Queen Mother is one of the loveliest people I have ever met.' Augustus John, on the other hand, was perplexed by her and unable to finish his portrait, saying that it was 'the most endearingly deficient picture of my life'. Graham Sutherland's was hard and severe, which distressed some people, but Roy Strong, one of the Queen's admirers, thought he had captured her true character: 'Typically upright posture . . . alert turn of the head and eyes – together with the determined set of the lips which revealed a robustness behind a perpetual beguiling mask of humorous charm.' Later portraitists, striving to get behind the 'chocolate-box image', were controversial to the point of caricature.

Certainly she was no intellectual, reading widely rather than deeply and having few innovative ideas and some idiosyncrasies. But the spell she wove and the great influence she wielded did not depend on books or ideas but rather on charm, determination and sheer hard work. Above all, her achievement was historic. As much as anyone she rescued the monarchy and restored its reputation.

FURTHER READING

Airlie, Mabell, Countess of, *Thatched with Gold*, Hutchinson, London, 1962

Battiscombe, Georgina, *Queen Alexandra*, Constable, London, 1969

Black, Jeremy, *The Hanoverians*, Hambledon, London, 2004

Bloch, Michael, *The Duchess of Windsor*, Weidenfeld and Nicolson, London, 1996

Bradford, Sarah, *George VI*, Weidenfeld and Nicolson, London, 1989

Channon, Sir Henry, *Diaries*, Weidenfeld and Nicolson, London, 1993

Chevenix-Trench, Charles, *George II*, Allen Lane, London, 1974

Clarke, John, *Life and Times of George III*, Weidenfeld and Nicolson, London, 1972

Creston, Dormer, *The Regent and His Daughter*, Eyre and Spottisforde, London, 1952

Donaldson, Frances, *Edward VIII*, Weidenfeld and Nicolson, London, 1974

Duff, David, *Alexandra: Princess and Queen*, Collins, London, 1980

—— *Queen Mary*, Collins, London, 1983

Fraser, Flora, *The Unruly Queen*, John Murray, London, 1996

Friedman, Dennis, *Ladies of the Bedchamber*, Peter Owen, London, 2003

Fulford, Roger, *George IV*, Duckworth, London, 1935

—— Royal Dukes, Collins, London, 1973

Hatton, R., *George I*, Thames and Hudson, London, 1970

Hedley, Olwen, *Queen Charlotte*, John Murray, London, 1975

Hibbert, Christopher, *Edward VII: A Portrait*, Allen Lane, London, 1976

—— George IV, Penguin, Harmondsworth, 1976

Higham, Charles, *Wallis*, Sidgwick and Jackson, London, 1988

Hopkirk, Mary, *Queen Adelaide*, John Murray, London, 1946

Hough, Richard, *Edward and Alexandra*, Hodder and Stoughton, London, 1992

Jordan, Ruth, *Sophia Dorothea*, Constable, London, 1971

Lloyd, Alan, *The Wickedest Age*, David and Charles, Newton Abbot, 1971

Longford, Elizabeth, *The Queen Mother*, Weidenfeld and Nicolson, London, 1983

Magnus, Philip, *King Edward VII*, John Murray, London, 1964

Marlow, Joyce, *George I*, Weidenfeld and Nicolson, London, 1973

Mortimer, Penelope, *The Queen Mother*, Viking, London, 1986

Nicolson, Harold, *George V*, Constable, London, 1952

Plowden, Alison, *Caroline and Charlotte*, Sidgwick and Jackson, London, 1969

Plumb, J.H., *The First Four Georges*, Batsford, London, 1956

Pope-Hennessy, James, *Queen Mary*, Allen and Unwin, London, 1959

Rose, Kenneth, *King George V*, Weidenfeld and Nicolson, London, 1983

Thornton, Michael, *Royal Feud*, Michael Joseph, London, 1985

Tisdall, E.E.P., *Wanton Queen*, Stanley Paul, London, 1939

Vickers, Hugo, *Elizabeth the Queen Mother*, Hutchinson, London, 2005

Wilkins, W.H., *Caroline, the Illustrious Queen-Consort of George II*, Longmans Green, London, 1904

Windsor, Duchess of, *The Heart Has Its Reasons*, Michael Joseph, London, 1956

Windsor, Duke of, *A King's Story*, Cassell, London, 1951

Young, Sir George, *Poor Fred*, Blackwell, Oxford, 1937

Ziegler, Philip, *King William IV*, Collins, London, 1971

—— *King Edward VIII*, Collins, London, 1990

NOTES

Chapter 1: Sophia Dorothea of Celle, Wife of George I

1. A morganatic marriage is one between two people of unequal rank whereby the one of lower degree, and any issue, have no rights of succession to the titles and properties of the higher-ranked party.
2. Confusingly, seven years later George William took the title of Duke of Celle and another brother, John Frederick, became Duke of Hanover, a title which on his death fourteen years later passed to Ernest Augustus.
3. A *maitresse-en-titre* was a permanent mistress of official standing.
4. Lüneburg had been divided among four brothers by the Treaty of Westphalia at the end of the Thirty Years' War.
5. With the exception of music. He had a love of opera, and when he came to England he became a patron of Handel.
6. Sophia had not yet acceded to this title, but it is used here to distinguish her from her daughter-in-law, Sophia Dorothea.
7. One of the difficulties in sorting out the Hanoverian Royal Family is the number of women called Sophia. Apart from Sophia Dorothea and her daughter there was her mother-in-law, the Electress Sophia, and her sister-in-law, Sophia Charlotte, who married King Frederick I of Prussia. Similarly, among the men there were a bewildering number of Georges: George William (Sophia's father), George Louis (her husband) and George Augustus (her son).
8. In one of his more bombastic passages Macaulay recorded how when Frederick William took a walk in the streets of his capital the citizens dispersed terror-stricken as if a mad tiger had been let loose among them, as he was liable to let fly with his boot or his cane at anyone who came within striking distance.
9. In the words of Horace Walpole: 'She was as corpulent and ample as the other was long and emaciated. Two fierce black eyes, large and rolling beneath two lofty arched eyebrows, two acres of cheeks spread with crimson, an ocean of neck that overflowed and was not distinguished from the lower part of her body, and no part restrained by stays.'
10. Her descendants occupy the throne of England to this day, although it was found advisable during the First World War to exchange the Germanic title for the more acceptable House of Windsor.

Chapter 2: Caroline of Anspach, Wife of George II

1. Charles II said of Prince George that he had tried him drunk and tried him sober and there was nothing in him.
2. He was in fact five-eighths German, a quarter French and an eighth Scottish.
3. A writ requiring a person to be brought before a judge or into court to investigate the lawfulness of his detention.
4. Including Joseph Addison, Richard Steele and Alexander Pope.
5. His death was said to have been expedited by a surfeit of watermelons.
6. An outbreak of manic speculation which brought ruin to many.
7. Notably in the case of a Bill to extend the power of excisemen which caused a wave of irrational uproar.
8. Quoted from *Caroline the Illustrious* by W.H. Wilkins.
9. Giving rise to the formation of the 'Rumpsteak Club', qualification for membership of which was that the King should have turned his back on one.
10. Similar to rumours spread by Whig politicians at the time of the birth of James Stuart, son of James II, that a baby had been smuggled into his mother's accouchement in a warming pan.
11. It was not only Hanoverians who mistrusted their sons. The Russian Tsar, Peter the Great, did away with his eldest; and King Frederick William I of Prussia treated his heir (later Frederick the Great) with ferocious brutality.
12. Tablecloths were the only things available as swaddling clothes.
13. She became convinced when the baby turned out to be a rather puny girl. If it had been a bouncing boy she might have had suspicions.
14. 'Only girls and fools resent conjugal infidelities,' she had once declared.
15. It was made worse by a particularly virulent attack of piles, to which painful and undignified complaint he was always susceptible.
16. Which soon afterwards on the death of her husband she was. She bravely made a second marriage, which was short-lived but not unhappy.
17. Because it was initiated by a none too reputable character who called himself Captain Jenkins and carried around with him a gruesome object in a bottle which, he claimed, was an ear of his that had been cut off by the Spanish while he was trading off the coast of South America.
18. The last English king to lead an army in battle.
19. Not least in the manner of his death, which occurred while he was in the lavatory.

Chapter 3: Charlotte of Mecklenburg-Strelitz, Wife of George III

1. Saxe-Coburg was another minor German state, brought into closer contact with England when Queen Victoria married Prince Albert of Saxe-Coburg.
2. Popular opinion was summed up by an epitaph which appeared at the time of his death:

Here lies Fred . . .
Who was alive and is dead.
There's no more to be said.

3. Later, after marriage to the daughter of a large Yorkshire landowner, he became extremely wealthy.
4. Father of the great Whig leader Charles James Fox.
5. This involved advancing the date by four days, which caused some to think that they had been deprived of four days of their lives, and the cry was raised: 'Give us back our four days!'
6. Including, so it was maliciously rumoured, some of the King's more intimate garments.
7. One of her main concerns was a Hospital for the Reception of Penitent Prostitutes.
8. Including the popular song about 'The noble Duke of York, he had ten thousand men. He marched them up to the top of the hill and marched them down again.'
9. Roger Fulford, *Royal Dukes*.
10. For a long time the only legitimate grandchild of George III was Princess Charlotte, daughter of the Prince Regent. When she died in childbirth in 1817 several of the younger sons of George III set about making legal marriages in order to provide heirs to the throne.

Chapter 4: Caroline of Brunswick, Wife of George IV
1. She was also the daughter of a bishop.
2. Well might George have reiterated the words of Henry VIII to Thomas Cromwell at his marriage to Anne of Cleves: 'My lord, if it were not to satisfy the world and my realm I would not do that which I must do this day for none earthly thing.'
3. Perceval was the only prime minister to be assassinated (in 1812).
4. The first, and for a long time the only, commander to inflict a defeat on Napoleon when his successful defence of Acre prevented Napoleon's threatened invasion of India.
5. Since his recovery from his second bout of porphyria, which affected his mind, George III's behaviour had often been strange. Once, having eluded his attendants, he rode down to Blackheath and insisted on being alone with Caroline, who had difficulty in warding off his advances. Ladies about the Court also felt themselves threatened by him.
6. They, too, distressed Caroline's ladies, who nicknamed them 'the Squallinis' and called the son 'Chanticleer' and the father 'the old orang-outang'.
7. She was deeply shocked by a report that he had come back from the races at Ascot incapably drunk.
8. This was not the only sign of sympathy Caroline showed towards

Napoleon. Later she paid a prolonged visit to Elba, staying in Napoleon's house there and coming away with a book of his and his favourite billiard cue which she treated as treasured possessions. She also dallied with Napoleon's brother Lucien, from whom she accepted a number of kindnesses.

9. Conditions were made worse by the presence on board of a menagerie which included Arab horses and lion cubs, gifts from well-meaning rulers, but the stench from them was overpowering.

10. After imposing 'strict' economies she continued to employ a domestic staff of over eighty as well as maintaining a ship with a captain and a crew at the ready.

11. Notably of how the Princess and Pergami had shared a tent on board ship and how Pergami accompanied her everywhere, not only to her bedroom but also to the bathroom, giving rise to the ribald doggerel:

> The Grand Master of St Caroline
> has found promotion's path.
> He is made both Night Companion
> and Commander of the Bath.

12. Wood was the son of a West Country clothmaker, he had had a successful career in the City of London as a chemist and hop merchant and had twice been Lord Mayor. It is probable that he knew little of Caroline's background and was unaware of the risks he was taking.

13. Not quite all the lords were present. A few were excused on compassionate grounds.

14. Although even at Brighton it was found that 'God Save the King' could not be played without fears of a riot.

15. 'Back to Como' and 'Back to Pergami', among other taunts.

16. Affected but not afflicted', as an onlooker remarked.

Chapter 5: Queen Adelaide of Saxe-Coburg Meiningen, Wife of William IV

1. Apart from being accompanied by a classical tutor, Midshipman the Reverend Henry Majendie, whose role on a man-of-war must have been ambiguous.

2. Duke of Clarence was hardly a propitious title. The last Duke of Clarence (Shakespeare's 'false, fleeting, perjured Clarence') had been drowned in a butt of Malmsey wine during the Wars of the Roses for being unfaithful to his brother, Richard III.

3. Especially as Jordan was another name for a chamber pot, which gave great scope to cartoonists.

4. The last time a monarch was to do such a thing.

5. In the interests of economy even Adelaide's crown was made up out of her own jewellery.

Chapter 6: Queen Alexandra, Wife of Edward VII
1. Christian IX was the first monarch to be elected by popular vote.
2. The condition of the drains at Windsor Castle is a more likely cause.
3. Nothing like it perhaps since the return of Charles II in 1660 after the demise of Cromwell and the Commonwealth.
4. Osborne was the Queen's residence in the Isle of Wight – hardly the most romantic location, described by the Crown Prince of Prussia (Victoria's son-in-law) as 'one great gloomy vault with relics of the Prince Consort'.
5. Causing a particular sensation by his performance of a Scottish reel in full Highland outfit.
6. But such was her hold on society that for some time fashionable ladies, imitating her in everything, felt compelled to adopt the 'Alexandra limp'.
7. Lord Esher was one of the most brilliant and enigmatic of contemporary politicians. He was the confidant of both Queen Victoria and Edward VII. Behind the scenes he wielded considerable power, which he relished but kept dark.
8. It was not, however, totally covered up, as Minnie's sister wrote an account of it which was printed privately and read by some.
9. But there were, of course, reasons of a more personal nature for this. In Paris, where he liked to mix with the *demi-monde*, he would have been unduly constrained by her presence, and in Biarritz he was usually accompanied by Mrs Keppel, who would not mix with Alix.
10. Fisher was deeply devoted to her and just as belligerent and anti-German. For some years they had been hatching unrealistic plots for the recapture of the Danish provinces.

Chapter 7: Queen Mary of Teck, Wife of George V
1. 'Her size is fearful, it is really a misfortune,' Queen Victoria wrote to her eldest daughter.
2. Including a bizarre occurrence when she and others were dabbling in the psychic and trying to make a table levitate by invoking powers from the spirit world. In this they were all too successful, but when the table came down to earth again it trapped Mary Adelaide and it took several strong men to free her.
3. In this she was sometimes helped by her mother's unpunctuality. Often left waiting for an hour or more, she always kept a volume by her so that the time would not be wasted.
4. Not dissimilar to Queen Salote of Tonga in the coronation procession of Queen Elizabeth II who almost obliterated the other occupant of her coach.
5. Maples was a large London furniture emporium.

6. Edward Albert, later King Edward VIII, then Duke of Windsor.
7. Princess Mary, later Countess of Harewood; Albert, later King George VI; and Henry, later Duke of Gloucester.
8. George, later Duke of Kent, and John, who died at the age of fourteen.
9. This was the residence of the Duke and Duchess of York in St James's Palace.
10. This may have been because he himself had held the title for so long that he could not think of it belonging to anyone else.
11. Quoted from *Queen Mary* by James Pope-Hennessy.
12. 'Abroad is awful,' George once said. 'I know because I've been there.'
13. There is a story, which may or may not be true, that he once said he had been afraid of his father and his father had been in terror of his mother, so he was determined that his children should be afraid of him.
14. This was recognized by the man in the street, as shown by the music-hall song beginning: 'There'll be no war, not so long as there's a king like good King Edward.'
15. In the event he had to do no more than threaten to create the new peers. In face of this the Tory peers climbed down.
16. For all her life until 1914 Queen Mary had maintained a regular and intimate correspondence with her aunt Augusta, Grand Duchess of Mecklenburg-Strelitz, the elder sister of Mary Adelaide. A lady of strong character and firm reactionary views, the Duchess more than any other was the person to whom Queen Mary could express herself freely and frankly.
17. Quoted from *King George V* by Kenneth Rose.
18. Perhaps the only comparable occasion in history was the so-called Field of the Cloth of Gold in 1520 when King Henry VIII of England and King Francis I of France sought to outdo each other in magnificence, but none the less it was not on the same scale.
19. As might be expected, not all of these were of professional standard; they were sent up in the popular song 'Sister Susie's Sewing Shirts for Soldiers':

> Some soldiers send epistles
> Say they'd sooner sleep in thistles
> Than the saucy, soft, short shirts
> For soldiers Sister Susie sews.

20. In the course of the war he undertook 450 visits to troops, 300 to hospitals, about the same number to factories and shipyards, and presented some 50,000 awards for gallantry.
21. A line from his favourite hymn 'Abide with me' epitomized his attitude: 'Change and decay in all around I see.'
22. MacDonald was born out of wedlock in a cottage in the north of Scotland; for most of his life he had been an impecunious clerk and journalist.

23. Maria Louise was the first cousin of George V.
24. Bernard Shaw was a marked exception.
25. The first of these, delivered in 1932, was written by Rudyard Kipling.
26. He complained at the time that he had never even seen a state paper.
27. This was contrary to precedent for the Queen Dowager. Queen Adelaide had not attended the coronation of Queen Victoria, nor Queen Alexandra that of George V.
28. It has been alleged that some of the diamonds with which Mary was ablaze should have been passed on to her daughter-in-law, but she was reluctant to part with them.
29. The Duchess was the daughter of the Queen's brother Adolphus, Duke of Teck and later Marquis of Cambridge.
30. Dispatch riders were permanently at the ready not only to keep her in touch with London but to conduct her to a secret hiding place in the event of a German invasion.
31. These sometimes included still serviceable agricultural implements which later had to be returned to their owners.

Chapter 8: Wallis Simpson, Wife of Edward VIII
1. He was of Jewish descent, having changed his name from Solomons, but this was always kept secret.
2. By a curious coincidence in the house of a Mrs Kerr-Smiley, sister of Ernest Simpson.
3. A royal folly in the form of a mock medieval castle dating from the reign of George III.
4. Son of the fabulously wealthy Aga Khan and a philanderer of great repute.
5. Simpson was reported to have been asked to perform in a play called *The Unimportance of Being Ernest* in which he would declaim: 'My only regret is that I have but one wife to lay down for my king' (quoted from *Ladies of the Bedchamber* by Dennis Friedman).
6. Ironically with a lady Wallis had provided to look after him while she was away with Edward.
7. Reno was where Americans went for a quick divorce. Cardinal Wolsey, chief minister of Henry VIII, came from Ipswich.
8. During the war Bedoux was imprisoned in America for trading with the enemy.
9. In negotiating a financial settlement with George VI he was less than candid about the large sums he had saved as Prince of Wales from the revenues of the Duchy of Cornwall.
10. Later the editor of *Burke's Peerage* wrote of 'this most flagrant act of discrimination in the whole history of our dynasty'.
11. Hoare was one-time Foreign Secretary, noted for his appeasement policies.

12. In 1943 he was brutally murdered in mysterious circumstances. The investigation into the crime was bungled and never solved, for which much of the blame was levelled at the Duke.
13. In a typical temper he was said to have kicked her sharply on the shins, drawing blood.
14. 'Why should I,' she is said to have remarked later, 'when she stopped people curtsying to me?'
15. At the graveside she told the Archbishop of Canterbury that the place reserved for her coffin beside her husband was too narrow and insisted on a hedge being removed to make more room.
16. It was even rumoured that her body had turned black.
17. Strangely, in the order of service there was no mention of her name.

Chapter 9: Queen Elizabeth the Queen Mother, Wife of George VI

1. Duff Cooper was politician, author and later Lord Norwich.
2. Apart from the procession being held up briefly by a Presbyterian minister fainting, a bishop standing on the King's train so that he could not move at the requisite moment and the Archbishop holding a text in front of the King for him to read but obscuring an important part with his thumb.
3. They were even knocking off policemen's helmets, it was alleged.
4. A dance culminating in partners bumping each other's backsides.
5. The King did not lose his sense of humour, however. He had no ear for music, but he once attended a concert conducted by Malcolm Sargent in which the orchestra played a rousing version of 'Rule Britannia', which so delighted the King that at the end he gave a royal command to Sargent that it must be played at every concert, to which Sargent demurred, 'Might there not sometimes be a problem with that, sir? Suppose, for example, the concert was the B Minor Mass.' 'No problem,' replied the King. 'I shouldn't be there.'
6. Princess Anne was born on 15 August 1950.
7. Sometimes she might startle them into silence. On one occasion she was receiving a group of American students soon after Princess Anne had been held up by a gunman in the Mall, and one of the group had asked how the Princess had felt. 'Oh, I expect she was all right,' said the Queen. 'After all, the British monarchy is accustomed to being shot at.' And then, after a pause, 'Often justifiably.'
8. Notably Woodrow Wyatt, chairman of the Tote and one-time Labour Member of Parliament, although he had strong Tory tastes.
9. His work for charity should not be underestimated. By the time he was thirty he was associated with more than two hundred charities.
10. Photographs of her topless appeared in the tabloids, as did one of her 'financial adviser' sucking her toe.

INDEX